ABOUT THE AUTHOR

After escaping from his first career in law, Warwick Hirst qualified as an archivist. As curator of manuscripts at the Mitchell Library, he researches, appraises, values and catalogues historical manuscripts relating to Australia, as well as giving talks and curating exhibitions. His first book, *My Dear, Dear Betsy: A Treasury of Australian Letters*, was published in 1993.

Warwick's other interests include cricket, rugby, films and theatre, and he also enjoys surfing the waves in his home town of Sydney, where he lives with his wife and two children.

GREAT CONVICT ESCAPES IN COLONIAL AUSTRALIA

REVISED EDITION

WARWICK HIRST

Kangaroo Press

For Anne, Robert and Catherine

All illustrations courtesy of the Mitchell and Dixson libraries,
State Library of New South Wales.

First published in Australia in 1999 by Kangaroo Press
an imprint of Simon & Schuster (Australia) Pty Limited
20 Barcoo Street, East Roseville NSW 2069
This edition published 2003

A Viacom Company
Sydney New York London Toronto Tokyo Singapore

Visit our website at www.simonsaysaustralia.com.au

National Library of Australia
Cataloguing-in-Publication data

Hirst, Warwick.
  Great convict escapes.

  New rev. ed.
  Bibliography.
  Includes index.
  ISBN 0 7318 1202 6.

  1. Escapes – Australia – History. 2. Convicts – Australia –
  History. 3. Australia – History – 1788–1851. I. Hirst,
  Warwick. Great escapes by convicts in colonial Australia.
  II. Title.

994.02

Cover design by Jason van Genderen, Treehouse Creative
Typeset by Darrel Hope, Asset Typesetting Pty Ltd
Typeset in 11/14 ITC Legacy Serif
Printed in Australia by Griffin Press

10 9 8 7 6 5 4 3 2 1

Contents

Voyages of Mary Bryant, the Cyprus and the Wellington

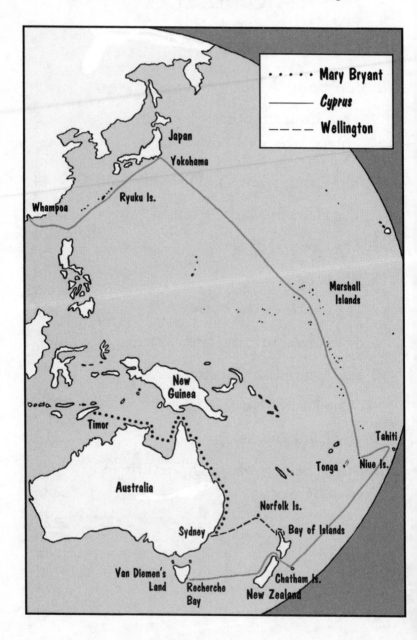

Introduction

Roosting on the highest shelf in my study is a rather scruffy collection of World War II books which I acquired during the early 1960s from the second-hand bookshops which then proliferated in Sydney between Circular Quay and Haymarket. My initial and lasting preference was for personal narratives of captivity and escape. In quick succession I consumed titles such as *The Wooden Horse* by Eric Williams, *Boldness Be My Friend* by Richard Pape and *The Great Escape* by Paul Brickhill. With fascination I read of the ingenuity of escaping prisoners of war in making use of the most unlikely material to fashion false identity cards, civilian clothes, compasses, maps and all the other paraphernalia needed to evade their captors, and then how they made their way through occupied territory, often with the assistance of local resistance groups, to eventual safety or in many cases recapture.

In later years my interest in stories of escape was rekindled when, in the course of my work as an archivist, I came across a number of memoirs written by convicts who had made daring escapes from colonial Australia. These, to my mind, were equally as exciting as those from World War II. While lacking the legitimacy of escapes by prisoners of war (whose duty it was to escape), they are still remarkable examples of human endeavour and resourcefulness.

Unlike the prisoners of war who were confined by barbed wire, it was remoteness and isolation that challenged the convicts. Admiral Sir George Young, who proposed a plan to the British Government in 1785 for settling convicts at Botany Bay, was of the opinion that 'the remoteness of its situation' promised a place 'from whence it is hardly possible for persons to return, without permission'.[1] From the admiral's point of view, escape was inconceivable.

And so, in the main, it proved. Despite the absence of stone walls and iron bars, to escape from the colony and get clear away to a safe haven was a difficult proposition. The formidable barriers of distance, trackless bush inhabited by hostile Aborigines, and the vast Pacific Ocean formed an effective natural prison whose perils relatively few convicts managed to overcome, although many made the attempt.

Nevertheless the desire to escape was strong and even before the First Fleet had arrived in Botany Bay the first attempt had been made. While the ships were moored at Tenerife in the Canary Islands, a convict named John Power lowered himself over the bow of the *Alexander* and swam to the jolly-boat lying astern. He climbed in, cut her adrift and floated across the harbour on the current. He attempted to board a Dutch East Indiaman but was rejected by the crew and next morning was discovered by a search party as he was preparing to row to the Grand Canary, 50 kilometres away.

The establishment of the first settlement at Sydney Cove in 1788 provided increased opportunities for escape by land and sea. Within a matter of days a group of convicts had evaded their marine guards and cut across country to Botany Bay where the ships of the French navigator La Perouse lay at anchor. He refused to take them on board and they had little choice but to straggle back to Sydney Cove. Over the next few years convicts occasionally took to the bush 'one or two people at a time' but this changed with the arrival of a boatload of Irish convicts in 1791. 'They went off in numerous bodies, few of whom ever returned,' reported David Collins, then the colony's first Judge-Advocate.[2] In explaining this unforeseen situation to his superiors in London, Governor Arthur Phillip observed that 'as these people work daily in the woods, the prevention of such desertions is impossible; but this is an evil which will cure itself'.[3] However, as the colony's records reveal, his optimism was unfounded.

2

Ignorance of their whereabouts in the world led one party of 21 Irish convicts to conceive the notion that China was situated only 240 kilometres to the north on the other side of a fordable river. In November 1791 they set out on their journey with provisions for a week, but as Surgeon Peter Cunningham wryly commented:

> through want of sign-posts, or some other essentials, on the way, they became bewildered in the woods, and returned to the settlement so squalid and lean that the very crows would have declined the proffer of their carcases.[4]

This evident failure did not deter further attempts by other 'Chinese travellers', nor did the gruesome discovery of 50 convict skeletons in the bush. In the convict imagination, China was a land of mystery and fabulous wealth, of almond-eyed girls and quaint palaces; above all it was a land that offered respite from oppression and the lash.

In 1798, ten years after settlement, the convict William Noah noted with some incredulity that this geographical ignorance was still common. 'The Situation and Extent of this Country is layd Down by several geographers,' he wrote,

> where they make it certain of being an Island of the length of 4000 Miles but it is not the Opinion of the Common people & so Obstinate they are of its Joining India that several have been lost in Indeavoring to find it out.[5]

Even as late as 1803 four convicts left Castle Hill for China. Only one survived. He was found by a kangaroo hunter 21 days later, exhausted and starving on the banks of the Hawkesbury River.

Another misguided belief which drew escaping convicts (colloquially called bolters or runaways) inland was disparagingly reported by Governor John Hunter:

> In addition to their natural vicious propensities, they have conceived an opinion that there is a colony of white people in some part of this country, in which they will receive all the comforts of life without the necessity of labour.[6]

A Chain Gang. Convicts going to work, Hobart Town, Van Diemen's Land, c. 1831, after Charles Bruce (Mitchell Library).

In 1798 some 60 men set out for this fabled paradise, supposedly 500 to 600 kilometres south-west of Sydney, supplied with the figure of a compass drawn on a scrap of paper to guide them through the bush. Perhaps even more bizarre was the belief held by some convicts that if they travelled south they would reach Ireland, 'knowing that as Ireland is a colder country than New South Wales, and that the cold winds blow from the south, therefore Ireland must lie in that direction!'[7]

More realistic in his objectives was an enterprising character from the Second Fleet named John Crow who was on a fourteen-year sentence for burglary. After breaking out of the lockup at Parramatta he made his way to Sydney where he swam out to an American vessel anchored in the harbour. He was detected climbing on board and as punishment was thrown in 'the black hole' at the guardhouse at Sydney. A night or two later he escaped by untiling part of the roof. He was apprehended back at Parramatta and for this and other offences was sentenced to death. A few hours before his execution he tried to effect another escape by jumping down the privy. Later it was discovered that he had removed some bricks from the wall of his cell, and it was David Collins's opinion that 'had he gained the respite of another day, he would easily have escaped'.[8]

These, then, were the first convict escapers, unsophisticated, no doubt, but all driven by a vision of freedom. Most of them headed west or north into the interior — it was far easier to simply walk into the bush than to steal a boat or stow away on a departing ship. For some years only relatively few convicts understood that true freedom lay to the east beyond the Pacific Ocean, but gradually this realisation burgeoned. Between 1803 and 1820 over 40 escapes and attempted escapes by sea were recorded involving more than 250 men and women.

The pioneers of the sea route to liberty were probably the five men who seized a punt at Rose Hill in September 1790 and proceeded to pass undetected down the Parramatta River to South Head. There they stole a small boat and put to sea with the intention of sailing to Tahiti. It was assumed by David Collins, 'from the wretched state of the boat wherein they trusted themselves', that the ocean 'must have proved their grave'.[9] His confidence turned out to be misplaced, for they were picked up five years later living with Aborigines at Port Stephens. However, once the way had been shown other attempts rapidly followed.

The stories in this book tell of escapes by women as well as men, of escapes overland and escapes by sea. In their efforts to flee the colony, convicts stowed away on visiting vessels, built their own boats and even hijacked fully rigged ships. Without the assistance of a sympathetic populace or an organised resistance movement, they demonstrated startling determination and enterprise. For them escape was not just a bid for liberty, it was a challenge to authority and an end to the degradation and dangers of transportation.

1

The Girl From Botany Bay

The most successful of the early escapers, and the most celebrated, was undoubtedly Mary Bryant, the heroine of an epic voyage from Sydney to Timor in an open boat. She was born Mary Broad in Fowey, Cornwall, in 1765, the daughter of a mariner. In 1786, at the Exeter Assizes, she was sentenced to death for assaulting a spinster and robbing her of a silk bonnet and other goods valued at eleven guineas. The sentence was commuted to transportation beyond the seas for seven years and she was sent to the prison hulk *Dunkirk* at Plymouth. There she remained until the following year when she was put on board the transport *Charlotte* bound for Botany Bay as part of the First Fleet under the command of Captain Arthur Phillip. According to her prison record she was 5 feet 4 inches (1.63 metres) tall with grey eyes, brown hair and a sallow complexion.

The prospect of exile in an unknown land situated at the ends of the earth was cause enough for fear and despair but Mary had a more immediate concern: she was pregnant, the result of a liaison formed on the *Dunkirk*, probably with a warder. The fleet sailed on 13 May 1787 and four months later the Surgeon-General, John White, noted in his journal, 'Mary Broad, a convict, was delivered of a fine girl'.[1] She was christened Charlotte Spence after the ship. The voyage finally ended for Mary when she stepped ashore at Sydney Cove on 6 February 1788. Four days later she was married to William Bryant, a fellow convict from the *Charlotte*. He, too, was from Cornwall, a 31-year-old fisherman and suspected smuggler. In 1784 he had been sentenced to seven years' transportation for receiving contraband goods and using a false name. Joining them in Australia's first marriage ceremony were four other convict couples, some of whom, remarked Lieutenant Ralph Clark with disgust, had left wives and children back in England. William signed his name in the marriage register but Mary was only able to make her mark.

With the nascent colony desperately short of fresh food, Bryant's skills as a fisherman were put to immediate use. He 'was given the direction and management of such boats as were employed in fishing', recorded Judge-Advocate David Collins.

> Every encouragement was held out to this man to keep him above temptation; an hut was built for him and his family; he was always presented with a certain part of the fish which he caught; and he wanted for nothing that was necessary; or that was suitable to a person of his description and situation.

However, the temptation to take advantage of his privileged position was too great for him to resist. Within a year he was convicted of selling privately some of the fish intended for the Government Store. He received 100 lashes and was ejected from his hut. Yet, Collins wrote:

> as notwithstanding his villainy, he was too useful a person to part with and send to a brick cart, he was still retained to fish for the settlement; but a very vigilant eye was kept over him and such steps taken to prevent him from repeating his offence, if the sense of shame and fear of punishment were not of themselves sufficient to deter him.[3]

For over a year he seems to have avoided trouble as his name does not appear again in the colony's records until April 1790 when he became the father of Mary's second child, Emanuel. By this time the situation of the colonists was becoming desperate. The failure of supply ships to arrive from England had brought the settlement near to starvation. 'Famine,' wrote Captain Watkin Tench of the marines, 'was approaching with gigantic strides, and gloom and dejection overspread every counten-ance.'[4] The weekly food ration was drastically reduced but the pittance each person received was distinctly unappetising. The pork 'had been salted between three and four years, and every grain of rice was a moving body, from the inhabitants lodged within it'.[5] One man collapsed and died outside the storehouse with his daily ration in his hands. When his stomach was opened by the surgeon it was found to be empty. The emotional Ralph Clark, languishing for his wife in distant England, considered that only God could ensure the colony's survival. In these conditions escape for the Bryants and their fellow convicts must have been doubly attractive.

The crisis was relieved, at least temporarily, by the arrival of the Second Fleet in June, carrying plentiful provisions but also another 950 convicts to be fed. In October the storeship *Supply* returned from a voyage to Batavia fully laden with additional provisions and equipment. But the long-term viability of the colony was still in doubt. 'I do not think that all the showers of the last four months put together, would make 24 hours rain,' wrote Tench in November. 'Our farms, what with this poor soil, are in a wretched condition.'[6] For the Bryants nothing had really changed — escape was still the best option.

The arrival of the Dutch trading vessel *Waaksamheyd* in December provided the opportunity. Bryant befriended the captain, Detmer Smit, and from him acquired a chart with navigational notes of the northern passage home as well as a compass, a quadrant, two muskets and quantities of pork and rice. These he carefully secreted under the floorboards of his hut. However, his preparations almost came to nothing when, according to Collins, he was:

> Overheard consulting in his hut after dark, with five other convicts, on the practicability of carrying off the boat in which he was employed. This circumstance being reported to the governor, it was determined that all his proceedings should be narrowly watched, and any scheme of that nature counteracted.[7]

On the following day Bryant's plans were shaken by another mishap. He was returning from a fishing expedition in the governor's six-oared cutter when it was struck by a sudden squall, dismasted and swamped. The occupants had no choice but to swim for the shore. The boat was retrieved by some Aborigines who paddled out in their canoes and towed it into the cove. It was damaged severely enough for Collins to be confident that 'the execution of his [Bryant's] project was for the present prevented'.[8] Doubtless on this score Collins slackened his surveillance of the Bryants but he reckoned without their determination and resourcefulness.

During the early months of 1791, the Bryants and their fellow conspirators continued to accumulate provisions and equipment for the voyage. According to marine Private John Easty they got these 'from time to time by work'.[9] And by theft, it can probably be assumed. It is known that Mary hoarded sarsaparilla leaves, which she collected from a vine that grew prolifically along the rocky foreshores of the harbour. From these the colonists made a variety of tea with a sweet astringent flavour. 'To its virtues,' Tench observed, 'the healthy state of the soldiery and convicts may be greatly attributed. It was drank universally.'[10] In addition to the equipment Bryant had obtained from Captain Smit, he and Mary also managed to acquire in one way or another a seine (fishing net), cooking utensils, 100 pounds of flour, bedding, two tents, carpenter's tools, fishing lines, hooks, nails, rosin and a new set of sails. Bryant also busied himself repairing and overhauling the damaged cutter.

Although Bryant's sentence had recently expired (Mary of course would not be free for another two years), his resolution to escape had not. To be a freed convict in Sydney had little meaning as Private Easty explained:

Thoughts of Liberty from Such a place as this is enoufh to induce any Convicts to try all Skeemes to obtain it as they are the Same as Slaves all the time thay are in this Country allthough thare times are Expired for which thay are Sentanced by Law thare is no difference between them and a Convict that is jest cast for Transportation.[11]

Further motivation for escape, if any were needed, was supplied by Governor Phillip himself who proclaimed that permission to leave the colony would be denied to any freed convict with a dependent wife or children.

According to Collins this measure had been prompted by William Bryant and others frequently stating that they did not consider their colonial marriages to be binding. Holding such a flexible view of his marriage, why, Collins later puzzled, would Bryant want to encumber himself on this perilous enterprise with a woman and two children, one of whom was not his own? It could only be accounted for, he reasoned, 'by a dread of her defeating his plan by discovery if she was not made personally interested in his escape'.[12] Any evidence to support this conjecture is, however, lacking.

The departure of the *Waaksamheyd* had been delayed while her opportunistic captain argued with Governor Phillip over the terms of a charter. Finally, on 28 March 1791, she cleared the Heads bound for England. With the *Supply* already on her way to Norfolk Island there were no vessels left in Port Jackson capable of overhauling a boat once it reached the open sea. The situation was not lost on the Bryants. That night, together with seven compatriots, they stole the governor's cutter and with muffled strokes crept fearfully down the harbour. There was no moon to betray their flight and they ghosted undetected past the lookout on South Head and out into the Pacific.

In such a small, enclosed community, where the only news was local news, it is scarcely believable that no inkling of Bryant's preparations had reached the ears of the authorities. Most of his companions 'were connected with women' who, if they knew anything at all, apparently kept silent. Collins's cynical explanation was that these liaisons were matters of convenience only and 'had the women been bound to them by any ties of affection, fear for their safety, or the dislike to part, might have induced some of them to have defeated the enterprise'.[14] As it was they did not care whether their men stayed or left.

It was not until daylight next morning that the alarm was raised. Sergeant James Scott on duty at the South Head lookout only became aware of the escape when, as he recorded in his journal:

A Serjt. & a party of Marines in the Long boat came to the look Out [Camp] Cove At Six Oclock this Morning in persute of Bryan (a Convict) the principal fisherman (for Government) Who was to fish on the foregoing Night; but on his getting the Boat in readiness to proceed, he has thought propper to put to Sea in order to make his escape.[15]

Investigations got under way and Collins reported that the fugitives had been:

traced from Bryant's hut to the Point [probably Bennelong Point or Mrs Macquarie's Chair] and in the path were found a hand-saw, a scale, and four or five pounds of rice scattered about in different places, which, it was evident they had dropped in their haste. At the Point, where some of the party must have been taken in, a seine belonging to the government was found, which, being too large for Bryant's purpose, he had exchanged for a smaller that he had made for an officer, and which he had from time to time excused himself from completing, and sending home.[16]

Also found was a letter which one of the escapees, a smash-and-grab artist named James Cox, had left for his lover, Sarah Young, affectionately:

conjuring her to give over the pursuit of the vices which, he told her, prevailed in the settlement, leaving to her what little property he did not take with him, and assigning as a reason for his flight the severity of his situation, being transported for life, without the prospect of any mitigation, or hope of ever quitting the country, but by the means he was about to adopt.[17]

Meanwhile the 'desperate adventurers'[18] were steadily steering north for Timor. In addition to the Bryant family and Cox, the other convicts on board were James Martin, who had come out on the *Charlotte* with the Bryants; Samuel Bird (alias John Simms), a stoutly built thief described by Collins as a waterman; William Allen, a 50-year-old shoplifter; red-haired Samuel Broom (alias John Butcher), who had been convicted of stealing pigs; Nathaniel Lilley, a Suffolk weaver-turned-burglar; and William Morton, on a seven-year sentence for obtaining money under false pretences. Of these, Morton, who had served as second mate on an East Indiaman, had some knowledge of navigation, and Bryant, Allen and Bird were experienced sailors. Mary, too, brought up on the harsh, rock-bound coast of Cornwall with a mariner for a father, can be assumed to have known how to handle a boat.

In Collins's estimation 'there was little reason to doubt their reaching Timor, if no dissension prevailed among them, and they had but prudence enough to guard against the natives wherever they might land'.[19] Private Easty had a less sanguine, and rather more realistic, view of their chances. 'Its a very Desparate attempt,' he confided to his journal, 'to go in an open Boat for a run of about 16 or 17 hundred Leags and in pertucalar for a woman and 2 Small Children the oldest not above 3 years of age.'[20]

The only extant first-hand account of their voyage is the *Memorandoms* by James Martin, written after his return to England. William Bryant also wrote a journal, but unfortunately its whereabouts are a mystery. When, in October 1792, Captain William Bligh visited Timor in the *Providence* during his second breadfruit voyage, he was shown the journal by the governor. 'This journal,' wrote Bligh in his log book, 'was very distinctly kept and titled Rem[ark]s on a Voyage from Sydney Cove New South Wales to Timor.'[21] In his opinion 'the writer must have been a determined and enterprising Man'. He arranged for a copy to be made, but with time running out his copyist 'did not get a fourth part through it'. All that remains is Bligh's own brief summary and a few quotations which he entered into his log. Martin's narrative is spare and un-emotional. It is uncluttered with personal references and, like Bryant's, 'the latitude and distances run are not regularly kept up so as to ascertain the different places they stopt at'.[22]

After coasting for two days Martin recorded that they put into 'a little Creek about 2 Degrees to they Northward of Port Jackson'[23] where they found coal. Bryant wrote that:

> Walking along shore towards the entrance of the Creek we found several large pieces of Coal — seeing so many pieces we thought it was not unlikely to find a Mine, and searching about a little, we found a place where we picked up with an ax as good Coals as any in England — took some to the fire and they burned exceedingly well.[24]

According to Bryant, 'it was with difficulty he got the boat into the creek, there being shoal water across it, but he tacked the Boat in without receiving any damage'. In all likelihood this was the mouth of Glenrock Lagoon just south of Newcastle, and to the Bryants and their companions can be attributed the discovery of coal in Australia. They camped there for two nights, feasting on cabbage trees which grew abundantly and 'avarse Quantity of fish which [was] of great Refreshment to us'. At some stage they were visited by a group of curious Aborigines who were given 'some cloathes and other articles and they went away very much satisfied'.

A further two days' sail to the north brought them to 'a very fine Harbour Seeming to run up they Country for Many miles and Quite Comodious for they Anchorage of Shipping'. This description fits well with Port Stephens and in Bryant's opinion it was superior to Port Jackson. They beached the boat 'to repair her Bottom being very leaky'. While some of them commenced work caulking the seams with rosin and beeswax, the others replenished the water supply. Their work was interrupted by a band of hostile Aborigines 'which meant to Destroy us'. Retreating to the boat they hastily launched it and rowed hard until they were out of spear range. Another attempted landing lower down the harbour next day was also foiled 'by natives in Vase Numbers with Speers and Sheilds'. Martin and several others attempted 'by signes to pasify them' and when this failed they tried firing a musket over their heads. The effect of this, however, was to anger the Aborigines whose hitherto threatening behaviour now showed signs of boiling over into violent action. Once again the fugitives were forced to pull hurriedly out into the middle of the harbour.

Having been twice frustrated in their attempts to repair the cutter they decided to move further up the harbour in the hope of outdistancing their assailants. After covering 15 or 16 kilometres, they landed on a small sandy island. Here they stayed for two days and were able to complete the repairs without further interference. Growing in confidence they made a foray to the mainland to fill the water cask and collect more cabbage tree leaves before putting to sea again.

Continuing to hug the coast they made good time, favoured by a lively south-westerly breeze. But that night a strong offshore wind drove them far out to sea. When they finally beat back to within sight of the coast they were prevented from landing by huge surf and 'Making no harbour or Creek for nere three weeks we were much Distressed for water and wood'. In desperation the boat was anchored beyond the breakers while two of the men swam ashore with the water cask. Before they could fill it they were spotted by Aborigines and, fearing for their lives, returned empty-handed. Finally, with the boat leaking so badly that they could scarcely keep her above water, they managed to creep inshore and make a landing in a small river.

The leaking seams were plugged satisfactorily with soap but they 'could get no Shell Fish or Fish of any kind' and were forced to put to sea again after only a short stay.

They made about 30 kilometres before the wind strengthened and the seas rose. Tall black waves leaned over them as they struggled to stay afloat. The boat began to fill and they were obliged to throw their spare clothing overboard to lighten it. That night they ran into an 'Open Bay' but with the surf still running high they decided to anchor beyond the line of breakers and attempt a landing in the morning. At two o'clock, the anchor cable snapped and they were swept helplessly into 'the Middle of the Surf Expecting every Moment that our boat wou'd be Staved to Pieces and every Soul Perish'. The men laid down their oars in despair and gave themselves up for lost. But Mary snatched up a hat and began to bail. Shamed by her example the men pulled themselves together and 'got our boat save on Shore without any Loss or damage excepting one Oar'. This time they were overjoyed to discover fresh water and plenty of shellfish. A large band of Aborigines who threatened them was easily dispersed by musket fire.

Their next landing was 'White Bay being in Lattd 27d 00', probably Moreton Bay, which they reached after a rough three days during which the cutter shipped 'many heavy Seas, so that One Man was always employed in Bailing out the Water to keep her up'. They ran down the bay for 7 or 8 kilometres until they found a safe place to land. For two days they enjoyed a respite, gathering their strength for the next leg of the voyage. The inevitable band of Aborigines made an appearance but a single musket shot drove them back into the bush.

On leaving, they were swept out to sea by a gale:

The Sea running Mountains high we were Under a Close reeft Mainsail and kept so untill Night and then came too under a droge [sea anchor] all the Night with her Head to the Sea thinking every moment to be the last, the sea Coming in so heavy upon us every now and then that two hands were Obliged to keep Bailing out and it rained very hard all that Night the next Morng we took our droge in but could see no Land but Hawling towards the Land to make it as soon as possible the Gale of Wind still Continuing we kept under Close reeft mainsail but could make no Land all that day — I will Leave you to Consider what distress we must be in, the Woman and the two little babies was in a bad Condition, everything being so Wet that we Cou'd by, no Means light a Fire, we had nothing to Eat except a little raw rice.

Their ordeal came to an end when they made a hazardous landing on a small coral island '30 leagues from the Main'. (From Martin's description and his estimated latitude of '26d 27m' it seems likely that this was Lady Elliot Island.) There was no fresh water to be found but while exploring a reef they came upon some turtles, one of which they killed and that night enjoyed 'a Noble Meal'. During the night it rained and by spreading out the mainsail they were able to collect two kegs of water. They supplemented their diet with a kind of fruit they found growing there 'like unto a Bellpepper which seemed to taste very well' and there was also 'a great Quantity of Fowls which stayed at night in Holes in the ground'. They remained six days and when they left were well provided with dried turtle meat.

Proceeding cautiously northwards they put in at numerous islands. Fresh water was plentiful but no more turtles were seen and edible shellfish were scarce. 'Being very Hungred' they eventually rounded Cape York, only to face further danger in the Gulf of Carpentaria. Following the coast south for 15 or 16 kilometres they came to a group of islands. As they steered towards one of them, two canoes put off from the beach, each containing a native 'very Stout and fat and Blacker' than any they had so far seen. When the fugitives approached them 'they seemed to stand in a posture of defence against us'. They fired a musket in the air, but far from being frightened, the natives each produced a bow and arrows and began firing at the cutter. Most of the arrows ('about Eighteen Inches long') fell short and no-one was hit. They immediately sheered away, hoisted the sails and left the canoes behind. From Martin's account it would appear that their assailants were Torres Strait Islanders rather than mainland Aborigines.

Shaken by this encounter they pushed further south, and being gravely in need of water they decided to attempt another landing. Once ashore they had no difficulty in filling their water casks but dared not risk the possibility of another attack by staying there. Instead they spent the night riding at anchor 5 or 6 kilometres out in the gulf. Morning brought them renewed confidence and they determined to return to the same place for more water. It was a mistake. As they approached the shore two large canoes appeared bearing down on them fast. 'We were Afraid to meet them,' wrote Martin.

> There seemed to us to be 30 or 40 Men in each Canoe, they had Sails in their Canoes seemed to be made of Matting, one of their Canoes was a Head of the others a little Way Stopt untill the other Came up and then she Hoisted her Sails and made after us, as soon as we saw that we Tack'd about with what Water we had — Detirmined to Cross the Gulf which was about five Hundred Miles Across which as God wou'd have it we Out run them, they followed us untill we Lost sight of them.

To elude these people, known for their ferocity and seamanship, was a considerable feat. A year later Lieutenant George Tobin, while exploring in the *Providence*'s cutter, was the object of a similar attack by Torres Strait headhunters in canoes he described as being 35 to 50 feet (11 to 15 metres) long, with an outrigger on each side and a kind of fighting platform on which was erected a low barricade. Unlike the Bryants he could not outsail them and it was only a destructive musket volley from his well-armed crew that allowed the cutter to escape.

It took the escapees four days to cross the gulf. Then from the shores of Arnhem Land, where they replenished their supplies, they moved out into the Arafura Sea for the final run of 800 kilometres to Timor. On 5 June they finally sighted their destination and after sailing along the southern coast of the island put into the Dutch settlement of Koepang. It was ten weeks, less a day, since they had stolen apprehensively through Sydney Heads, and in Bryant's opinion Mary and the children had borne 'their sufferings with more fortitude than most among them'. They had covered over 5000 kilometres in a voyage which, as a feat of navigation, endurance and survival, ranks with Captain Bligh's celebrated open-boat voyage across the Pacific to Timor in 1789 after he had been cast adrift by the *Bounty* mutineers. Indeed it is probable that the Bryants actually gained inspiration from Bligh's achievement for their own desperate venture. In December 1789 Bligh had written from Koepang to Governor Phillip in Sydney giving him an account of the mutiny, and this remarkable story would have flowed rapidly throughout that isolated, news-impoverished colony.

When the Bryants and their companions stepped ashore they found themselves in a settlement:

> of no great extent but its situation remarkably pleasant, a fine stream on whose banks are the Mangoe plantain, Breadfruit, Cocoa-nut and other trees, running through the town. A Fort of no great strength but in good repair, commands the mouth of the river. Including military, the Dutch inhabitants did not reach an hundred.[25]

To the exhausted and half-starved fugitives it must have seemed as though they had fetched up in paradise. According to Bryant he passed himself off as the 'Mate of a Whale Fisher that was lost, and in which all but themselves perished'.[26] The governor, Timotheus Wanjon, readily accepted this tale. 'We went on Shore to the Governors house,' wrote Martin, 'where he behaved extremely well to us, filled our Bellies and Cloathed Double with every that was wore on the Island.' This was the second boatload of distressed Englishmen that the 'worthy' Mynheer Wanjon had welcomed in recent years (Bligh was the first); within a short time there would be a third, with disastrous consequences for the convicts.

Meanwhile they happily reacquainted themselves with civilisation. They obtained work of some sort and no doubt enjoyed whatever limited social amenities Koepang offered. They financed themselves by impudently drawing bills on the British Government and were well supplied with everything they needed. Two months passed and then something unaccountable happened. In Martin's words, 'Wm Bryant had words With his wife, went and informed against himself Wife and Children and all of us which we was immediately taken Prisoners and was put into the Castle.' That Bryant would deliberately place his family and himself in jeopardy in this way is scarcely believable. His own version of the facts, as reported by Bligh, is as follows: 'one of the party informed through peek at not being taken so much notice of as the rest'.[27] It is unlikely that the full truth will ever be retrieved. Indeed there are several other versions of what happened. David Collins, relying on information from the 'Calcutta papers', stated that 'by their language to each other, and by practising the tricks of their former profession, gave room for suspicion; and being taken up, their true characters and the circumstances of their escape were divulged'.[28] A more reliable source was Watkin Tench, who had his information from the escapees themselves when he met up with them seven months later. 'Their behaviour giving rise to suspicion, they were watched; and one of them at last, in a moment of intoxication, betrayed the secret.'[29] Here perhaps lies a kernel of truth: whatever the mechanics of the betrayal, it may well have been generated by an overindulgence of rum.[30]

Prison conditions at Koepang under the genial governor were a far cry from the hulks of England. 'After been Examined,' wrote Martin, 'we were allowed to Go out of the Castle 2 at a time for one Day and the next Day 2 more and so we continued.' Confinement, however, even of this limited nature, was calamitous and within weeks their situation would worsen.

On 17 September the Arafura Sea disgorged another lot of stray English seamen in open boats. In command was Captain Edward Edwards, who had sailed from England in November the previous year under orders to seek out and arrest the *Bounty* mutineers. He succeeded in wrenching fourteen of them from their sanctuary on Tahiti, but during the return voyage his ship, HMS *Pandora*, foundered on the Great Barrier Reef. The survivors, 99 in all, including ten mutineers, scrambled into the ship's boats and in the wake of Bligh and the Bryants passed through the Endeavour Straits and on to Timor.

Governor Wanjon received them with his usual generous hospitality and informed Edwards of the English prisoners he was holding in the castle. Under Edwards's interrogation they confessed. 'We told him we was Convicts,' wrote Martin, 'and had made our Escape from Botany Bay which he told us we was his prisoners.' They were joined in the castle by the mutineers and remained there until 5 October when they were embarked on the *Rembang*, a Dutch vessel Edwards had chartered to convey them and the *Pandora* survivors to Batavia (present-day Jakarta). 'The Botany Bay men were also brought on board by a party of Dutch Soldiers and put in Irons with us in the same manner,' wrote James Morrison,[31] one of the mutineers. Martin made particular mention of the irons, describing them as 'bilboes', a long iron bar fastened to the floor with sliding shackles for the ankles.

According to Morrison, the ship leaked so badly that the prisoners were released two at a time to work the pumps in two-hour shifts. Six days out from Koepang they were overtaken by a tremendous storm. 'In a few minutes every sail of the ship was shivered to pieces,' wrote Surgeon George Hamilton.

> The pumps all choked, and useless; the leak gaining fast upon us; and she was driving down, with all the impetuosity imaginable, on a savage shore, about seven miles under our lee. This storm was attended with the most dreadful thunder and lightning we had ever experienced. The Dutch seamen were struck with horror, and went below; and the ship was preserved from destruction by the manly efforts of our English tars.[32]

On 7 November the *Rembang* lurched into Batavia. While Edwards was arranging transport to England the mutineers and convicts were detained on an old Dutch hulk lying in the harbour. 'We remained here till 23 of December,' complained Morrison, 'during which time we were permitted to come on Deck, but twice, each for about half an hour at a Time to Wash ourselves.' What seemed cruelty was in fact an unintended favour as Morrison himself acknowledged: 'yet we enjoyd our Health, tho the *Pandora*s people [who could go ashore] fell sick and died apace'.[33]

In 1770 Captain Cook had warned of Batavia's 'unwholesome air', which he claimed 'is the death of more Europeans than any other place upon the globe',[34] and twenty years later nothing had changed. Morrison observed that the river which fed the city's canals and then emptied into the harbour teemed 'with such filfth that the Road where the large Ships lye is little better than a Stagnate Pool'. The prisoners were allowed to smoke tobacco and it was his belief that this 'freed us from headachs &ca, which we supposed to be occasioned by the pestilential Vapours'.[35] Surgeon Hamilton was in complete agreement. In his professional opinion 'all the mortality of that place originates from marsh effluvia, arising from their stagnant canals and pleasure grounds'. In this disease-ridden port, this 'golgotha of Europe',[36] the chances of all the prisoners being spared were slight, and so it proved. In December William Bryant and little Emanuel succumbed to the 'unwholesome air' and died. The sick had all been removed to the Dutch hospital and it was there that father and son spent their last days, comforted, one hopes, by Mary.

Captain Edwards succeeded in procuring passage on four ships for the homeward voyage. Mary, Charlotte, William Allen and probably James Cox were assigned to the *Horssen* while the remainder of their companions sailed on the *Hoornwey*. On Edwards's instructions all the prisoners were to be kept below in irons, only coming up on deck briefly for exercise. For Hamilton the voyage was 'tedious', not quite the word the convicts and mutineers would have chosen to describe their own experiences. 'Our lodgings were none of the Best,' wrote Morrison,

> as we lay on rough logs of Timber, some of which lay Some inches above the rest and which our small portion of Cloathing would not bring to a level, the Deck also over us was very leaky, by which means we were continually wet, being alternatively drenched with Salt water, the Urine of Hogs or the rain which happened to fall.[37]

To make matters worse Batavia fever had followed them on board and there was 'great death and sickness'. Two of the victims it carried off were William Morton, the man whose navigational skills had got the escapees to Timor, and Samuel Bird. And then while passing through the Straits of Sunda, James Cox disappeared overboard. Hamilton reported that he 'jumped over board in the middle of the night, and swam to the Dutch arsenal of Honroost'.[38] Martin remarked simply that he died.

When Edwards sailed into Cape Town in March 1792 he found a British man-o'-war, HMS *Gorgon*, anchored there. At once he determined 'on account both of expedition and greater security ... to remove the pirates late belonging to His majesty's armed vessel, the *Bounty*, and the convicts, deserters from Port Jackson into His Majesty's said ship'.[39] When the convicts were transferred to her later in the month they were surprised to discover on board the marine detachment from Sydney which was returning to England after being relieved by the newly formed New South Wales Corps. 'We was known well by all the marine officers,' declared Martin happily, 'which was all Glad that we had not perished at sea.' Among the familiar faces was the sympathetic Watkin Tench. 'I confess that I never looked upon these people, without pity and astonishment,' he enthused.

> They had miscarried in a heroic struggle for liberty; after having combated every hardship, and conquered every difficulty. The woman, and one of the men, had gone out to Port Jackson in the ship which had transported me thither. They had both of them been

always distinguished for good behaviour. And I could not but reflect with admiration, at the strange combination of circumstances which had again brought us together, to baffle human foresight, and confound human speculation.[40]

The *Gorgon* put to sea early in April. Her commander, Captain John Parker, showed himself to be a more humane man than Edwards, whose cruelty towards his prisoners has few apologists. 'Our treatment became less rigourous,' observed Morrison with satisfaction, 'and 2/3rds Allowance of Provisions was now thought feasting ... only one leg in Irons and every Indulgence Given.'[41] However, before the convicts reached England another name was added to the mournful list of fatalities. On 6 May Lieutenant Ralph Clark noted in his journal:

> Squaly weather with a great dele of Rain all this day. Last night the child belonging to Mary Broad, the convict woman who went away in the fishing boat from P. Jackson last year, died about four o'clock. Committed the body to the deep.[42]

On 18 June 1792 the *Gorgon* arrived in Portsmouth. For the five remaining fugitives the long voyage which had commenced at Sydney fifteen months previously was over. They had survived storms, starvation, headhunters, treacherous waters and fever only to return home still prisoners. At the end of the month they were brought before a magistrate at the Public Office in Bow Street, London. They were committed to Newgate for trial but not before

> it was remarked by every person present, and by the magistrate, that they never saw people who bore stronger marks of a sincere repentence, and all joined in the wish that their past sufferings may be considered as a sufficient expiation of their crimes.[43]

The prisoners responded by declaring that 'they would sooner suffer death than return to Botany Bay'.[44]

On 7 July they appeared at the Old Bailey and were ordered 'to remain on their former sentence until they should be discharged by due course of law'.[45] They were extremely fortunate to avoid the hangman, as the usual penalty for escapees from transportation was death. The government's policy, according to Evan Nepean, the Under-secretary of the Home Office, was that it 'would not treat them with harshness, but, at the same time, would not do a kind thing to them, as they might give encouragement to others to escape'.[46] They were returned to Newgate facing an indefinite term of imprisonment, but as they told a reporter, 'the prison [was] a paradise, compared with the dreadful sufferings they endured on their voyage'.[47]

The story of 'The Girl from Botany Bay' received enthusiastic coverage from the press. 'The resolution displayed by the woman is hardly to be paralleled in the annals of ancient Rome,' trumpeted the *London Chronicle*.[48] The *Dublin Chronicle* called the escape 'perhaps the most hazardous and wonderful effort ever made by nine persons (for two were infants) to regain their liberty',[49] while the *Birmingham Gazette* considered it 'miraculous'.

One man who agreed with the *London Chronicle* that 'His Majesty who is ever willing to extend his mercy surely never had objects more worthy of it'[50] was James Boswell, the great biographer and friend of Samuel Johnson. In the summer of 1792 he was a practising lawyer with an absorbing fondness for the bottle and a sincere interest in poor, undefended criminals. Acting promptly he visited Newgate and interviewed the five returned convicts. Then presuming on a former friendship he petitioned Henry Dundas, the Secretary of State for Home Affairs, for clemency for 'the unfortunate adventurers from New South Wales'. Dundas replied with a promise to duly consider the matter.

Apparently the Home Secretary's considerations were a long, weighty process, for it was not until the following year that he reached a conclusion. On 2 May 1793, six weeks after Mary's original sentence had expired, Dundas signed an unconditional pardon authorising 'Mary Bryant otherwise

Broad' to be 'forthwith discharged out of custody'. After her release Mary settled in London in lodgings paid for by the kindly Boswell. He also invited his friends to assist her and in at least one case was successful. The former Lord Chancellor, Lord Thurlow, although at first reluctant – 'Damn her blood, let her go to a day's work',[51] was his initial response – finally agreed to help her. Boswell was a regular visitor at Mary's place and on one occasion he was introduced to her sister Dolly, who was in service as a cook: 'A very fine, sensible young, woman,' whose tenderness towards her sister impressed him so much that the warm-hearted man resolved to 'get her a place more fit for her.'[52]

Despite his continuing concern for Mary, Boswell had not forgotten her four companions still languishing in Newgate. He went to see them in mid-August 'to assure them personally that I was doing all in my power for them'.[53] And indeed he was. He peppered Evan Nepean with letters urging clemency and called repeatedly at his office only to be told that the great man was either too busy to see him or was away. He even sought out Governor Phillip, who had recently returned to England, in the hope that he might be an advocate for them. One of the convicts, Samuel Broom, made an attempt to effect his own release. He wrote to the Home Secretary asking to be sent back to New South Wales where, he claimed, his knowledge of agriculture would be very useful. Unfortunately the authorities did not agree.

Meanwhile it was decided that Mary should return home to her family in Fowey. Boswell made all the arrangements and paid for her passage on the *Ann and Elizabeth*. On 12 October he accompanied her in a hackney coach to the wharf at Southwark where she was to embark. He remained with her for two hours, first in the kitchen of a tavern on the wharf and then in the public bar where they shared a bowl of punch with the landlord and the captain of the *Ann and Elizabeth*. Mary was depressed and unsure of her welcome at home and 'to make her mind easy' Boswell, in a typically generous gesture, 'assured her of ten pounds yearly as long as she behaved well'. He then 'saw her fairly into her cabin, and bid adieu to her with sincere good will'.[54] For the former convict and her benefactor it was a final farewell, and with her return to Cornwall Mary slipped quietly from history's grasp.

Boswell was a dedicated womaniser, and inevitably his relationship with Mary had become a subject of ribald interest among his intimates. One of them, William Parsons, composed a poem called 'A Heroic Epistle from Mary Broad in Cornwall to James Boswell, Esq., in London', in which she is represented as pining away in a second exile, bemoaning her separation from Boswell, her true love. Far better, she proclaims extravagantly, to have:

> stayed, the willing prey
> Of grief and famine in the direful bay!
> Or perished, whelmed in the Atlantic tide!
> Or, home returned, in air suspended died![55]

However, there is no evidence to support the poet's salacious contention that Boswell's involvement with Mary was anything other than altruism and friendship.

Boswell's efforts on behalf of the four convicts still 'miserable in Newgate' were eventually rewarded. On 2 November he returned home to his dinner to find them waiting at his doorstep. They had been released that day by proclamation. After thanking Boswell they too disappeared from his world.

2

Into the Blue

As Sydney, with its deep-water harbour, developed from an isolated gaol into an important Pacific trading centre, more opportunities for leaving the colony illegally by sea opened up. Bluff American and British whaling captains, coming in for repairs and provisions, were not averse to replacing sick and injured crewmen with willing runaways. On 9 November 1794 the *Resolution* left Sydney on a whaling voyage but was observed the next day hovering about the coast — waiting, as it turned out, to pick up a boatload of convicts. 'The impropriety of the conduct of the *Resolution*'s master,' thundered Judge-Advocate David Collins, 'was so glaring there was not any doubt of his having received on board, without permission, to the number of twelve or thirteen convicts whose term of transportation had not been served. To take clandestinely from the settlement the useful servants of the public was ungrateful and unpardonable.'[1] But he raged in vain. To the tough, lawless whalers, such sentiments were laughable, and convicts continued to be absorbed into their crews as required. Governor William Bligh was able to report in 1807 that there had been some abatement in the 'practice of Merchant Ships taking Prisoners', but he did add that 'it still exists when opportunity offers'.[2]

When the American brig *General Gates* sailed from Sydney in July 1819 there were eleven convicts on board, 'all good mechanics',[3] illegally procured by the master, Captain

Abimelech Riggs. One of the convicts described how he was wrapped up in a sail and hidden in the hold within the forecastle bulkhead, which was then nailed up. The other convicts were concealed on the opposite side of the hold behind rows of bread casks. At risk was a bond of £500, but Riggs had made careful preparations. Because the ship was carrying a cargo of gunpowder she was not smoked — by then a common procedure for forcing stowaways out of hiding. Nor was she searched, an omission that smelt strongly of collusion between Riggs and the chief constable. In fact, Reverend Samuel Marsden, who was a passenger on the brig, saw the police boat in the harbour and was surprised that it kept well away. The *General Gates* headed for New Zealand, where Riggs indulged in some gun-running to the Maoris. As part of the deal he offered to sell them two of the convicts, skilled in repairing firearms, in return for supplies of pigs, potatoes and wood. Eventually Riggs was arrested, brought back to Sydney and fined £6500, which included £500 for each convict.[4]

The majority of convicts who escaped from the colony by sea did so as stowaways, sometimes with the assistance of sympathetic seamen, a practice which, Governor Phillip was forced to admit to Under-secretary Evan Nepean in 1791, 'cannot be prevented by any steps which can be taken at present'.[5] When the *Endeavour* sailed from Sydney for India on 18 March 1795 an astonishing 50 runaways were secreted on board.[6] A year earlier, the *Indispensable* was a day or two out of Sydney when a passenger found a convict lurking in his cabin. Three weeks later another one was flushed from the hold, where, it was suspected, he had been concealed by the boatswain.

The escape of four convicts from Norfolk Island in the South Sea whaler *New Zealander* without her captain's knowledge prompted Governor Lachlan Macquarie to warn Earl Bathurst in 1813 that:

the facility with which convicts may effect their Escape by Means of Shipping from any of the frequented Harbours of this Colony or its

Dependencies, Notwithstanding every Exertion to prevent it, is Still so great that Unless Measures are adopted at Home to terrify these Fugitives from revisiting their Native Country in this Manner, by Stealth, such Desertions will become every day more frequent, as the Commerce and Shipping increase, and it will be a Serious Evil unless speedily Checked.[7]

Macquarie's pessimistic forecast was well founded. Writing in 1827, Surgeon Peter Cunningham, veteran of five voyages to Australia, observed that:

a somewhat considerable number of convicts escape annually by concealing themselves in vessels about to sail from the colony ... Sometimes these people are concealed by the master to be useful to him on his voyage; but occasionally they slip on board, stow themselves away there, and slip on shore in like manner at the end of the voyage, without a single individual ever knowing that they had been in the vessel.[8]

The *Dromedary*, on a return passage to England from Sydney in 1821, was within a few weeks' sail of the English coast when a soldier happened to glance down through the main-hatchway gratings one morning and notice a man he had never seen before, pacing the deck below. When the stranger became aware that he was being watched, he coolly asked the soldier to pass him down a glass of water. The soldier was nonplussed but still reported the matter to the captain. At first he was laughed at, but when he persevered with his story a search of the ship was made and a scrawny figure bundled in rags was dragged out by the heels from under a pile of planks. On being questioned as to how he had survived the long voyage, the man said, 'We suffered much for want of water for some time at first; but always had plenty of prog.'[9] As he continued to use the word 'we' it was put to him that he was not alone. This he strenuously denied, explaining with admirable quick-wittedness that it was just the way people from his part of England spoke. Despite the plausibility of this explanation, the ship was searched again and a second runaway was hauled out. It turned out that the first man had only been spotted because he had become overconfident after drinking the contents of a cask of rum.

One convict who successfully stowed away left an anonymous account of his experiences in the form of an undated and unsigned petition [10] written in the hope of saving his life and avoiding re-transportation. It was probably addressed to Lord Denman, Lord Chief Justice of England, as it is associated with a letter to him dated 18 August 1844. The document has no addressee or signature, and has several insertions and one deletion in the text, suggesting that it was a draft.

The convict began his tale by relating how he was transported to Sydney for burglary (for which he wisely said he blamed neither the judge nor the jury), and how he spent more than four years cutting wood in the bush where 'the least murmur brought us to the triangle and the lash'. Conditions were so insufferable that he resolved to abscond. Together with another convict, named Mahony, he slipped away during the night to Botany Bay, where he and his companion lay concealed among some rocks. At daybreak they spotted a ship lying offshore. 'We determined to swim to her,' stated the convict in his petition. 'We reached her, climbed by a line to which some pork was hanging, into the hold and I hid myself in a water cask.' After a while they heard the sound of a tarpaulin being hauled across the deck. This plunged them into a state of fright, for Mahony believed the crew was about to smoke the ship. However, their fears were groundless, and for twelve days they remained in the hold, existing solely on a handful of mouldy biscuits. Eventually they were discovered. Fainting and half-starved, they were dragged before the captain, who appeared to accept their claim that they were not escaped convicts. 'Being acquainted with naval matters,' explained the convict, 'I took the helm and got the favour of the sailors, but at night I heard with despair the order "about ship" for I knew we were to be taken back again.' Knowing that the perils of Norfolk Island awaited them, they preferred to take their chances in the sea and jumped overboard, even though it was night and they were several miles from an unknown shore.

After they had swum for some time, with Mahony barely managing to stay afloat, they had the extraordinary good fortune to come across an upturned canoe. This they righted and clambered aboard, and eventually they were washed up on an island – possibly one of the Fijian group. At dawn they were discovered by a band of natives, and when Mahony showed some fight he was dragged off. In the fracas our anonymous protagonist was wounded in the shoulder by a poisoned spear, but according to the narrative was rescued by a native woman who had apparently succumbed to his charms. He wrote:

> The woman stayed with me, she was the sister of the Chief one day her Brother came down upon me in anger and raised his tomahawk, his sister saved my life for she snatched it from his hand and threw it away. She took me to a grove of trees and there showed me poor Mahony's dead body They had eaten most of the flesh from his bones. I buried him and felt that I was performing a good action ... I was informed by the woman by signs that her tribe would kill me for I had buried Mahony on ground consecrated to their chiefs.

With the woman's help he fled in a canoe to another island. Here he lived alone, sustained by fish brought to him on occasional visits by the woman. Eventually he was picked up by a French ship and landed at Tahiti, from where he took passage for Liverpool. Unable to find any work, and faced with the prospect of starving, he joined a ship bound for Quebec. There he was paid off and was on the point of joining HMS *Buffalo* when he learned that she was bound for New South Wales with Canadian rebels who had been sentenced to transportation for life for their involvement in armed uprisings against the British colonial government. Not daring to venture where he would almost certainly be recognised, he shipped on board a merchantman sailing for Hull. Ironically, at Manchester, while on his way to Liverpool in a second attempt to seek employment, he was recognised and detained by the police.

The convict concluded his petition with an extravagant yet pitiful plea — designed, no doubt, as a final attempt to catch the Chief Justice's sympathy:

> Now my lord I beg your mercy. Do not for the sake of God send me back to that dreadful land where chains and darkness must be my lot. Condemn me to death, with a few hours preparation I shall die peacefully. Sentence me to be hanged rather than go back to live like a dog and to die like a dog.

Whether this plea was successful is unknown, as the convict's fate is unrecorded.

Pirating a large vessel and escaping to sea was another option for the more ambitious and desperate convicts, and the first such attempt occurred in 1797 with the seizure of the *Cumberland*. This vessel, rated by Governor John Hunter as 'our largest and best boat, belonging to Government',[11] was in Broken Bay delivering stores to the Hawkesbury River settlements when she was hijacked by some of her convict crew in collaboration with a party who rowed out from the shore. They threatened the coxswain with death, then landed him, and three others who were unwilling to accompany them, in Pittwater before sailing out past Barrenjoey Head into the Pacific. Meanwhile, the stranded men made their way overland to Sydney and raised the alarm. Governor Hunter dispatched two whaleboats in pursuit, each of them crammed with well-armed men, one northward along the coast and the other south. Both returned without finding any trace of the fugitives. However, the first, under Lieutenant John Shortland, did derive some benefit from the fruitless chase. He went as far as Port Stephens, 96 kilometres to the north, and on the return voyage put in to the Hunter River where, like Mary and William Bryant before him, he came across deposits of coal lying near the shore — a discovery that would later reap huge financial benefits to the country.

Following the successful seizure of the *Cumberland*, convicts became emboldened and ships began disappearing from ports along the eastern seaboard with increasing frequency. The second vessel to be spirited away was the sloop *Norfolk*. Originally one of the longboats of HMS *Sirius*, she had survived the wrecking of the First Fleet's flagship on Norfolk Island in 1790 and, on the orders of the lieutenant-governor, had been decked over (using local pine) and rigged as a sloop. Eight years later she became famous as the ship in which Matthew Flinders and George Bass circumnavigated Van Diemen's Land. In 1800, while returning to Sydney from the Hawkesbury with a cargo of wheat, the *Norfolk* was seized by fifteen convicts. Their intention was to sail her to a Dutch settlement among the Moluccas, but she ran aground on the coast north of Sydney and was lost, thus ending her short colonial life. The convicts managed to get ashore, and stole a small boat lying in the Hunter River. They had not got very far, however, when they were overtaken by a boat that had been sent in pursuit by Governor King. Nine of the escapees were recaptured and brought back to Sydney. Two of them were executed and the other seven received life sentences.

In May 1808 the brig *Harrington* was moored in Sydney Harbour when she was boarded by more than 50 escaping convicts. This vessel had arrived in Sydney at the end of March with a curious history of privateering and intrigue behind her. Originally owned by Chace, Chinnery & Company, Merchants of India, the *Harrington* carried thirteen guns and had been provided with letters of marque from Lord William Bentinck, Governor of Fort St George, for a voyage to South America. The letters of marque gave her captain, a resourceful Pacific trader named William Campbell, authority to seize ships belonging to France and Holland, with whom England was then at war. However, off the coast of Peru, Campbell, in cavalier disregard of this restriction, attacked and captured two Spanish vessels: the merchant brig the *St Francisco and*

St Paulo, and the cruiser *Estramina*. The crew of the brig was put ashore, while the *Estramina*, outgunned in a brisk engagement, was run aground and set ablaze. The *Harrington*'s crew managed to extinguish the fire and the cruiser was got off.

The *Harrington* sailed to Sydney in March 1805 by way of Tahiti and Norfolk Island with a cargo of copper 'pigs' taken out of Guasco. Campbell made no mention of his privateering exploits, and to all appearances he had completed a successful trading voyage. He was about to sail for Madras when Governor King received a report that a strange vessel was lurking in Jervis Bay, about 160 kilometres south of Sydney. It turned out to be the *Estramina* flying British colours, and on King's orders she was brought to Sydney under escort. Campbell had no qualms in immediately claiming her as his prize, stating that before reaching the South American coast he had been informed by American sealers that Spain and England were at war. While these claims were being investigated, news came that another mysterious vessel had been sighted hovering off the coast of Van Diemen's Land. This ship was also brought to Sydney and proved to be the *St Francisco and St Paulo*. It seemed that Campbell, having learned at Norfolk Island that England and Spain were not actually at war, had sent his prizes south to wait for him while he revictualed the *Harrington* before escorting them to Madras.

Governor King gave orders for the *Harrington* to be detained while he attempted to get to the bottom of Campbell's machinations. Her topmasts were struck, her rudder removed and she was placed under armed guard. The investigations dragged on until the following year, when news was received that hostilities had finally broken out between England and Spain. This was good enough for King, who declared that the matter was now resolved. He claimed the two ships as lawful prizes of war and sold them at auction on behalf of the Admiralty. Meanwhile, Chace, Chinnery & Company had failed, and in March 1807 Campbell was directed to return to

Madras for the benefit of the company's creditors. Instead, having entered into an agreement with the opportunistic pastoralist and businessman John Macarthur, Campbell sailed to Fiji where he picked up a cargo of sandalwood. He traded this in China for another valuable cargo, which he brought to Sydney, arriving on 30 March 1808. By this time the colony had been shaken by the overthrow of the new governor, William Bligh, who had replaced King. Government was in the hands of the military, closely advised by Macarthur, who had been appointed colonial secretary and would make a handsome profit from the sale of the *Harrington*'s cargo.

The *Harrington* dropped anchor just outside Farm Cove and within sight of Campbell's harbourside residence. For over a month she lay there while she was fitted out for another voyage to Fiji. The night of Sunday 16 May was no different from any other. Few people were abroad, and in the darkness no-one noticed several boats rowing silently out from the shore. They came alongside the *Harrington* and a 'body of desperadoes'[12] swept over the bulwark and down the companionway. The chief officer, Mr Fisk, was asleep in his cabin but awoke suddenly to find two men standing beside his bunk, one of them holding a pistol to his head. The rest of the crew was confined in the steerage by men armed with firelocks, which they banged in menacing fashion on the deck. The convicts cut the anchor cables and towed the brig cautiously down the harbour, past the South Head lookout and out to sea. At the wheel was William Jackson, a short, stout seaman who had been discharged from the *Harrington* 'on account of his repeated depredations against his shipmates'.[13] For some days he had been observed hanging around the waterfront; he had clearly thrown in his lot with the convicts, no doubt having provided them with useful information about the brig. When the *Harrington* was about 30 kilometres offshore, Mr Fisk and his crew were brought on deck one by one, ordered into two of the ship's boats and cast off.

The leader of this coup was a 33-year-old Scotsman named Robert Stewart (alias Michael Seymour, alias Robert Seymour), who had 'had the benefit of a liberal education and was respectably connected'.[14] Formerly a lieutenant in the Royal Navy commanding a sloop, he had been convicted of forging and counterfeiting a bill of exchange with intent to defraud, and was sentenced to transportation for life. He would later claim that, in fact, it was a far more romantic crime that had brought him to New South Wales. He had become enamoured of an heiress, he said, but found that his attentions to her were opposed by some of her friends. Consequently the young lovers eloped to Gretna Green, where they were married. That night they were surprised in their apartment by one of the bride's friends, a baronet, who threatened to take her back with him. Stewart responded by shooting him in the arm with his pistol. It was a capital offence, and there was no difficulty in securing a conviction. Despite the shame of a prison sentence, Stewart maintained that his wife remained loyal to him, constantly visiting him in his cell until she died giving birth to his child.[15]

Whatever the truth of the matter (and his early life is obscure), Stewart was among the 300 convicts who were sent out in 1803 in HMS *Calcutta* to establish a settlement at Port Phillip. When the settlement failed they were moved to Sullivans Bay in Van Diemen's Land, where Stewart was made an overseer with the responsibility of keeping the camp clean and the stream free from filth. He was soon in trouble and was dismissed from his post after receiving 50 lashes. In June 1805 he and six others stole the Reverend Robert Knopwood's boat and absconded. Their intention was to hijack the schooner *Governor Hunter* on her passage to the Schouten Islands, but the plan failed and within weeks Stewart was up before the magistrate. Undeterred, he escaped into the bush less than three months later, along with three companions, but they returned after only three days, having exhausted their provisions. This latest effort brought him to the attention of Lieutenant-Governor David Collins, who wrote to Governor King in Sydney that 'that truly *vaurien*, Stewart, has made another attempt to escape'.[16] It seems that this was not his only offence, for Collins went on to say:

> He says now he has seen his error, and assures me I may trust him, but fortunately I know exactly how far. I have in my possession the paper containing the forgery of your initials, which, as he never betrayed anyone by it, I have promised him not to bring forward against him. No possible evil can accrue from it now, and it shall be destroyed when I hear from you that you have not a wish to use it.[17]

In February 1806 Stewart was on the run again. With four equally desperate convicts he stole a small boat, intending to use it to seize the *Estramina*, which had been put into government service. However, he was captured with 'two of his deluded companions' by the *Estramina*'s crew and brought to Hobart.[18] After this escapade he was transferred to Sydney and placed in confinement, but this sentence was rescinded after Bligh's overthrow. Bligh would later describe him as 'a determined Man, who had frequently endeavoured to leave the Colony in open Boats',[19] the implication being that he would not have released such a desperate character had he remained in power.

So it was that in May 1808 Stewart led William Jackson and the band of convicts in what may or may not have been his last attempt to take a boat by force. The *Harrington* sailed out of Farm Cove by night, but it wasn't until nine o'clock the next morning that Captain Campbell reported the disappearance of his ship to the authorities, having unaccountably failed to notice at first daylight that she was missing. At once the sloop *Halcyon* was prepared for the chase. Ten privates of the New South Wales Corps under a sergeant filed on board, and she was towed down the harbour accompanied by a flotilla of boats manned by more members of the military, plus some citizen volunteers. At the Heads they waited in vain for a wind and at nightfall were obliged to turn back. Earlier in the afternoon Mr Fisk and his crew had come in after rowing for eight backbreaking hours. In his report he mentioned a significant fact: the convicts were apparently without a timepiece for navigation. They had 'demanded of him his watch,' he said, 'and as he had left it on shore, they afterwards went below to search for the cook's watch, but he being on shore at the time, had it with him'.[20]

On Wednesday the *Pegasus* sailed in pursuit of the *Harrington*. It had taken a day to prepare her for sea, as only her standing rigging was up, but when she cleared the Heads she was fully provisioned for a voyage of six weeks. On board were Captains Ebor Bunker and Symonds, as well as William Campbell and Mr Fisk — an indication of the seriousness with which the matter was viewed by the government, for it was hoped that their combined experience and knowledge of the South Seas would give them an advantage over the fugitives, despite the lateness of their start. Also on board was a military detachment made up of twenty privates, a corporal and two sergeants. Urged on by Campbell, the *Pegasus* headed east for New Zealand. It was his belief that the convicts would attempt to seize the American brig *Eliza*, which had left Sydney a few weeks earlier for the Bay of Islands, with money in coin on board. The *Eliza* could also provide them with replacements for the anchors and boats they had left behind, as well as a timepiece.

The *Pegasus* made good time to the Bay of Islands but found no evidence that the *Harrington* had called in there. However, Captain Ceroni of the sealer *Commerce*, who was there at the same time, reported that two days after the *Pegasus* left a strange brig stood into the bay but then suddenly hauled her wind and went eastward. Her suspicious actions led him to believe that it might have been the *Harrington*. Meanwhile, the *Pegasus* sailed for Tongataboo before returning to Sydney via New Caledonia. After a cruise of nine weeks, no intelligence was gained of the runaways.

The fate of the *Harrington* remained a mystery until April of the following year, when the *Sydney Gazette* announced that the ship had been intercepted by the frigate *Dedaigneuse* while heading towards Manila. A party of seamen was sent on board to take possession, but the *Harrington* ran aground and was wrecked. In the confusion, many of the convicts made their escape. Whether or not Robert Stewart was among them is uncertain. According to a report in the *Calcutta Gazette* of 23 March 1809, he was taken out of the *Harrington* before she was wrecked and transferred to the *Dedaigneuse*, whose commander, 'affected by the gentleman-like appearance of his prisoner, allowed him every reasonable indulgence, and forbore to place him under personal restraint'.[21] The report went on to say that Stewart took advantage of this situation and made an attempt to escape, after which he was placed in close confinement. He was landed on Prince of Wales Island, where he was transferred to the *Phaeton* and brought to Calcutta. On 24 August 1809 the *Calcutta Gazette* carried a brief notice stating that, after being embarked on the *Union* for Sydney, he disappeared and was supposed to have jumped overboard and drowned.[22] However, four years later, in a petition to the government for £4000 compensation for the loss of the *Harrington*, William Campbell stated that Stewart was among the convicts who escaped from the wreck and was believed to be at large in India. There is no doubt that some of these convicts did reach India, for two of them, Terence Flynn and Thomas Dawson, were apprehended there and shipped to Hobart. On arrival they both evaded the authorities, but Flynn was subsequently arrested for the murder of Dawson and hanged. The *Sydney Gazette* devoted several columns to the trial over two editions,[23] but had nothing more to say about Stewart.

So did he drown while attempting to escape in Calcutta, or was this final escape attempt successful? Or had he already escaped from the wreck of the *Harrington* as Campbell claimed? To compound the matter, one of his fellow convicts from HMS *Calcutta*, John Fawkner, believed that Stewart did in fact return from India but escaped from the ship, with the assistance of the captain, as it entered Port Jackson.[24]

This was not the only mysterious circumstance associated with the loss of the *Harrington*. At the time of its seizure there was speculation about a number of matters. Who was the real owner of the brig? Why did Captain Campbell take so long to raise the alarm? Why was the brig lying outside Farm Cove, fully provisioned and ready for sea, yet no watch was kept? How had the convicts got hold of their arms? No answers to these questions were ever forthcoming, and a feeling remained that some sort of skulduggery had been involved, but no-one was quite sure what or why.

In 1813, the same year that Campbell was making his petition, the schooner *Unity* was cut out of the River Derwent in Van Diemen's Land by seven convicts, five of them lifers. After landing the owner and his crew at Frederick Henry Bay, the convicts vanished over the horizon. However, as they had little experience of the sea and there were insufficient provisions on board for a long voyage, Governor Macquarie thought it probable that they would be 'either totally lost or Cast on some Unfriendly Shore where they may all perish'.[25] This may have been wishful thinking on his part, but the chances of success were certainly not high. The majority of convicts who hijacked ships either perished at sea or were eventually captured. As an article in the *Sydney Gazette* pointed out:

> Should they even escape the present pursuit whither must they fly; where hope security? Can they weakly imagine that by even running into an enemy's port they are to regain the freedom they have so unhappily forfeited? If so, how illusive have their conjectures been; how impotent their reasoning? They must find an enemy in every port, if they should ever gain one; for to countenance a pirate would be a disgrace to any Power.[26]

Despite his pompous tone, the writer's argument was well founded, as the two gangs of convicts who hijacked the brig

Trial and later the schooner the *Young Lachlan* would discover. The *Trial* was lying at anchor near the Sow and Pigs rocks in Sydney Harbour in September 1816 when she was boarded by thirteen convicts from a working party at Macquarie Lighthouse. It was a dark night and the ship's crew was taken by surprise. The convicts cut the anchor cable and by sunrise the brig was well away. Some months later a party of soldiers from the colonial vessel *Lady Nelson* came across the wreck of the *Trial* in an inlet (now called Trial Bay) at South-West Rocks, 350 kilometres to the north. The local Aborigines indicated by 'descriptive signs and gesticulations' that the convicts had built a boat from the wreckage but that it had been swamped in heavy surf and they had all drowned.[27] The captain, passengers and crew of the *Trial*, including a woman and child, had taken to the bush in an attempt to reach Newcastle, but were never heard of again.

In 1819 the schooner *Young Lachlan* was cut out of Sullivans Cove, Hobart, by 'a band of thirteen Piratical Convicts'.[28] Contrary to port regulations, the sails were bent and the rudder had been left on board. The convicts had crept up over the side, secured the crew below decks, and with a strong northerly behind them ghosted past Mulgrave Battery and out to sea. At daybreak two government boats and a sloop were dispatched in pursuit, but they returned without having sighted the schooner — although they did recover the crew, who had been landed on Bruny Island. With only a limited supply of water, and no charts, the convicts were not expected to survive a long voyage. However, they in fact turned up off the coast of Java, where they abandoned the *Young Lachlan* after setting her on fire. An attempt to convince the Dutch authorities that they were shipwrecked sailors failed, and they were imprisoned as suspected pirates. Over half of them died of gaol fever and the remainder were returned to Hobart.

For absconders intent on leaving the colony by sea, stowing away or securing a passage with a compliant whaling captain offered the best odds. The dangers and difficulties inherent in hijacking a ship were far greater, and the success rate was not encouraging. Not too many escapees made it back to Britain, in any case. Those who weren't recaptured were more likely to end up on a South Sea island or in one of the ports on the Pacific rim.

By 1800 there was already a number of runaways living in Calcutta. Their establishment there was considered so prejudicial to the 'British Character and Interest' that the governor-general wrote to his counterpart in New South Wales exhorting him to take stern measures to prevent any more 'convicts from Botany Bay from repairing to India'.[29] In the late 1840s, San Francisco was host to the 'Sydney Ducks', a community of lawless adventurers from Australia, many of them escaped convicts, who had been attracted to the Californian goldfields. One of them, James Heartzoke, who had been transported for 'shooting with intent', claimed to have amassed a fortune there. He planned to return to England in disguise and 'had thoughts of entering Parliament by the purchase of an Irish borough'.[30] Peter Cunningham wrote in 1827 of small colonies of runaways who had established a precarious existence on Kangaroo Island and the islands of Bass Strait, living on seals, kangaroos and shellfish and trading with passing vessels for 'European necessaries'. He noted with some wonder their readiness to 'submit to live in a state of the most abject wretchedness, in the enjoyment of liberty'.[31] Captain Andrew Cheyne, a trader in sandalwood and bêche-de-mer, was appalled by the 'European reprobates' living on Bornabi (or Ascension) Island in the Carolines. 'The majority of them,' he wrote in his journal, 'is made up of runaway convicts from New South Wales and Norfolk Island, and deserters from Whale ships. These men, the outcasts and refuse of every maritime nation, are addicted to every description of vice and would be a pest even in a civilised community.'[32] A similar situation existed in the Society and Friendly islands, which were 'overrun with escaped convicts and deserters from merchant ships, to the great injury of the natives and insecurity of trade in those parts'.[33]

New Zealand's proximity to Sydney had always made it a popular haven for runaways, being particularly valued as a convenient stepping stone for travels further afield. In 1830 Samuel Marsden informed Governor Darling that:

> it will be impossible to prevent the Convicts from making their Escape to these Islands, where they Commit every Crime, until an opportunity offers for them to return to Europe or America, which is not difficult for them to meet with from the Number of Vessels which put into the different Harbours; at present they go where they like, and none can interfere with them.[34]

Whether they had stowed away, hijacked a ship or been cast ashore by unsympathetic whaling captains when their usefulness was over, the number of these escapees has gone unrecorded, but over time there must have been many hundreds of them scattered among islands and in ports all around the Pacific.

3

The Cannibal of Van Diemen's Land

On 19 July 1824 a small, pockmarked Irishman named Alexander Pearce was hanged in Hobart Town, his insignificant appearance at odds with his gruesome reputation. He had twice escaped from the penal settlement of Macquarie Harbour and in doing so had committed crimes shocking even to the hardened frontier society of Van Diemen's Land. Officially he was executed for murder, but it was the circumstances accompanying the offence which had horrified both the authorities and the public. In the words of the court reporter for the *Hobart Town Gazette*, this was a man who was 'believed to have banqueted on human flesh!'.[1]

Pearce arrived in Hobart on the *Castle Forbes* in February 1820, transported for seven years for stealing six pairs of shoes. During the next eighteen months he was seldom out of trouble. Assignment to farmer settlers was interspersed with stints of hard labour on the town gang as punishment for theft, drunkenness, disorderly behaviour and absconding. This, and a few doses of the cat-o'-nine-tails, failed to reform him. In June 1822 he was charged with forging a money order and being absent in the bush for several months. His guilt was easily proved and, with so many misdemeanours crowded into his short colonial career, his fate was assured. The magistrates ordered him to be sent to Macquarie Harbour for the remainder of his original sentence.

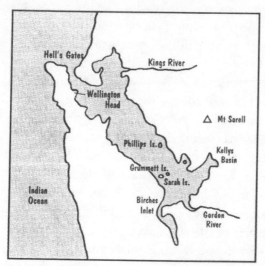

Macquarie Harbour

To some, death may have been preferable because Macquarie Harbour, situated on the remote west coast, was a place of the utmost misery seemingly designed by nature and man for the reception of the most intractable and dangerous convicts. Complementing the pitilessness of its discipline were the towering mountains and damp, impenetrable forests which hemmed it in on the east, and the storm-wracked Antarctic winds which lashed it from the west, bringing rain for more than 300 days a year. The commandant, Lieutenant John Cuthbertston, was at pains to carry out Lieutenant-Governor William Sorell's orders:

> that the constant, active, unremitting employment of every individual in very hard labour is the grand and main design of your settlement. They must dread the very idea of being there ... You must find work and labour, even if it consists in opening cavities and filling them up again.[2]

In short, it was to be a place of 'rigid penal restraint and coercion'.[3] The main settlement was on Sarah Island in the middle of the harbour, but the worst offenders were quartered on the smaller Grummet Island, about 800 metres away. Most

45

of the convicts were employed in the heavy, backbreaking toil of timber-getting, while a few of the more fortunate ones were placed in the shipbuilding yards, where ships of up to 100 or so tonnes were built from the Huon pines cut by their comrades. Six days a week they worked, all year round, felling the giant trees that fringed the mainland, dragging them down to the water's edge and then floating them across to Sarah Island. There they were received by men wading waist and neck deep in the icy water with every chance of being crushed by the massive logs as they bumped and jostled towards the shore.

Pearce arrived at Macquarie Harbour in August 1822 to be quickly initiated into the harsh craft of survival. Doubtless he soon learned of the six convicts who, earlier in the year, had attempted to escape overland. No trace of them had been found and it was assumed that they had perished miserably in the unforgiving bush. This discouraging story had little effect on him, however, as in little more than a month he made his own bid for freedom. On 20 September he joined seven other desperates in seizing a boat at Kellys Basin at the head of the harbour where they had been sent to cut timber. They rowed east along the shore to the coalmine at Coal Head where another convict, Robert Greenhill, the brains behind the escape, was waiting for them. In company with another of the escapees, Matthew Travers, he had been sent to Macquarie Harbour for attempting to hijack a schooner in the Derwent estuary. The remaining members of the party were Alexander Dalton, a cashiered soldier and perjurer, another experienced escaper named William Kennely (alias Bill Cornelius), Thomas Bodenham, a highwayman, John Mather, a 22-year-old Scot with convictions for theft and forgery against his name, and 'Little Brown', whose history is unknown.

They broke into the miners' hut with axes, and secured all the provisions they could find, chiefly flour and beef. To prevent the miners alerting the main settlement they poured water on their signal fire and then set out for the harbour entrance. They had proceeded only a short distance when they noticed a column of smoke rising astern and realised that their efforts to extinguish the fire had been ineffectual. Escape by sea was now out of the question, as there was little hope of making the open sea before being overtaken. Hastily they revised their plans. They beached the boat, smashed a hole in it and took to the bush with the intention of traversing the island on foot and stealing another boat at Hobart. Forcing their way through the smothering forest they headed away from the shore and up the flanks of Mount Sorell, 1100 metres high. They spent the night on the summit huddled around a fire, taking the precaution of setting a regular watch in case their flight had been observed.

The next day they continued their easterly course, keeping to the high ground north of the Gordon River. The going was difficult and Brown struggled to maintain the pace. Several times he fell behind and it was only the threat of being abandoned that gave him the will to continue; as night fell he was still with them when they camped beside a small creek. At daybreak the escapees moved on, anxious to outdistance any possible pursuit. They were now travelling through some extremely rugged country where giant sassafras and eucalyptus trees grew so closely together and put out so much foliage against the sun that penetrating them was like entering a dimly lit room. A direct route was impossible as they stumbled over rotting, moss-covered logs, which often collapsed under their weight, tripped over coiling vines, and fought through dense nets of fern. Their progress was worryingly slow and the situation was aggravated by constant rain, which lowered their spirits even further. As Pearce remembered,

> It was excessively cold particularly at nights & they not having sufficient nourishment & being exposed so much to the night dews greatly impaired their Constitutions they durst not use that Freedom with their provisions that they would wish to have done allowing themselves scarcely sufficient to keep themselves alive.[4]

They battled on in this way for another three days:

> plunging themselves into greater miseries & hardships than ever could be experienced at that place [Macquarie Harbour] by them & not the least prospect of ever arriving at any place from whence they might expect to find releif.

On the seventh day the weather cleared and they passed over 'a Tier of Mountains near to that one called Frenchmans Cap'. From this height Macquarie Harbour could he discerned at a disheartening distance of only '20 or 30 Miles' (about 30 to 50 kilometres). At nightfall they cut branches to make shelters as protection from the icy winds that came barrelling across the mountain tops. Food was now becoming a serious problem and 'they lived for eight or nine days on the tops of tea-tree and peppermint, which they boiled in tinpots to extract the juice'.[5]

Next morning they pushed on, 'the Brush being so excessively thick' that one of them had to go ahead to clear a way for the others. Brown continued to straggle, complaining incessantly of weakness. By mid-morning he had dropped out of sight. At the same time it was discovered that Kennely and Dalton had also gone missing. The others 'stop'd frequently coohincy [cooeeing]', but there was no reply from the drab forest depths. Fearing that if any of the three found his way back to Macquarie Harbour a military search party would soon be on their trail, the remaining five gave up the search and 'hurried themselves on their Journey'. Brown and Kennely did in fact make the punishing trek back to Macquarie Harbour but, exhausted and starving, they expired in hospital several days later. Dalton's fate is uncertain.[6]

On the evening of the eleventh day they came to a river, probably the Franklin, in spate from the torrential rains. For a day and two nights they tried to find a way of crossing this formidable barrier. They attempted to bridge it with two fallen trees but these were instantly swept away. Eventually Pearce, Greenhill and Mather swam out to a rock projecting from the far bank into the middle of the river. With the aid of a long wattle pole they hauled the other two, who couldn't swim, safely across. Their provisions were exhausted and they were suffering terribly from the extreme cold, their clothes were in shreds and 'their shoes being totally worn out gave them considerable pain', but still they struggled on, at times making only 7 or 8 kilometres a day. During this time they existed 'on wild berries, and their kangaroo jackets, which they roasted'.[7] They 'saw plenty of Kangaroos, Emus and Game of all Kinds',[8] but lacking firearms they had no chance of killing them.

On the fifteenth day they struck another river but were too feeble to venture a crossing:

> Here they sat down and being almost famished for the want of food began to intimate to each other that it would be much better for One to be sacrificed as food for the rest than the whole of them to perish for want.

Consensus for 'the horrid Ceremony' was reached and lots were cast. The choice fell upon Thomas Bodenham who accepted his doom with remarkable calmness. Far from 'soliciting their Compassion' he merely requested 'a few minutes to implore pardon of his offended Maker for past offences'. Greenhill sent Pearce and Mather into the bush to gather firewood judging them too squeamish to witness the 'Execution'. Then taking up his axe he 'gave the unfortunate Culprit Bodenham a Severe blow on the Head which soon deprived him of his life — then taking his knife began to cut the Body to pieces'. When the others returned, a fire was kindled and 'several pieces of the Body placed thereon to Cook which they soon devoured greedily'.

During the next week they climbed wearily through the rugged Deception and Surveyor ranges 'subsisting on nothing but the Carcass of unfortunate Bodenham which scarcely kept the Faculties in motion'. All this time Pearce and Mather were nervously watching the violent Greenhill and his mate Travers, aware that when the last pieces of Bodenham had been consumed their own lives would be at risk. On about 12 October they descended to a small valley dotted with ferns and watered by a thin, dark creek. While the others rested, Mather dug up some fern roots which he boiled in a billy and attempted to eat. But he brought the 'Mess' up and 'while in the act of discharging it from his Chest, Greenhill still showing his spontaneous habit of bloodshed seized the Axe & crept behind him and gave him a blow on the head'. Mather was only stunned. He leapt up and wrested the axe away from the surprised Greenhill. Pearce and Travers quickly intervened and pacified Mather by agreeing that from now on their only axe would be kept from Greenhill.

In this state of tension and mistrust they travelled on for another two days until 'having not the least morsel of anything to satisfy their appetites with being dreadfully fatigued & near a Creek of Water they agreed to take up their abode from the night'. They built up a fire and sat round it 'in a very pensive & Melancholy mood'. During that day's march Pearce seems to have formed an alliance with Greenhill and Travers, and Mather, sensing this shift, settled down some distance away from this murderous group. It was a wise precaution but it proved ineffective, for:

> The other Three consulted to take his life to satisfy their hungry appetites with accordingly one of them under the pretence of gathering wood for the fire drew near to where he sat & seized him & drag'd him to the ground the others perceiving immediately rush'd on him striking him with the Axe on the Head which soon terminated his Existence they then began to dissect him which was soon accomplised, they then placed several pieces of him on the fire which they very soon devoured & having appeased their cannibal appetites laid themselves down by the fire.

Greenhill attempted to convince the other two that the real reason for killing Mather had been to prevent him informing on them when they finally reached Hobart. Openly, Pearce and Travers agreed with him, but in their own minds they knew that it was hunger only 'that drove them to the Commission of such Horrid & Barbarous Actions'. They were afraid that 'by appearing different with him in their opinions [they] might incur his displeasure he would embrace an opportunity of Murdering them when asleep'.

All three were still alive next morning. They packed up the remains of the body and continued their easterly journey. The travelling became easier as the forest began to thin and the weather improved. On the fourth day after Mather's death, Travers was bitten on the foot by a snake. He was soon unable to walk and implored the others to abandon him. He was terrified that he would now form the basis of their next meal and urged them to press on with the remaining portions of Mather while he made 'his peace with his Maker before he expired'. Even the alarming Greenhill was moved by his friend's distress. He and Pearce remained with the stricken man for five days in the hope that he would recover. Remembering their longstanding friendship 'both in days of Prosperity as well as in the present days of Adversity', Greenhill 'rendered him all the assistance that Circumstances would then allow'. This care and attention did little to reduce Travers's agitation and, distrusting their intentions, he watched their every movement warily.

> He was not so much afraid of Greenhill as he was of Pearce for seeing nearly the whole of their provisions expended was apprehensive that the same Measures would be adopted which had been & he was confident that he would be the Victim — the unfortunate Man all this time had but little or no sleep.

Eventually Greenhill's compassion withered when Travers's condition failed to improve. He was impatient to move on, and the half-delirious Travers, his swollen foot brimming with pain, had to keep up as best he could with whatever help the others could give him. They dragged themselves across 'a lofty teir of Hills' and at night came to a wide river where, weak and brittle with exhaustion, they resolved to set up camp. Sleep finally overwhelmed Travers, and:

> the others perceiving this began to Comment on the impossibility of ever being able to keep Traviss up with them for their strenth was nearly exhausted it was impossible for them to think of making any Settlement unless they left him as they were quite out of provision it would be folly for them to leave him for his flesh would answer as well for Subsistence as the others.

At this point Travers woke up and, alarmed to see them talking together, he begged them once more to leave him 'for it was morally impossible for him to attempt travelling any more & therefore it would be useless for them to attempt to take him with them'.

Travers's pleas only served to strengthen the designs of his companions and when he fell asleep once more 'one of them took the Axe & gave him a blow on his head ... he only stretched himself in his agony & then expired'. The body was carved and several chunks were rapidly roasted and devoured 'and having appeased their appetites [Greenhill and Pearce] lay themselves down to sleep'. For two days they remained at this spot doing 'nothing but Gorge themselves on the Carcass — & sleep'. Then having vowed 'the greatest Fidelity & Friendship' to each other they 'gather'd all that remained of the flesh & after packing it up very carefully proceeded on their Journey'.

From the heights of another range they were overjoyed to see 'a very beautiful and extensive plain' opening out before them, probably the King William Plains. In the optimistic belief that it was a stock run, they wasted a day in a fruitless search for traces of cattle or sheep before moving out across the grassy expanse, 30 or 40 miles (about 50 or 60 kilometres) long in their estimation. In the distance a wavering smudge of smoke caught their eyes and they turned towards it. The source turned out to be an Aboriginal camp; they formed the desperate resolve of attacking it and in the ensuing melee of escaping with the Aborigines' food supply. Arming themselves with a heavy stick as well as the axe, they snaked cautiously to within 20 metres of the camp. Fuelled by hunger they cranked their courage up a few notches and launched their suffering bodies into the midst of the startled Aborigines, 'each exerting his utmost strength, striking several of these unfortunate Blacks some severe blows which so terrified them that they all Immediately dispersed in the greatest Confusion leaving behind all they were possessed of'.[9] The jubilant convicts prudently burned all the spears they could find, gathered up a good supply of kangaroo meat and skins, and faded into the bush before their victims could recover and set up a pursuit, for as Pearce, with unconscious irony, remarked, 'although these Natives are not Cannibals, there has been several instances of people being Babourously Murdered by them in several parts of the Colony'.

As soon as they considered themselves safe they stopped to devour some of their booty and to rest. After their 'decisive victory' and with stomachs bulging they felt like 'monarchs', but the next day they were soon robbed of their high spirits when they resumed the endless bush-bashing slog towards civilisation 'being nearly naked & quite barefoot, their flesh was dreadfully lacerated & torn by the rocks & Briars'. Day merged into day and they began to blame each other for losing the way. Concern grew into wary antagonism. 'Greenhill always kept the Axe in his possession', carrying it on his back by day and at night laying it under his head:

> Which made Pearce very shy, he would not associate with him as usual & when they Halted at nights Pearce always made a fire at such a distance from Greenhill as he considered far enough to prevent any attack that might be made by him.

The escalating tension between them was eased following another successful attack on an Aboriginal camp. After making off with 'the whole of their Store of Provision', Pearce and Greenhill slept that night 'nearer to each other than they had done for Several days'. In the morning they arose 'apparently on the strongest terms of Friendship'. Further mountains lay ahead and from the summit of one they saw what they joyfully took to be the grey bulk of Table Mountain, in whose shadow Pearce had once worked as a shepherd under assignment. They hastened towards it for their salvation might be found among the stock runs and shepherds' huts of Pearce's memory. It seemed to them that they had finally reached 'the Summit of their hope', and their disappointment was bitter when after two days' walking over some difficult terrain they realised that it was not Table Mountain after all and that they were lost. In their distress their newfound friendship evaporated and Pearce became distrustful of 'the Murderous disposition of Greenhill ... seldom or ever sleeping at night [and] he also acted with the same precaution lest I should act by him as I considered he would by me'.

In this fashion they travelled for several days, crossing two large rivers (one of which was probably the Upper Gordon) and passing through 'a most delightful country' of open grassy levels with stands of gums providing shade from the languid spring sun. Pearce was encouraged to think that they must be approaching an inhabited part of the country but Greenhill 'began to fret, and said he would never get to any port with his life'. He continued to cherish the axe and Pearce 'began to discover Something of an eviller Tendency in the disposition' of his companion. At night they eyed each other uneasily across the camp fire.

'One evening,' Pearce recalled:

when we were both lay down he pretended to be asleep & I just in the act of slumbering when I perceived him raise himself up taking the Axe with him in his hand on discovering this I immediately rose as though out of Slumber appearing as I had not perceived him fortunate it was for me that I was not asleep for had I been I should have shared the same fate as the others this piece of Treachery, on the part of Greenhill so much affected me that I was determined to embrace the first Opportunity of leaving him but he having possession of the Axe at this time Made me form a resolution of getting possession of the Axe we proceeded on traveling for a few Days Continually watching each other during which time he made several attempts to effect his purpose but I always guarded against such attempts & frustrated his design one evening I crept slily to the brush where he lay and took the Axe from under his head gave him a Severe blow on the head which deprived him of his life.

Pearce sliced off part of a thigh and an arm which sustained him for another two days. Then for several days more he walked on without any sustenance at all. In his intense loneliness he was contemplating suicide when he stumbled across a marsh inhabited by a family of ducks. He floundered into the water and somehow managed to catch two of them 'which greatly added to relieve my then distressed and deporable condition'. Pearce's whereabouts at this point are uncertain (as indeed is his precise route from the time of his escape). He may have already crossed the Derwent River and continued east to follow the Ouse River, or he may have still been wandering along the banks of the Derwent. As he moved downstream he 'was Suddenly Surprised at hearing the noise of Sheep'. Tracing the sound, he came across a flock which he drove against a rocky wall until they were piled on top of each other and he was able to grab hold of one. But his strength failed and the furious animal dragged him down a slope for 20 or 30 metres until he gave up and let it go. When he recovered his breath he herded the flock together again and this time selected a lamb which was more his size. He cut its throat and being so famished began to wolf it down raw.

He was still crouching over his bloody meal when a shepherd, armed with a musket, appeared behind him and threatened to blow his brains out. When Pearce cried out in alarm the shepherd, whose name was McGuire, recognised the filthy scarecrow tucking into one of his flock as an assigned stockkeeper he had met months before in this same district. 'Is it possible that this is Pearce?', McGuire exclaimed, and distressed by the runaway's dilapidated condition — 'being almost naked my clothing being torn from my back my flesh being almost torn from my bones by the Brush my beard 3 or 4 inches in length' — he took him back to his hut where he cooked the lamb for him. For five days McGuire cared for Pearce 'with the tenderness of a Saint' before passing him on to another hut-keeper.

It had been mid-November when Pearce finally emerged from the wilderness into the settled districts of the middle Derwent. He had succeeded in crossing some of the most inhospitable country in Australia and indeed was the first to do so. And the feat had been accomplished without adequate provisions and clothing, without maps or even a compass. In all the circumstances of his ordeal he had shown himself to be a tenacious and resourceful survivor.

During the next few weeks he moved from hut to hut, sheltered and fed by sympathetic convict stockkeepers. One evening as he was settling down for the night he heard someone whistling. When he went outside to investigate he was bailed up by two 'desperadoes ... armed with Muskets having Knapsacks on their backs and 3 or 4 Kangaroo Dogs'. With some difficulty he managed to convince them that he 'was the Person who effected my escape from the New Settlement' and not 'one of the Military'. The reason for their suspicion was soon revealed — they were bushrangers with a price of £10 on their heads, and if apprehended could confidently expect the hangman's noose. Their names were William Davis and Ralph Churton, both former convicts. Having satisfied themselves as to Pearce's credentials they invited him to 'associate with them where I should be enjoying a life of ease and plenty, than to go to Hobart Town to surrender myself for I should perhaps be sent to Macquarie Harbour again'.

Persuaded by this argument Pearce agreed to join them. He accompanied them to their hideout where they had 180 stolen sheep hidden, which they were preparing for sale by altering their ear markings. Pearce was armed with a musket and pistol, and when the sheep were ready the gang set out with them for a place called the Lovely Banks near the Jordan River. Within 20 kilometres of their destination, however, they were surprised by a patrol of the 48th Regiment. They escaped only by abandoning the sheep and throwing off their knapsacks, 'which was a great loss to us, being stored well with Articles that we mostly wanted'. They fled to 'Daviss place', somewhere nearby, where they remained for two days. For another week or so they roamed the bush relying for food and shelter on friendly hut-keepers, most of whom were themselves living on the edge of the law. At some stage Pearce went off on his own for a while to steal some sheep, but he was detected by a shepherd who gave the alarm. Pearce escaped 'into a cave ... but I was very near being caught'.[10]

Early in the new year the bushrangers were near the town of Jericho, 'resting ourselves beneath the Shade of a Tree', when once again they were surprised by soldiers of the 48th Regiment. Davis attempted to flee but was shot through the thigh and arm; Pearce and Churton were secured before they could rise. All three were taken to Hobart and lodged in the town gaol. Their capture was briefly noted by the *Hobart Town Gazette* a week later:

> Wm Davis and Ralph Churton, who made their escape in April last from a military guard while being conveyed to town on a charge of sheep-stealing, were apprehended on Saturday last in company with an absentee, named Pearse, by a party of soldiers near Jericho — Davis was severely wounded.[11]

Some time in February the three men were examined by the Reverend Robert Knopwood in his capacity of magistrate. Knopwood's generally expansive diaries contain no reference to this, but he was not so reticent about the fate of Churton and Davis. Within a matter of weeks they were tried, found guilty of sheep stealing and sentenced to death. Knopwood visited them on their last night 'and perform'd D.V. service before them and read them a condemned sermon'.[12] He also attended them on the scaffold and was pleased to record that 'they were all very penitent'.

Although Pearce had confessed to murder and cannibalism, he was spared the gallows and merely ordered back to Macquarie Harbour. The reason for this startling decision is that the authorities simply did not believe his outrageous confession. To their minds he was loyally protecting his companions who must still be roaming the bush. After all, the only evidence against him were his own words, and no bodies had been produced to confirm his grotesque claims.

He was returned to Macquarie Harbour towards the end of February. He was now something of a celebrity, being the first man known to have made it across the western mountains to the settled districts. No doubt the commandant, Lieutenant Cuthbertson, was concerned that Pearce's success would encourage others to follow in his footsteps. As a consequence, Pearce was closely watched and forced to work in heavy irons. According to Pearce, a young hero-worshipping convict named Thomas Cox 'constantly entreated him to run away with him from that Settlement'.[13] Cox was a farm labourer who had been transported for life in 1819. He arrived in Van Diemen's Land the following year and soon chalked up a variety of local convictions including two for absconding. This earned him 50 lashes and a trip to Macquarie Harbour. Escape was still on his mind and he set about scrounging 'fishhooks, a knife and some burnt rag for tinder'[14] in order to be ready when the chance came. Eventually, Pearce succumbed to Cox's entreaties, but this time he planned to head for the north coast and Port Dalrymple rather than attempt to repeat his nightmare crossing of the mountain ranges to the east.

Towards the middle of November the two men fled into the bush, each carrying an axe and a small quantity of food. Cox knocked Pearce's irons off and following the harbour shore they pushed their way through a mesh of thick, sodden scrub.

For several days they struggled on. At night it was too wet to make a fire to warm themselves. Wisely they supplemented their meagre supplies with 'the tops of trees and shrubs',[15] and on the fifth day arrived at the Kings River, which empties into the northern reaches of the harbour. Here, according to Pearce, a quarrel erupted:

> I asked Cox if he could swim; he replied he could not; I remarked that had I been aware of it he should not have been my companion; we were enabled to make a fire; the arrangement for crossing the river created words, and I killed Cox with the axe. I ate part of him that night, and cut the greatest part of his flesh up in order to take on with me. I swam the river with the intention of keeping the coast round to Port Dalrymple; my heart failed me and I resolved to return and give myself up to the Commandant.[16]

On 21 November the crew of the schooner *Waterloo*, heading for the harbour entrance, observed a lone figure on the shore capering around a signal fire. A boat was sent to investigate and at the same time another boat set out from Sarah Island where the lookout had also spotted the fire. Both boats returned before nightfall bringing the remorseful Pearce with them. When he was questioned by Lieutenant Cuthbertson, he calmly stated that he had murdered Cox two days earlier and had been living off his body ever since. There could be no doubting his story this time, for 'a piece of human flesh, about half a pound, was found upon his person'.[17]

Early next morning a search party, with Pearce as a willing guide, found Cox's remains on the bank of the Kings River about 400 metres upstream 'in a dreadfully mangled state'. According to one report the body had been:

> cut right in two at the middle, the head off, the privates torn off, all the flesh off the calves of the legs, back of the thighs and loins, also off the thick part of the arms, which the inhuman wretch declared was most delicious food; none of the intestines were found; he said that he threw them behind a tree, after having roasted and devoured the heart and a part of the liver; one of the hands was also missing.[18]

When Thomas Smith, the commandant's coxswain, horrified at what he had seen, asked Pearce how he 'could do such a deed as this? He answered no person can tell what he will do when driven by hunger.'[19] This statement sits uneasily with the fact that 'when he was taken there was found upon his person a piece of pork, some bread, and a few fish ... which he had not tasted, stating that human flesh was by far preferable'.[20] Probably Pearce did kill Cox in a moment of anger, but one is left with the grisly thought that when he agreed to take Cox with him he was viewing him as a sort of mobile larder of fresh meat.

Within a week Pearce was packed off to Hobart to stand trial in the Supreme Court. There was a delay of seven months, though, while the authorities waited for the arrival from England of the colony's first Chief Justice, in May 1824. On 20 June Pearce appeared before the court and pleaded not guilty to the charge of murdering Thomas Cox. This was the only charge — no mention of cannibalism or the murder of his companions during his first escape was included, although his reputation as a man-eater was a matter of public horror. The court report for the *Hobart Town Gazette*, after colourfully alluding to 'the vampire legends of modern Greece', wrote that 'our eyes glanced in fearfulness at the being who stood before a retributive Judge, laden with the weight of human blood'.[21] In this prejudicial atmosphere the prosecutor felt constrained to warn the jury:

> to dismiss from their minds all previous impressions against the prisoner; as however justly their hearts must execrate the fell enormities imputed to him, they should dutiously judge him, not by rumours — but by indutible evidence.[22]

It is not known whether Pearce defended himself, but having, pleaded not guilty it is likely that he did offer some sort of defence although having willingly confessed to the murder on several occasions it is difficult to imagine what this could have been. The evidence of these confessions and of the men who had viewed Cox's mutilated body was compelling. The jury, comprising seven commissioned officers, was in no doubt.

After retiring briefly they returned a verdict of guilty. The automatic sentence of hanging was pronounced, with the additional refinement that the body was to be made available for dissection at the Colonial Hospital.

Pearce spent his last weeks in Hobart Gaol. On 16 July he was visited by the Reverend Knopwood, who informed him that he was to be executed in three days' time. This was the extent of Knopwood's duty towards the prisoner, whose tormented soul was in the care of the Roman Catholic chaplain, the Reverend Philip Conolly. During these last days Pearce dictated another confession to Father Conolly who, it was agreed, would read it from the scaffold.

Early in the morning of the appointed day, Pearce was led from his cell to the place of execution within the gaol. His arms were pinioned and the noose placed around his neck. Father Conolly delivered the confession to the assembled crowd. He concluded by stating that the condemned man was 'weary of life, and willing to die for the misfortunes and atrocities into which he had fallen'.[23] Then after a final prayer the trapdoor was opened and Pearce dropped into oblivion. The *Hobart Town Gazette* recorded the event in a piece of florid and moralising prose:

> We trust these awful and ignominious results of disobedience to law and humanity, will act as a powerful caution; for blood must expiate blood! and the welfare of society imperatively requires, that all whose crimes are so confirmed, and systematic as *not* to be redeemed by lenity, shall be pursued in vengeance and extirpated with *death*![24]

After his body had hung for the usual time it was taken down and delivered to the hospital for dissection in accordance with the court's sentence. The head was separated from the trunk and it turned up 30 years later in a collection of over 1000 skulls assembled by Dr Samuel Morton, an American scientist with an abiding interest in phrenology.[25] Today Pearce's skull, minus the lower jaw and teeth, may be seen in the Museum of the University of Pennsylvania.

4

The Heirs of Mary Bryant

Mary Bryant (see Chapter 1) was not the first female convict to attempt an escape. On 12 February 1788, only a week after landing in Sydney Cove, Ann Smith absconded into the bush, never to be seen again. Two years earlier she had been charged at the Old Bailey with the theft of a pewter pint pot. Her plea that she was merely looking after the pot for someone else failed to impress the judge, and he sentenced her to seven years' transportation. During the voyage out to New South Wales with 101 other women on the *Lady Penrhyn*, Surgeon Arthur Bowes-Smyth reported that Ann 'always behaved amis[s]' and was heard to say that she would run away as soon as she could after arriving.[1] True to her word, she did just that. On 12 February, Lieutenant William Bradley wrote in his journal that 'a Boat belonging to the *Sirius* being up the Harbour found 4 Convict Women straggling about the Rocks, one of whom made her escape into the Woods & no doubt perished'.[2] The identity of this woman was confirmed at a general muster of convicts a fortnight later when nine men and one woman — Ann Smith — were found to be missing. It seems that she may have cherished hopes of being taken on board one of La Perouse's vessels then anchored in Botany Bay. After referring to those convicts who scrambled back to Sydney Cove following their rejection by the French, Surgeon John White mentioned that 'a woman named Ann Smith and a man, have never since been heard of. They are supposed to have missed their way as they returned, and to have perished for want.[3]

Over the years it has been claimed that two convict women actually did escape on the French ships. This unsubstantiated story may have arisen from Bowes-Smyth's report on 11 March 1788 that 'this day 2 of the Convict women elop'd from the Camp & took their beds & baggage wh them'.[4] However, as the French sailed on 10 March these women could not have been on board, and like Ann Smith must be presumed to have met their ends in the bush.

Almost two years later, in December 1789, Judge-Advocate David Collins noted that some convicts had found a scrap of linen 'said to have formed part of a petticoat which belonged to Anne Smith, a female convict who absconded a few days after our landing in this country'. He went on to surmise that it 'might have been carried thither and dropped by some natives ... but it gives a strong colour to the supposition of her having likewise perished, by some means or other in the woods'.[5] In 1796 Anne Smith's escape was brought to Collins's mind again when he received a report that a white woman had been seen with Aborigines to the north of Sydney. He mused:

> There was indeed a woman, one Ann Smith, who ran away a few days after our setting down in this place, and whose fate was not exactly ascertained; if she could have survived the hardships and wretchedness of such a life as must have been hers during so many years residence among the natives of New Holland, how much information it must have been in her power to afford![6]

These first escape attempts by women offered little in the way of hope to other like-minded convicts. Mary Bryant's escape, however, was different. Her ground-breaking voyage achieved legendary status, and according to Governor Hunter 'may have contributed to encourage similar attempts'.[7] Her success certainly spurred Governor Phillip to take steps to improve the colony's security. A sentry was promptly posted on every wharf at sunset, and no vessel was permitted to leave Sydney Cove without the authority of the officer of the guard. In addition, the private construction of boats longer than 14 feet was prohibited. But these precautions failed to dampen what David Collins called 'the spirit of Emmigration'[8] among convicts, a spirit which infected women as well as men.

Among 21 Irish convicts who took off from Rose Hill for China in November 1791 was a woman. Within days the group was recaptured, starving and bewildered. The woman had become separated from her companions and was found by a wooding party from the *Albermarle* wandering along the north shore of the harbour, not knowing where she was.

Far more successful in their bid for freedom were the two women encountered in Calcutta in 1794 by Jacob Nagle, an adventurous American seaman who had sailed on the First Fleet. He wrote in his journal:

> I fell in with two ladies that new me. [They] had made there escape from Port Jackson. They were rejoice'd to see me and invited me home. I was astonished to see the grand situation they ware in, sedans and chairs at all calls. They treated me very hansomely, I suppose that I might keep my tounge to myself, as they kept no company excepting mates and capt[ains] of ships or those that appeared as gentlemen, though sailors when there are all gentlemen. The weather being hot, they must have a sedan with two Negroes to carry them wherever they wish to go and a boy a long side to fan them.[9]

Unfortunately Nagle does not name these two high-class courtesans, nor does he describe how they had reached India. The most likely possibility is that they had stowed away on one of the transport ships leaving Sydney on the voyage home, probably with the willing help of some members of the crew. This certainly appears to have been the case with Elizabeth Hervey, Mary Ann Fielding and Mary Briant (or Brian), who escaped to Calcutta on the *Marquis Cornwallis* and were reported to be living there in 1800 with three men who had sailed on the same ship.[10]

In 1794 Mary Morgan, commonly known as Molly, failed in

an attempt to stow away on the store-ship *Resolution* as the boat was preparing to sail, or so Judge-Advocate David Collins was led to believe. Molly had come out to Sydney in 1790 in the *Neptune* with the Second Fleet, having been sentenced to seven years' transportation for stealing some linen yarn from a bleaching factory. A year later she was joined by her husband, and after she had earned a ticket-of-leave they opened a small shop. However, on 9 November 1794 she was reported missing, together with another female convict. At once Collins sent out a boat to search the *Resolution*, but no illegals were found and the boat came back for further orders, leaving a sergeant and four privates on board. Unwilling to wait any longer, the master, Mr Locke, ordered the marines off his ship, got under way and stood out to sea.

During the next few years various theories circulated around the colony as to what had happened to Molly Morgan. Then, in July 1796, Collins heard from the crew of a fishing boat that a white woman was believed to be living with Aborigines to the north of Broken Bay. 'This unfortunate female,' he wrote, 'was conjectured to be Mary Morgan, a prisoner who it was now said had failed in her attempt to get on board the *Resolution* which sailed hence in 1794.'[11] He sent a boat crewed by volunteers with orders to 'bring her away, unless she preferred the life that she now led; upon which more than three years experience of it would certainly enable her to decide'.[12] After searching Broken Bay for a week, the party returned with nothing to report. And no wonder, for while they were looking for her in New South Wales she was living in Plymouth, working as a dressmaker. She had, as originally suspected, been taken from Sydney by Mr Locke in the *Resolution* store-ship, together with thirteen other convicts. In 1804 she was back in Sydney, re-transported for another seven years for arson. The charge had been laid by her second husband — whom, presumably, she had married bigamously. There is no record of her attempting another escape, and by the late 1820s, through resourcefulness and hard work, she had become one of the largest landholders on the Hunter River. She died in 1835.

Another successful escapee was the mysterious Jane Lambert, one of a party of convicts who escaped in the American ship *Otter* in 1796 and reached North America. Her past, even her real name before she adopted 'Lambert', is unknown. All that can be stated with certainty is that she was a convict from London. Her story begins in January 1796, when the American vessel *Otter* arrived in Sydney from Boston on a fur-trading voyage to the north-west coast of America. During the course of provisioning his ship, the captain, Ebeneezer Dorr, made the acquaintance of a number of residents. Among them was Thomas Muir, a Scottish political reformer, who had been shipped out to Sydney in 1794 on a fourteen-year sentence for sedition. He was one of a group of five radicals known as the Scottish Martyrs.

As a political prisoner Muir enjoyed an unusual degree of freedom. He was permitted to purchase a small holding at Cockle Bay on the north shore of the harbour, and to employ several convict servants. For over a year he occupied himself with farming and preparing documents in defence of the ideals that had brought him to the far side of the world. Early in February 1796 he began planning his escape on the *Otter*. With the greatest care he sounded out Captain Dorr, who, it turned out, had no scruples in offering him a passage to Boston provided Dorr himself was not placed in any danger. Thus encouraged, Muir completed his plans in the utmost secrecy. On the evening of 17 February, the day before the *Otter* was due to sail, he stole a small boat and, accompanied by two servants, pushed off down the harbour intending to rendezvous with the American ship several kilometres off the coast. He had nothing with him but the shirt and coat on his back. Muir never revealed the identity of his servants, who he tells us only learned of his plan at the last moment, but it is quite possible that one of them was Jane Lambert. There is no doubt that she came on board the *Otter* at Sydney, and it seems unlikely that Captain Dorr, about to embark on a lengthy voyage, would have readily countenanced the inclusion of a convict woman among his crew of 30 hardened sailors. However, if she was one of the two servants who turned up with Muir in his boat, Dorr would surely have been obliged to take her on board.

By dawn the three runaways had passed through the Heads and were well out to sea. But there was no sign of the *Otter*. For 24 hours they kept on the agreed course, with the coast gradually receding until it dropped over the horizon. By noon of the second day they were exhausted. A heavy sea was running and they had almost lost hope of being picked up when they sighted a sail. Frantically they hoisted a shirt on an oar, and after a few moments of suspense the vessel swung around towards them. It was the *Otter*, and within a short time they were hauled safely on board, where they were greeted by another group of escaped convicts who had been taken on by Captain Dorr as additional crewmen.

Captain Dorr shaped a course to the north-east, passing to the north of New Zealand and reaching the Tongan group of islands in early March. For over a week the *Otter* nudged cautiously through the reef-strewn waters, moving from island to island while the crew set up a keen trade with the natives, bartering scissors and knives for coconuts, bananas and yams. Attracted by what appeared to be an earthly paradise, six of the runaways elected to remain behind, preferring a beach-combing life to the hardships and uncertainties of a long sea voyage. Then, with her decks laden with fresh fruit and vegetables, the *Otter* moved out into the open sea. Niue and Samoa were sighted, and finally the north-west coast of America. By mid-June they were anchored in Nootka Sound, an inlet on the western shore of Vancouver Island first discovered by Captain Cook in 1778. During the voyage Jane had formed an attachment to the ship's carpenter, Andrew Lambert, who was part of the original crew that had signed on at Boston. She would later claim that years earlier they had been married there and had left their thirteen-year-old daughter behind in the care of grandparents. This is plainly untrue, as it is certain that she boarded the *Otter* in Sydney. It was probably an attempt to retrospectively legitimise their liaison, and is made even more unlikely when we consider their ages at this time — Andrew 25 and Jane 27. Whether or not they were later married is not clear, but at some time as they crossed the Pacific she assumed his name.

At Nootka, Captain Dorr learned that a British warship had been seen cruising in the area. Fearful of being captured if he continued north with the *Otter*, Thomas Muir, together with five of the convicts, transferred to a Spanish gunboat which took them down the coast to Monterey in Spanish California. Since the 1770s Spain had claimed sovereignty over much of the north-western seaboard as far north as San Francisco, and foreign visitors to this wild, largely unexplored region were viewed with alarm and suspicion. Regardless of this, Muir posed no obvious threat to Spain's territorial ambitions, and as a gentleman of culture and learning he was received sympathetically by the governor of Monterey. After a congenial stay of four weeks he travelled under escort to Mexico and then Cuba, eventually returning to Europe and ending his life in France.

Meanwhile, Captain Dorr was coasting slowly northward, trading with the Indians for sea otter skins. By September provisions were short and he turned south to California. He arrived off Monterey in late October and, having received the governor's permission to land, entered the harbour firing a seven-gun salute which was answered by the Spanish fort guarding the entrance. While he was provisioning his ship, Dorr became aware that there was dissatisfaction among the convicts and some of the crew: they were unprepared to face another long voyage, this time to China, where he intended to sell his otter skins. Eleven of them deserted but within days six had been rounded up by the Spanish and returned to the ship. However, the day after the *Otter* sailed, Dorr returned clandestinely to a nearby bay and put another six of them, including Andrew and Jane Lambert, ashore at gunpoint. 'To Monterey!' were his brief parting words to his shipmates of over eight months. No doubt unwilling to risk their disaffection contaminating the rest of the crew, he probably figured that they had served their purpose — as he had theirs.

For a year the little band of eleven refugees (the five earlier deserters had come out of hiding as soon as the *Otter* had sailed) lived at Monterey under the tolerant eye of the governor. They found paid work and were quietly integrating themselves into the community when orders came from the Viceroy in Mexico that they were to be repatriated. In March 1797 they were shipped on the frigate *Concepción* to the southern port of San Blas. Their reception there was very different from the one they had received in Monterey. For four months they lived in extreme poverty, regarded as outcasts by the Spanish inhabitants. One of their number died of malaria, while another managed to stow away on a ship bound for South America. Finally, after a year of uncertainty, new orders came through that they were to be moved across Mexico to Veracruz. The journey was taken in easy stages over three months and they were given a modest daily allowance for living expenses. Although they were not treated as prisoners, they were made aware that their movements were being closely watched.

At Veracruz the group was broken up. Six of them sailed to Havana and from there to their own countries. The three who remained behind were Andrew and Jane Lambert and an English convict from Liverpool named Peter Pritchard. The Lamberts, at their own wish, were received into the Catholic Church, and both the men found jobs at the royal shipyards. For some time they lived happily enough, but then the two men fell ill and were unable to work. Without any income, Jane was reduced to begging for alms in the streets. The situation improved when the Lamberts were granted permission to travel to Mexico City, whose more congenial climate restored Lambert to full health. Pritchard, who did not accompany them, was later transferred to Havana, but the Lamberts were allowed to remain in Mexico for another four years. Andrew resumed his work as a ship's carpenter at Veracruz, but Jane seems to have found difficulty in settling down. She developed a drinking problem and moved around the country, never staying very long in one place. Finally, in September 1802, the Spanish authorities decided that the couple should be sent to Spain. At this point they disappear from official records. Where did the Lamberts go? Did they go to Spain, and if so did they eventually reach England, there to live out their lives in obscurity, or did they take another direction and make their way to Andrew's home port of Boston?

The fate of another escapee, Charlotte Badger, is also open to conjecture. On the night of 16 June 1806 the colonial brig *Venus* was forcibly seized in Port Dalrymple, in the north of Van Diemen's Land, by six of its crew acting in conjunction with four convicts. Among them were Badger and her friend Catharine Hagarty, who were being sent to Hobart as assigned servants. The *Venus* had sailed from Sydney in April with supplies of meal, flour and salt pork for the settlements at Hobart and Port Dalrymple. Having put into Twofold Bay to collect further stores of flour, the ship had become weather-bound there for five weeks. During this time the master, Samuel Rodman Chace, discovered that the crew had been plundering the cargo and he accused the first mate, a former American whaler named Benjamin Kelly, of having broached a cask of spirits, a charge that Kelly denied. There was further trouble after the *Venus* put to sea. Chace noticed a small deal box floating away from the ship; however, by the time he sent a boat to recover it, it had disappeared. On investigation he found that the box contained official documents belonging to Captain Kemp of the New South Wales Corps, and had been thrown overboard by Catharine Hagarty. Chace would later state that he believed 'the vessel was in danger of being run away with ... and from the general behaviour of the people on board he did not think his life safe'.[13] He also accused the crew of drunkenness and vandalism, and Kelly of cohabiting with Hagarty.

On the morning of 16 June the *Venus* dropped anchor off Lagoon Beach, just inside the mouth of the Tamar River. Ignoring his own concerns about the security of his ship and its cargo, Captain Chace left her to go 16 kilometres up the river to deliver dispatches to Lieutenant-Governor Paterson — conduct later held to be 'imprudent and unjustifiable'.[14] Chace's decision not to return until the next morning compounded this recklessness, for late that night, while he was being entertained by the port's naval officer on board the schooner *Governor Hunter*, Benjamin Kelly was setting in motion a plan to take over the *Venus*. With Richard Evans, the pilot, and Richard Thompson, a corporal in the New South Wales Corps, Kelly knocked down and imprisoned the second mate. Then, brandishing a musket and pistol, they forced five of the crew ashore.

Early next morning, as he was being rowed down the river to rejoin his ship, Captain Chace was appalled to see her heading out to sea. At the helm was Evans, a former gunner's mate who had deserted from HMS *Calcutta* and was serving a fourteen-year sentence. Seven others had joined in the mutiny. Four of them were regular members of the crew: Joseph Redmonds, a stout mulatto who wore his hair 'tied in pigtails, and with holes in his ears, being accustomed to wear large earrings',[15] a Malay cook and two boys. The remaining three were Hagarty, Badger and another convict named John Lancashire, a thin, sallow-faced man who, before being transported, had been a painter and draughtsman. Charlotte Badger's brief career as a housebreaker had been curtailed when she was convicted at the Worcester Assizes in 1796 and sentenced to transportation for seven years, arriving in Sydney on the *Earl Cornwallis* in 1801. She was unflatteringly described by the authorities as very corpulent, with a full face and thick lips.[16] She was also said to have an infant with her. The official description of Catharine Hagarty made note of her fresh complexion, hoarse voice and that she was 'much inclined to smile'.[17]

The story of the mutiny as told by later writers has sometimes put Charlotte in an overly heroic role. In one account she personally flogged Captain Chace before setting him adrift in a small boat. Then, like the notorious eighteenth-century female pirates Anne Bonny and Mary Read, she dressed in men's clothes and, armed with a brace of pistols, led a raid on another vessel for supplies of food and firearms.[18] Such embellishments were added to titillate Victorian readers' tastes for tales of ruthless deeds and sensation, and cannot be substantiated.

After a stormy passage across the Tasman Sea, the *Venus* put into the Bay of Islands in New Zealand for shelter. This was a region well known to Kelly from a previous visit there in the South Sea whaler *Albion*, and he and Lancashire, together with the two women, decided to stay. Command of the *Venus* now fell to Redmonds, but lacking navigational skills he dared not take the ship out of sight of land. For some months the mutineers cruised down the eastern coast of the North Island. They had already kidnapped two young Maori girls from the Bay of Islands, and at Whangarai and the Thames River they added to this number. The subsequent movements of the *Venus* are uncertain, beyond making several calls in the Bay of Plenty. The last report of the mutineers came from the captain of the colonial schooner *Mercury*. According to him, Redmonds and his unsavoury shipmates had been lured ashore by vengeful Maoris, killed and eaten. The *Venus* had been hauled ashore and burnt for its iron.

Nothing was heard of the four who had remained at the Bay of Islands until April 1807 when the *Commerce*, putting into Sydney with a cargo of seal skins for the London market, reported that Kelly had been taken to England in the *Britannia* and that Lancashire had also been captured and taken to Sydney by the American ship the *Brothers*. Further news came with the arrival on the same day of the *Elizabeth* after a long whaling voyage. Her captain, Ebor Bunker, reported that Catharine Hagarty had died and that he had offered to take Charlotte Badger and her child with him, but that she had refused. What happened to her after this has never been satisfactorily established. In 1820, a white woman was reported to have been living for some years with a Maori chieftain in the Bay of Islands. This could well have been her. Then again, she may have been the 'very big stout woman'[19] encountered by the captain of an American whaler on the Tongan island of Vavau in 1826, who, to his surprise, spoke to him in English and claimed to have come there from New Zealand ten years earlier.

Instead of bolting overseas, another convict, Eliza Callaghan, managed a different sort of escape — she escaped into respectability. In 1820, aged only seventeen, she was convicted of passing a forged £1 banknote. Her sentence of death was commuted to fourteen years' transportation, and she arrived in Hobart in late 1821 on board the *Providence*. On disembarking she was assigned to John Petchley, a former convict who had been appointed keeper of Hobart Gaol. Her conduct during the voyage had been described as 'bad', and she was soon in trouble again.[20] In March 1822 she was found guilty of being drunk and disorderly, and then, three months later, of being absent from her master's house overnight. For the latter offence she spent three hours in the stocks. In January 1823 she absconded for a whole day and night and was sentenced to bread and water for a week, plus two hours in the stocks each day.

Some time in 1823 or 1824, Eliza Callaghan was reassigned to P.A. Mulgrave, Superintendent of Police in Launceston. Her next appearance in the colony's records was on a list of runaway convicts that appeared on 15 February 1825. A reward of £2 was offered for her capture, but the details of her escape were not included. For seven months nothing was heard of her. Then, in October, a convict assigned to John Batman (the future founder of Melbourne) reported that he had seen her in Batman's house at Ben Lomond in the north of the island. A constable was immediately sent to investigate this claim. Although a fire was blazing in the hearth, the constable found the house was empty. He did, however, find some women's gowns and slippers, a lace cap and some sewing equipment — items which confounded Batman's alleged bachelor status. A month later another of Batman's servants alleged that Batman had told him to treat Eliza Callaghan as mistress of the house. Batman denied these charges, even after another of his servants swore that he had seen 'a Female standing inside my master's House she was dressed in a white Gown she had black hair her complexion was pale and her face appeared to be pitted with the small Pox, she had no Cap on'.[21] In the end the authorities apparently found Batman's denial more persuasive than the testimony of his convict servants, for no further action was taken and Eliza Callaghan was never apprehended.

Of course, suspicion that the liaison was unofficially condoned by the authorities cannot be discounted. Batman was a large landowner and rendered the government a valuable service in 1826 by capturing the notorious bushranger Matthew Brady. By then Callaghan had borne Batman a daughter and was pregnant with another, and when in January 1828 Batman sought the governor's permission to marry her it was readily granted. After being at large for three years, Eliza Callaghan had finally escaped her convict status to become the wife of a man of influence and standing in the colony.

The story of another convict's escape appeared in a pamphlet published in England in 1850.[22] Penned by the convict herself, Jane Turner, it is a curious blend of authentic detail flawed by factual inaccuracies, and should be treated with some caution. She begins by relating how, encouraged by her lover — 'a dissipated character' — she stole a quantity of silver, valuable trinkets and cash from a house in Doncaster and was sentenced to fourteen years' transportation. After a voyage of four months she landed in Sydney and was sent upriver to the Female Factory at Parramatta, which she described as a 'scene of horror'. There this young daughter of a respectable grocer was thrown in with older women who 'were all adepts in every vice and crime, thieves, bawds, and prostitutes of the lowest description'. At length she was assigned to a settler on an outlying farm. However, her new master, far from being the kind, humane gentleman she had hoped for, worked her like a slave. She was a criminal, he informed her, and must expect to be treated as such.

Life became a burden for her, and when she was offered a chance to escape she was easily persuaded. With four other women from nearby farms she began hoarding a store of food. When all was ready they slipped away at night and headed into the bush, disguised as men. At dawn they rested up and only moved on again when darkness fell. After three days their food was gone and they were reduced to living off the 'herbage of the fields'. For another nine days they wandered aimlessly through the bush, not knowing where they were heading. Gradually Jane began losing her companions, two to sickness and exhaustion and two carried off by an Aboriginal hunting party. At last she stumbled down to a beach where she came across a boat's crew, from the ship *Hastings*, filling water casks. She wrote:

> On coming up to them they were surprised to think where I came from. I fell on my knees, imploring their assistance, relating to them my sad and melancholy tale, but I did not disclose my sex; they gave

me some biscuit and salt beef, which I devoured with voracious appetite. They promised me protection, and agreed at dusk to get me on board of the ship, without the knowledge of the captain. The got me on board and concealed in the forecastle.[23]

The ship was only two days' sail from England when Turner was discovered by the mate and brought before the master, Captain William Dobson. She revealed her identity to him and was given into the charge of his wife, who was also on board. On arrival in London, Dobson handed her over to the authorities and she was removed to Millbank Penitentiary, the huge prison built in 1816 to house convicts awaiting transportation. However, she was not to make a second voyage to New South Wales. The story of her 'surprising adventures and unparalleled sufferings' got out. The Home Office agreed that she had endured enough and recommended her to the clemency of the Crown, with the result that she received a free pardon.

Although these were not isolated examples, the records show that escapes by female convicts were not as numerous as those by men. This can be readily accounted for by the fact that female numbers were always considerably fewer than male numbers. Between 1788 and 1852, about 24 000 women were transported to New South Wales and Van Diemen's Land. The proportion of women to men for this period was only one in seven. The reasons for this disparity lay partly in the prevailing attitudes of the time towards female convicts, most of whom were widely regarded as prostitutes or otherwise depraved, worthless and a burden on the settlement. In Surgeon Peter Cunningham's opinion, 'the women are more quarrelsome and more difficult to control than the men, their temper being more excitable, and a good deal being calculated on by them in respect of the usual leniency shown their sex. They are certainly more abandoned in their expressions, too, when excited.'[24] A far stronger statement appeared in the *Sydney Gazette* on 9 January 1830 when it was claimed that the female convicts from the *Lady Davidson* 'have proved a profitless shipment. Most of the

Magdalens were assigned in Sydney and most of those have been returned by their masters as "incorrigibly bad characters".[25] Twenty years earlier Governor Macquarie had remarked in a dispatch to Viscount Castlereagh that 'the situation of the Colony requires that as many male convicts as possible should be sent thither, the prosperity of the country depending on their numbers; whilst on the contrary, female convicts are as great a drawback as the others are beneficial'.[26] This ignored the fact, as the Select Committee on Transportation was quick to point out, that from women only 'can a reasonable hope be held out of a rapid increase to the population; upon which increase, here as in all infant colonies, its growing prosperity in great measure depends'.[27]

There were, of course, other factors contributing to the relatively small number of women known to have escaped. In general, women didn't enjoy the same freedom as men. Most female convicts were employed as domestic servants and were closely supervised throughout the day and into the evening, whereas there were opportunities for men to work as shepherds and stockkeepers on the fringes of the settlements away from their masters' immediate control. Ships' captains needing to fill vacancies in their crews with escaped convicts wanted men, preferably with sailing experience, not women. Women, in any case, were always a potential source of friction in the overwhelmingly male environment of a ship.

Another interesting factor is that very few narratives written by convict women have survived. For some reason, possibly literacy, many more male convicts appear to have written about their experiences, including attempts to escape, than have women. (Even the story of Mary Bryant's extraordinary escape was written by one of her male companions.) This paucity of female narratives may well mean that some escapes by women have gone unrecorded.

The disproportionate number of women convicts in the colony and the fewer opportunities available to them inevitably meant that the bulk of the escaping was done by men. Nevertheless, Mary Bryant's legacy was potent, and there were enough determined escapers among the women to continually trouble the authorities.

5

The Council of Seven

In June 1825 Norfolk Island was resettled after having been abandoned twelve years earlier. This tiny island, 1600 kilometres north-east of Sydney, was to be reactivated as a sort of floating penitentiary for the reception of the most incorrigible offenders. Escape, it was believed by the authorities, would be impossible. The island's sole purpose was to punish and repress, and it quickly acquired a reputation of being a place where hope was forfeit and misery certain, thus fulfilling Governor Sir Thomas Brisbane's earnest desire: 'Port Macquarie for first grave offences; Moreton Bay, for runaways from the former; and Norfolk Island, as the *ne plus ultra* of Convict degradation.'[1]

On 10 December 1826 the brig *Wellington*, with 66 convicts on board, sailed from Sydney for 'Old Hell', the name given to Norfolk Island by its inmates. In command was Captain John Harwood with a detachment of twelve soldiers under a sergeant to guard his human cargo. For more than a week the brig proceeded steadily and smoothly across the flashing waters of the Pacific. The weather was indulgent, as was the convicts' conduct, which betrayed no hint of the conspiracy fomenting below decks. Perhaps the convicts' unusual mellowness of spirit and ready compliance with orders should have alerted the guards. They were, after all, men on the rim of a reputed earthly hell whose only hope of a reprieve was through their own actions.

At midday on 21 December, when they were within a day's sail of the island, the convicts put into operation a plan that was later shown to have been conceived before they came on board. The moment was carefully calculated. Six convicts were on deck with only two soldiers to watch them. The sergeant had just gone below to bring up another group of convicts for a regular session of exercise and fresh air; the rest of the platoon was off duty in the forecastle. Captain Harwood was busy taking the noon sighting. With feigned casualness the six convicts positioned themselves around their guards and on a predetermined signal pitched into them. After a brief scuffle the soldiers were overpowered and disarmed. At the same moment the captain was secured. Moving swiftly the convicts closed the forecastle hatch, but the soldiers confined there managed to get off a few shots, one of which wounded a convict in the shoulder. The unarmed sailors were rounded up without difficulty and forced into the prison hold in place of the other convicts, who had been liberated by their fellows. Aroused by the commotion, a passenger, William Buchanan, emerged from the cabin looking dangerous with a brace of pistols at the ready, but before he could bring them to bear on anyone he was slammed senseless by a blow from a musket butt. The soldiers in the forecastle continued to resist by firing through the bulkhead into the hold until they realised that it was the crew, rather than the convicts, who were their unseen targets. Reluctantly they surrendered their weapons and also their red coats which were soon adorning the backs of the leading mutineers. The wounded, including eight or nine of the soldiers, were examined, but none had suffered anything more dangerous than cuts and bruises.

With the *Wellington* now firmly under their control, the convicts gathered on the quarterdeck. They were probably surprised at the ease with which they had carried the vessel — it had taken less than fifteen minutes — and they were now faced with making some crucial decisions about what to do with their freedom. Leadership was the first issue to be canvassed. A democratic arrangement was arrived at with a former subaltern of the 48th Regiment, John Walton, who had been convicted of receiving stolen goods, being given the command. In addition, a 'council of 7 persons' was created 'to judge and punish misdemeanors, regulate the supply of provisions, water etc'.[2] Its composition is unknown, but presumably it included Walton, the convicts who had assumed the roles of first and second mates, William Douglass and John 'Flash Jack' Edwards, and Charles Clay, who had been allocated the position of steward.

Next on the agenda was their destination. It was decided that the best option was to make a run for South America after landing the soldiers and unwanted crew at the earliest possible landfall. About twenty of the convicts, fearful of the consequences of failure, refused to become further involved and were confined below with the soldiers. Some of the sailors were released to help work the ship, and Captain Harwood was persuaded to navigate. They got under way but on inspecting the ship's stores it was found that they contained only sufficient water to last a week at the most, not nearly enough for a crossing of the vast emptiness of the Pacific. Accordingly the brig was hauled round, and with the water creaming under her bow, a course was shaped for New Zealand, only 650 kilometres to the south, where the water supply could be replenished.

The voyage to New Zealand was remarkably harmonious. Among this disparate collection of petty thieves and thoroughgoing villains — most of them multiple offenders who had been thrown together at the whim of an autocratic government — brawling over plunder and attempting to beat up their former guards was to be expected. That order was in fact tautly maintained by the Council of Seven and challenges to its authority effectively quashed is evident in the following extracts from the log book kept by the mutineers:[3]

This day [22 December] regularly placed the men in watches; 14 centinels, and 7 to work, and the 4 sailors in each watch, enacted regulations to prevent irregularity and dissension ... regularity and good order is predominant, and a glow of satisfaction pervaded every countenance interested in the events; from this day the sheep slaughtered as required, 2, 3 or 4 per day.

This day [23 December] being an holyday, was big with the fate of two men, who were brought before the council; one charged with sleeping on his post, the other for getting into the hold, and breaking open a cask of wine, and getting drunk upon it; the first was sentenced a few extra guards, and his grog stopped; the other was sentenced — to be put in irons, and to be sent on shore at New Zealand, instead of proceeding with us to our ultimate destination, and at the same time cautioned everyone against the same acts, or they might expect the same fate; overhauled the whole of the government despatches and ships papers; returned all but the manifest and invoices; moderate breezes.

In all the excitement of their novel situation as masters of a government vessel, the convicts did not forget Christmas. It was celebrated in traditional style as the relevant log, entry, written with sly good humour, records:

This being Christmas Day, and the only deficiency we have at present found on the part of government, was in not supplying us with plums, issued an order, if any individual on board had any plums they must be given up for all hands; plums were procured, four geese killed, together with three sheep, spent a very comfortable day, moderately indulging ourselves with some gin and brandy.[4]

As the distance from Norfolk Island lengthened, life on the *Wellington* settled into a conventional shipboard pattern. The watches were rigorously kept, those of the convicts with carpentry and coopering skills were put to work making repairs, the brig's sides were scraped and it was cleaned and painted inside and out. 'Good order and content' prevailed and the council was called upon to enforce discipline on only three more occasions. The first two cases involved the theft of wine and drunkenness, and the culprits were put in irons and had their grog stopped. The third offender faced the far more serious charge of:

> attempting to breed discontent and dissatisfaction among the late prisoners. After a trial of two hours before the council, he was found guilty of attempting a revolt and mutiny, sentenced to two pairs of irons, to be landed at New Zealand, and to be kept upon deck day and night, and not allowed communication with any person whatever.[5]

As well as meticulously maintaining the ship's log, Walton also wrote a dispatch to Governor Darling. As might be expected, it was full of invective and contained a catalogue of grievances, chief among them being Walton's own claim that his life sentence had not been reduced to seven years' transportation as had been promised. He concluded on a defiant note 'by assuring His Excellency that he was quite aware what his fate would be should he ever be re-taken, and that a hempen cord would terminate his career'.[6] This document was eventually delivered to the governor, who ordered its immediate destruction in case its unflattering contents were made use of by the press.

Fortunately the ocean was empty of other ships to interrupt or, worse, terminate their flight. The winds were generally light — at one stage the brig wallowed in a calm for 24 hours — and it was not until New Year's Day that the west coast of New Zealand was sighted. Heeling before a brisk wind they rounded North Cape and coasted south until, on 5 January, they slid quietly into the Bay of Islands. The *Wellington* glided up the expansive harbour to the settlement of Kororareka. At that time the bay, with its deep coves and abundance of fresh water, pigs and sweet potatoes, was a haven for whalers, and two whaling vessels, the *Sisters* and *Harriet*, were already riding at anchor there.

On shore, the Reverend Henry Williams, superintendent of the nearby mission station at Paihia and a former British naval officer, noted in his journal:

> At 8 o'clock, obs'd a brig standing in for the Bay: at 10 she came to anchor. We obs'd a number of persons standing aft and were in hopes of news from Port Jackson, with an accession to the mission.[7]

Meanwhile Captain Robert Duke and Captain Clark of the two whalers had put off in a whaleboat to offer help as pilots. As they stepped on board they were surrounded by a squad of 'soldiers' and ushered aft to the quarterdeck where they were introduced to Walton, posing as the brig's lawful commander. He informed them that he was bound for the Thames River on government orders with troops, stores and equipment to found a new settlement, but having run short of water had put into the bay to replenish his supplies. Captain Duke replied with his offer to guide them to an anchorage close to the usual watering place. This, Walton 'politely accepted'.[8]

'No sooner was the Anchor down,' remembered Duke some years later,

> than the canoes came off in hundreds. There being no effort made to keep them off, she was soon swarmed with women as the prisoners were all dressed in Soldiers Clothing which was rather novel sight in those days; to the good folks of New Zealand they were very lavish in their presents.[9]

While all this fraternising with the Maoris was going on, Duke returned to his own ship, somewhat perplexed by the unskilled way the brig was being handled and the unmilitary bearing of the soldiers. A few hours later he was joined by one of the missionaries, William Fairburn, who was anxious to know if the *Wellington* carried any letters for the mission. Together they rowed across to the brig. Captain Duke's concerns were intensified when, on making his way to the cabin, he became aware that the brig 'was literally crammed [with people] below, upon Deck and even in the Rigging'.[10] And, he noted, the quantity of water they were taking on board seemed excessive for the short passage to the Thames River.

To his professional eyes the scene that confronted him as he entered the cabin was even more puzzling:

We found about a dozen seated round the Table regaling themselves upon the Governor's good wine and beer which they asked us to partake of. On getting the information we required, we had some difficulty in forcing our way thro' the crowds of Natives & Soldiers and get to the gangway to our boats. Such a scene I never before witnessed.[11]

Among the soldiers and crew bartering with the Maoris, Fairburn was surprised to recognise a convict he had known in Sydney. Then Captain Duke caught sight of a man he knew to have received a sentence of transportation to Norfolk Island. Thoroughly disturbed by what they had seen the two men hurriedly left the brig. In due course Fairburn reported to Reverend Williams his suspicion that the brig had been taken over by convicts from Port Jackson. With Captain Duke endorsing this opinion, Williams decided to see for himself in the company of Fairburn and the two whaling captains.

The unseamanlike confusion and absence of discipline that confronted him as he climbed on board were quite foreign to his own naval experience:

The brig certainly presented a very different scene from any I had ever before witnessed. The decks were crowded to excess, with very ill-looking fellows, about twenty under arms. The cabin was filled, and wine and spirits passed freely about. I did not say many words, but was soon fully aware what was the matter.[12]

Williams was equally unimpressed by Walton who, surprisingly, accepted an invitation to dine with them on board the *Sisters* that evening. As they left the brig one of the crew (who later proved to be Captain Harwood) managed to slip a hastily scribbled note to Fairburn which gave a true account of the *Wellington*'s situation, that en route for Norfolk Island she had been seized by convicts who intended to sail her to South America.

No doubt Walton was feeling very uneasy when he arrived on board the *Sisters*. He must have suspected that his imposture had not been entirely convincing. His composure slipped further under a barrage of questions from Williams, and when Fairburn produced Captain Harwood's note he did not attempt to deny its accuracy. According to Williams, 'He bid us all defiance: stating that every man would sell his life very dear; he also produced a letter written by him to the Governor, dictated in exceedingly impudent terms.'[13] After such a belligerent response, the prudent course would surely have been to confine Walton below decks, thus depriving the convicts of leadership, but unaccountably he was allowed to return to the *Wellington*. Duke's explanation was that as a heavy gale had blown up from the north-east the brig was effectively bottled up in the bay anyway.[14] Also on his mind was the risk involved in a confrontation with a ship full of armed desperadoes.

Reverend Williams, however, espoused a more positive policy. Reverting to his earlier life as a fighting lieutenant on a British man-o'-war during the Napoleonic era, he urged direct intervention to prevent the brig putting to sea:

> I proposed to fire some great guns and disable the vessel, but everyone appeared extremely fearful lest the vessels should in return be attacked. After much consultation, I left the ship, distressed at the idea that the vessel should escape. In the eveng. I made it a special point in prayer, that she might not be suffered to escape.[15]

During the next day, Saturday 6 January, he had no communication with the whalers or the *Wellington* but he noted 'Numbers of canoes going over to Kororareka desirous to attack the Brig. The prisoners very impudent; everyone much disturbed concerning the Brig; our thoughts all afloat.'[16] He was not to know that Captain Duke had finally roused himself into taking some action. At daylight 'we got all our Guns on Deck,' he recorded, 'which amounted to 8 long six pounders, which we ranged all on one side. With a spring upon our cable we could get our whole broadside to bear upon him.'[18] This, however, was a purely defensive measure and was taken, as the *Sisters*' log makes clear, 'in case the pirates should make any attack upon us'.[19]

If the convicts had in fact done so, they might well have carried the day. The artist and traveller Augustus Earle, who was in the area later that year and met Captain Duke, was firmly of this opinion. 'Had the pirates acted with promptness and spirit,' he noted in his journal,

> they might easily have made themselves masters of the whole, but while they were arguing and hesitating where they should make their first attack, the whalers were actively employed in getting their great guns out of the hold, and in preparing their vessels for defence; so that, by the time the pirates came to the resolution to attack them, the whalers were in good posture for resistance.[20]

Despite the arming of the *Sisters*, relations between the whalers and the convicts remained strangely cordial. At eight o'clock the *Wellington* came alongside the *Harriet*. Walton offered to trade provisions and tools — all government property of course — for various articles needed for the long voyage to South America. At midday an invitation was sent to Walton for dinner. He declined but responded with the following courteous note:

> Captain J. Walton's compliments to Captain Clark, and will be glad of his company to spend an hour or two this afternoon with himself, the late officers and passengers, in which he may rest assured nothing but sociability is intended. N.B. I canot with propriety allow Captain Harwood to go out of the vessel alone.[21]

Both Duke and Clark accepted and were amicably received onto the brig. They were able to converse with Mr Buchanan and the other passengers who assured them that 'they had been well used since the time of their capture by the prisoners in every respect, except plundering their property'.[22] They also agreed to witness a statement prepared by Walton in which he exonerated Captain Harwood and his crew from any complicity in the proposed voyage to South America. The statement also conveniently excused the whaling captains from failing to take any action against the convicts:

> their vessels being whalers, and too weak in force, without endanger-
> ing the lives of their crews, and of the troops on board the brig

Wellington, to recapture her from the hands of the prisoners or present crew, by whom she was taken on her passage to Norfolk Island.[23]

While the two captains were socialising with the convicts, Philip Tapsell, chief mate of the *Sisters*, was pushing matters forward rather faster than the cautious Duke, with his stance of neutrality, would have wished. A more pugnacious man than his captain, he was prepared to defy the convicts in the hope of effecting a rescue:

> He got a spring upon [the *Sisters*'s] cable, which when the pirates discovered, they called Captain Duke on one side and told him they observed the spring on the cable, and that they were told by the native girls the guns were loaded, and that the chief mate meant to fire four guns at them, if they got under weigh.[24]

Only when he gave his word not to use the guns against them was Duke permitted to return to his vessel. Once on board he was faced with a determined crew who informed him:

> that if it was agreeable, they would endeavour to stop the brig, rescue the poor fellows that were below and reinstate the Captain; and at 7 p.m. we resolved not to let the brig go out of the harbour, but to attack her the next morning. The brig having moved further in shore, and clear of the *Harriet*, we hove taut our spring and brought the ship's broadside on to her.[25]

By next morning the wind had moderated and the brig was observed making preparations to get under way. Captain Duke sent a message to Walton demanding the release of the passengers, soldiers and crew, otherwise he 'would bring all his Spars & Rigging about his ears'.[26] Walton's reply was to haul up the anchor and begin making sail. Duke raised his colours and without further warning 'let him have the whole Broadside'. The *Harriet* joined in and both ships continued firing at intervals for four hours 'which crippled his Main Mast and Bowsprit and shot away nearly the whole of his Standing Rigging'.[27] The convicts did not return the fire even though the brig carried two long 10-pounders on the quarter-deck. Instead, most of them scrambled below out of danger while a few others dived overboard. At nine o'clock one of them was brave enough to creep on deck and hoist a white flag. Taking this to be a request for a parley, Duke sent a boat across to hear their terms. It came back with the following note from Walton:

> It is with the greatest reluctance I have, on the part of the majority of the crew, to request that if they resign the vessel, they may be permitted to land some provisions, etc. etc. together with themselves. On these terms we will surrender, otherwise the passengers, crew, and soldiers must share our fate.[28]

Duke was happy enough to accept this offer and set about organising the evacuation of the *Wellington*. The convicts were afraid that once on shore they would be at risk of massacre by the Maoris, who had already shown signs of aggression towards them. To reassure them Duke sent a message to Reverend Williams asking him to come over to Kororareka and use his considerable influence to keep the warlike Maoris under control. Williams had been woken at five o'clock that morning by the first broadside and, though distressed that the peace of the Sabbath should have been disturbed in this way, he had nevertheless been excited by 'the shot flying about the Brig'.[29] On receipt of Duke's request he hurried across to the *Sisters*, eager to be involved in the action.

By five o'clock in the evening the last of the convicts had been landed (leaving 25 in irons on the brig). Williams proved powerless to protect them. As soon as they stepped ashore the Maoris fell on them, stripping them of their possessions and treating them as 'runaway slaves for whom one day or the other they would get a reward'.[30] Towards nightfall the brig was warped close to the *Sisters* and the *Harriet*, a precautionary measure in case she was attacked from the shore.

Next day after breakfast, Duke, Clark and Williams made a survey of the brig to determine what damage she had suffered. Her 'masts, hull and rigging were very much wounded', and the carpenters were set to work making repairs.[31] The convicts had broken into the stores and removed everything of value, and the soldiers, 'who had scarcely an article of Clothing, to cover them', had to be restrained 'from taking summary vengeance on the Prisoners who remained on board'.[32] Williams was greatly disappointed that Duke, when he returned to his own vessel, showed no inclination to recover the convicts he had landed. According to the missionary, 'the Cap. expressed himself afraid to put to sea with them'.[33]

Events, however, would soon cause Duke to change his mind. He was called on shore to the watering place where some of the convicts were reported to be destroying the *Sisters'* water casks. While dealing with this, two Maori chiefs of his acquaintance approached him with a story that they had caught William Douglass, armed with a musket, waiting to ambush him. When they produced the wretched fellow he did not deny the accusation and in fact threatened Duke with a pistol before somehow escaping into the bush. Duke's reaction was not to pursue the would-be assassin but to offer a reward to any Maori who brought him on board the *Sisters*, 'but he being a powerful man and resolute they were afraid of him and wanted to know if they shot him and brought his head would they be entitled to the reward'.[34] This, Duke said, he could not countenance.

The Maoris plunged eagerly into the task of tracking down not only Douglass but rounding up the other convicts as well. During the next fortnight the convicts were led on board the *Sisters* in small batches, their captors receiving rewards of gunpowder and muskets. When Douglass was delivered 'lashed from head to foot with rope',[35] Duke gave orders for him to be chained to a ringbolt on the deck, given an empty wine cask to sleep in and kept separate from the other prisoners. Fear of mutiny now took hold of the captain; muskets, pistols and cutlasses were issued to the crew, and the armourer was set to work making irons. 'A strong guard was kept over the prisoners, and double irons put on three of the most desperate characters.'[36] In spite of these precautions, a number of the more spirited convicts contrived to file through their manacles and 'were within a few hours of a murderous outbreak' when the plot was betrayed by an informer. The ringleaders were sent to join Douglass on the quarterdeck and they too were given a 'tun-butt as a sleeping room'.[37] The failure of this escape attempt in no way discouraged the convicts, understandable with the gallows waiting for them in Sydney. Less than 24 hours later, another 'diabolical conspiracy' was discovered. Eleven of them had cut through their irons and got hold of two knives, 'their intention being to rush up the hatchway, get possession of the vessel and put the crew to death if they did not comply with their wishes, and again take the brig'.[38] This time the punishment was far more severe — they each received two dozen lashes and the armourer was ordered to make handcuffs as well as leg irons.

On 28 January the *Sisters* finally weighed anchor and set sail for Sydney in company with the *Wellington*. Only six of the convicts had not been recovered. These appear to have been retained by a Maori chief as slaves. Some months later they were seen at Kororareka where one of them burned down a hut belonging to Captain Duke. At the time it was occupied by Augustus Earle, who wrote in his journal:

> I chanced to be in the house alone, and was amazed by seeing an Englishman enter the hut with his face tattoo'd all over. Not being aware he was one of the runaways from the 'Wellington', I spoke to him. He slunk into our cooking house on pretence of lighting his pipe, and before ten minutes had elapsed, the house was in flames.[39]

It was Earle's opinion that this action was prompted by a desire for revenge against Duke.

During the voyage the convicts made another despairing effort to take control of their own destiny. Once again they planned to seize the vessel and carry out their original scheme of sailing her to South America, and once again they were betrayed by an informer. The conspirators were handcuffed behind their backs but several days later were found with their hands in front again 'having drawn their legs up through their arms'.[40] Captain Duke was a vastly relieved man when, on 9 February, he sailed into Port Jackson and handed over responsibility for his dangerous and resourceful charges to the authorities.

Towards the end of February, 31 convicts were arraigned before the Supreme Court for the piratical seizure of the *Wellington*. (It was considered that the other 29 had not participated in the affair.) Their defence rested principally on their counsel's contention that the instrument authorising their transfer from the *Phoenix* hulk to the *Wellington* had been legally deficient and that therefore being in a state of duress they had a right to liberate themselves. While appreciating the ingenuity of this argument, the judge nevertheless overruled it. A total of 23 were sentenced to death, the remainder being acquitted. For two days the Executive Council deliberated over the sentences, eventually concluding that only six of the 23 would be required for execution. These were to be chosen by ascertaining 'which among the Prisoners seemed least deserving of clemency, either in consequence of their violent conduct whilst effecting their purpose, or from the vicious course of their former lives'.[41] On this extraordinary basis the six were selected. They included Douglass but not Walton. His sentence was commuted to hard labour in chains on Norfolk Island during his natural life. In sparing him, the council was influenced by the 'circumstances of moderation and humanity, which marked his conduct after the capture of the *Wellington*', and because his original offence had been his first and not a capital one. Governor Sir Ralph Darling disagreed; he considered the execution of Walton necessary to serve as an example but he was unwilling to act contrary to the unanimous wishes of the council.

A final attempt to escape by six of the convicts under the leadership of 'Flash Jack' Edwards was foiled when a gaoler overheard them estimating the height of the outer wall of their gaol. 'O! that's nothing,' said one, 'if only we had the irons off.' 'That,' replied Edwards, 'we'll soon manage.' At this point the gaoler burst in and began to search their cell. In a short time he discovered three knives, a file and some other tools 'planted in a situation where the prying eye alone of a gaoler would have thought of exploring – in the bottom of the night tub!'[42]

On 5 March, immediately after the names of the six were announced, the jury presented a petition for mercy on behalf of Douglass. It was supported by the sergeant of the guard and two of the soldiers, who stated that Douglass had 'been the means of preserving their lives when the prisoners seized the vessel'.[43] According to Captain Duke, Douglass was 'just on the point of being launched into eternity' when his reprieve arrived from Government House at Parramatta.[44] Instead of swinging, he too was to spend the rest of his life on Norfolk Island. No such mercy was extended to the other five who were duly hanged. The editor of the *Monitor* sternly condemned the government's action, claiming that they 'appeared too much the victim of policy, and too little of malefactors receiving a just and expedient doom'. An enthusiastic crowd which turned out for the executions agreed and roared its disapproval with cries of 'What are they hanged for; do they suffer for sparing men's lives?' and 'Is this the way to reward humanity?'[45]

Meanwhile Captain Duke had petitioned the governor for compensation for loss of profits in consequence of 'having to quit the Whaling Station at New Zealand at the commencement of the season, and which will be over before the return of your petitioner to that or any other Whaling Station'.[46] (In the light of this petition it seems likely that his reluctance to act against the convicts may have been prompted by commercial considerations rather than timidity.) His claim was referred to the Colonial Office in London, which awarded him £1800 as well as sufficient gunpowder and muskets to replace those he had given to the Maoris.

Curiously this was not the end of Duke's involvement with the *Wellington* pirates. In 1832 he was fishing for cod off Norfolk Island when a boat pulled out from the shore and made towards his ship. As it came alongside Duke was surprised to recognise his 'old friend Douglas' in the stern sheets. When he questioned the officer in command about him he was told that he 'was a well behaved man and the only one on the island who could take the boat out & in the surf'.[47] Two years later Douglass turned up at Duke's house in Sydney. Apparently he had received a conditional pardon for 'meritorious services as coxswain of the boat'[48] and was looking for work. All Duke could offer him was some advice 'as to his future good behaviour'. This Douglass seems to have ignored, for two months later he was charged with robbery and stabbing a constable. By chance Duke was attending the Supreme Court as a juror on the day he was tried, found guilty and once again sentenced to Norfolk Island for life.

6

Wild White Men

For convicts on the run, survival in the bush was always a hazardous business, as Alexander Pearce (see Chapter 3) and others before him discovered, often too late. Yet parties of runaways continued to stumble about in the unfamiliar and dangerous landscape, many to be claimed by hunger and exhaustion or picked off by hostile Aborigines. From the earliest days, convicts had provoked the Aborigines by souveniring unattended spears, clubs, shields and even canoes, which they sold to sailors on the transport ships. Naturally the theft of these implements, necessary for their daily subsistence, moved the Aborigines to retaliate. In May 1788, a week after a convict had been speared on the government farm, two more, who were cutting rushes for thatch near what is now Rushcutters Bay, were found dead, one of them transfixed by four spears.

In May 1804 the *Resource* picked up a man at the entrance to Newcastle. He had hailed the vessel from the north side of the river, and was naked, wearing only 'a beard that swept his breast'.[1] His right hand was crushed and he had a deep spear wound in his shoulder, as well as lacerations to his head. On examination he proved to be a convict named James Field who, with two companions, had made off in a boat in the hope of being taken on board an American ship that was about to leave Sydney. Failing in this endeavour, they had been swept northward to Port Stephens where they remained for three days. They then put to sea again, with the intention of reaching Timor, but a heavy gale drove them ashore. The boat was smashed to pieces, and they were on their way back to Sydney on foot when they 'were assaulted by a body of natives, who showered spears upon them with a barbarity only to be conceived by those that have witnessed the brutal ferocity of these unfeeling savages'.[2] Field's companions were killed and he himself was left for dead. He continued south along the coast and after three days came 'to the spot of his deliverance'. The commandant of Newcastle, Lieutenant Charles Menzies, who had survived a convict plot to assassinate him earlier in the month, publicly displayed Field to the convicts in the settlement in the hope that 'the truly miserable and wretched spectacle he exhibited, will prevent others from attempting the same with any of our boats that go up the River, by representing to them the punishment and misery that awaits their rashness and offence'.[3]

Apparently it was to no avail, for less than a year later two men and three women were taken into Parramatta after a parlous flight south from Newcastle. Within hours of escaping they had 'undergone the customary ceremony of being stripped and deprived of every morsel of provision by the natives',[4] and only kept their lives because one of them had previously shown some kindness to one of their assailants.

Petty thievery was by no means the worst offence to be suffered by Aborigines at the hands of convicts. 'A more serious evil to which Black men were subject,' wrote the missionary Lancelot Threlkeld in 1825, was 'the taking away of their wives ... for purposes which would not bear the light of day.'[5] Even children were not immune to convict lust. The horrified missionary continued:

> I have heard at night the shrieks of Girls, about 8 or 9 years of age, taken by force by the vile men of Newcastle. One man came to me with his hand broken by the butt-end of a musket because he would not give up his wife. There are now two government stockmen, that are every night annoying the Blacks by taking their little girls.[6]

Three years later the explorer and botanist Allan Cunningham noted the general hostility of the Moreton Bay Aborigines towards escaped convicts and attributed it to 'liberties having been taken with the women by the convicts'.[7]

Aborigines thus had much reason to despise the convicts, who in their black-and-yellow uniforms were easily disting-uishable from other white people. The convicts, too, at least in their own eyes, had cause to resent the Aborigines. The convict artist Thomas Watling, who was transported in 1792 for forgery, had this complaint:

[M]any of these savages are allowed what is termed a freeman's ration of provisions for their idleness ... and they are treated with the most singular tenderness. This you will suppose not more than laudable; but is there one spark of charity exhibited to poor wretches, who are at least denominated Christians? No they are frequently denied the common necessaries of life! wrought to death under the oppressive heat of a burning sun; or barbarously afflicted with often little-merited secondary punishment.[8]

Added to this was Governor Phillip's seeming refusal to bring to justice those Aborigines who attacked convicts in the bush. 'I have not the least doubt of the convicts being the aggressors,'[9] he wrote of one such incident, despite denials of provocation by the victims. And on another occasion he wrote, 'I did not mean to punish any of the natives for killing these people, which, it is more than probable, they did in their own defence, or in defending their canoes.'[10] This opinion was shared by Captain Watkin Tench, who concluded that 'the unprovoked outrages committed upon the [Aborigines], by unprincipled individuals among us, cause the evils we have experienced'.[11] The result was racial intolerance with its usual accompaniments of contempt, ignorance and violence. To Watling, the Aborigines were characterised by 'irascibility, ferocity, cunning, treachery, revenge, filth and immodesty', and their only virtue was the fact that they were not cannibals.[12] This view was echoed in 1830 by a Colonial Committee in Van Diemen's Land, which came to the conclusion that acts of violence by Aborigines proceeded 'from a wanton savage spirit, inherent in them, and impelling them to mischief and cruelty'.[13] With such opinions as these abroad, the chances of racial harmony were slight.

In October 1788, Governor Phillip had reported that 'the natives now attack any straggler they meet unarmed'.[14] In the same month Lieutenant Ralph Clark wrote that 'the natives have never Yet come into camp but are ready to attack the Convicts in the woods when ever the[y] think the[y] can get the better of them'.[15] Thirty years later the situation had not changed. Sergeant John Evans noted that the Hunter River Aborigines, 'when in the woods, will take the life of any person, soldier or other, who may happen to have given them offence in the settlement. They never forget anyone whom they have seen.'[16]

By the 1820s Aborigines were being rewarded with tobacco, sugar, blankets and even money for turning escaped convicts in, and their skills as trackers were being utilised. In his report on the colony Commissioner John Bigge wrote:

> They accompany the soldiers sent in pursuit, and by the extraordinary strength of sight that they possess, improved by their daily exercise of it in pursuit of kangaroos and opossums, they can trace to a great distance, with wonderful accuracy, the impressions of the human foot. Nor are they afraid of meeting the fugitive convicts in the woods, when sent in their pursuit, without the soldiers; by their skill in throwing their long pointed wooden darts they wound and disable them, strip them of their clothes, and bring them back as prisoners.[17]

In 1820 two runaways from Newcastle, John Kirby and James Thompson, were tracked by a band of Aborigines and surrounded. As they were being led back to the settlement, Kirby spitefully stabbed their chief in the stomach, mortally wounding him. Immediately the other Aborigines set up a great cry, which attracted the soldiers who had also been sent in pursuit. Kirby was brought to trial for murder, and even though the Aborigines were not permitted to appear as witnesses because, as non-Christians, they were unable to swear on the Bible to tell the truth, he was convicted on circumstantial evidence and sentenced to death.[18] When he was hanged on 18 December 1820 he became the first white man to be executed for the murder of an Aboriginal person. On all previous occasions the charge had been quashed or the death sentence commuted.

Not all encounters between Aboriginal people and convicts ended in violence. There are cases on record where absconding convicts were given shelter by Aboriginal tribes and protected from pursuit. Mention has already been made of the five convicts who, after bolting from Parramatta in 1790, headed out to sea in a small, leaky boat and were discovered five years later living with Aborigines at Port Stephens. On their return they spoke not of hostile savages but of a hospitable people who had accepted them as unfortunate strangers thrown up by the sea and therefore entitled to protection. They had been allotted wives, by whom several of them had fathered children, and were kept well supplied with fish and other food. Eventually they came to understand that the Aborigines regarded them as ancestors of relatives who, after death, had migrated to another world and had now returned.

After escaping from Port Phillip in 1803, William Buckley, a 2-metre-tall ex-soldier, lived for 32 years with the Wathaurong people. When he finally gave himself up he had forgotten how to speak English and was identified only by a tattoo on his right arm in the form of his initials, 'W.B.', part of a group of tatoos comprising a mermaid, a sun, a crescent moon, seven stars and a monkey. Over the next few weeks, as he gradually recalled his native tongue, his story began to unfold. It was an extraordinary tale and he became something of a celebrity, popularly known as 'the wild white man'. Seventeen years later he collaborated with a Tasmanian newspaper editor, John Morgan, to write his autobiography. The result was *The Life and Adventures of William Buckley*, which was published in 1852. As

Buckley could neither read nor write, and the narrative was composed from 'rough notes and memoranda, made at various times, and by conversations',[19] Morgan's own editorial input must have been considerable. It does not follow, however, that the book should be viewed as misleading or generally unreliable. No doubt Buckley's memory was faulty at times, and Morgan's embellishments fanciful, but it remains the most detailed contemporary account of Buckley's life available.

Buckley was born in Cheshire in 1780 and as a young man became apprenticed to a bricklayer before joining the King's Own Regiment of Foot. He was wounded in action in the Netherlands, and upon returning to England seems to have drifted into questionable company. He was convicted of stealing two pieces of Irish cloth worth 8/- from a shop, and was sentenced to death. Reprieved and sentenced to transportation for life instead, he found himself on HMS *Calcutta*, with 300 other convicts (including Robert Stewart), bound for Port Phillip in Victoria, where Lieutenant-Colonel David Collins had orders to found a new settlement.

The expedition reached this wild, unexplored corner of the British Empire in October 1803. A temporary camp was set up at a small sandy beach just inside the entrance to the bay (near present-day Sorrento), and the convicts were set to work. Buckley was drafted to help build a stone magazine and a storehouse. However, within weeks Collins realised that the site was totally unsuitable for a settlement — the soil was thin, there was little fresh water to be found, the heat was oppressive, and they were harassed by hordes of flies by day and given no respite from mosquitoes at night. So he was mightily pleased when on 13 December he received a dispatch from Governor King authorising him to abandon Port Phillip and transfer the colony to the Derwent River in Van Diemen's Land.

During these few months at Port Phillip, at least twenty convicts absconded from the camp at different times in the wild hope of meeting up with a South Sea whaler further along the coast. Most returned after a few days of freedom and received 100 lashes for their trouble. Among these hopeful escapers was William Buckley. On the night of 27 December, he and three companions slipped quietly into the bush, their desperate plan being to strike north for Sydney — a plan which even Buckley admitted was 'little short of madness'. They had with them a fowling gun, a kettle, some tin pots and enough rations for several days. However, before they could get clear they were challenged by a sentry, who, on receiving no reply, fired into the darkness and with more luck than skill succeeded in bringing one of them down with a bullet in the stomach. The other three fled for their lives and kept on running until they dropped from exhaustion.

For several days they followed the curve of the bay. They crossed the Yarra River and moved into the You Yang Hills where they ate the last of their rations and rested. Next morning, in search of food, they descended to the coast, eventually reaching Corio Bay where they found a freshwater spring and some shellfish. Another two days' march brought them to Swan Island, which they were able to reach at low tide. From here they could see the *Calcutta* on the opposite side of the bay. They had come practically full circle. Sydney was as far away as ever, and in despair they decided to give themselves up, for 'although the dread of punishment was naturally great, the fear of starvation exceeded it'. They endeavoured to attract the attention of the ship's crew by hoisting their shirts on poles. At night they lit a signal fire, but there was no response. After six days 'signalizing all the time, but without success', Buckley's two companions decided to retrace their steps around the bay and back to the encampment. Buckley, however, changed his mind and refused to join them, 'being determined to endure every kind of suffering rather than again surrendering my liberty'. Taking the gun with them, the two men set off, leaving Buckley to continue his solitary journey. Only one of them made it back to the camp; the other was never seen again.

On his first day's march westward along the coast, Buckley saw a group of about 100 Aborigines but managed to evade them by swimming across the Barwon River. That night he lay down to sleep in thick scrub, covering himself with leaves and broken boughs. At dawn he left his 'uncomfortable lodging, and took again to the beach'. For several weeks he continued in this way, finding plenty of berries and shellfish but little fresh water, until he came, in a state of exhaustion, to what he described as his 'first permanent resting place'. Here, in the shadow of a large rock, he built a shelter out of branches and seaweed. He remembered:

> It was a work of great labour for a sick man, but I persevered and finally completed my sea-beach home in about three or four days; there I remained several months. In addition to my supply of shell-fish, I found also in great abundance a creeping plant [pig-face], the flavour of which is very much like that of the common water-melon — rather insipid, but very refreshing. I also discovered a kind of currant, black and white, so that I fared sumptuously every day, and rapidly recovered my strength, mentally and bodily.

One day he was startled from an idle reverie about his Robinson Crusoe-like existence by the sound of human voices. Looking up he saw three Aborigines armed with spears standing on an overhang above him. His first thought was to hide, but realising he would be unable to escape their notice, he stepped out into the open. Amazed by his unusual height, they repeatedly grabbed his hands and beat their chests, at the same time making a strange whining noise. Buckley's initial trepidation proved to be unfounded, for after accompanying him to his hut they cooked and shared a meal of crayfish which they caught in the sea below. After this meal they indicated that they wished him to follow them, and reluctantly he did so, all the time looking for an opportunity to escape. They spent the night in 'small turf cabins', and next day Buckley indicated that he preferred to go his own way. After 'a warm discussion by signs' they apparently gave in and set off without him. As soon as they were out of sight he made a dash for the coast.

For some days he wandered through the bush subsisting only on a few berries and a little water that he scooped from clay holes. At night he was terrified by the howling of dingoes and the unearthly shrieks of koalas. His clothes were in tatters, his shoes were worn out, and he was lonely and cold — all in all, he was in a pitiable state, and he determined to try and make his way back to the *Calcutta*, supposing she was still at Port Phillip. Half-starved and only able to travel short distances each day, he began to retrace his steps. After a handful of hard-won miles he stumbled across a mound of earth surmounted by an upright spear, which he took to use as a walking stick. By now he was becoming seriously weak, and with winter fast approaching began to despair of surviving.

One morning, while fossicking for food, he was seen by two Aboriginal women. Unaware that he was being observed, he lay down at the base of a large tree to rest. The women slipped away, only to return shortly afterwards with their men, who seized his arms and beat their chests just as the others had done before. They pulled him to his feet, and with the women helping him to walk, led him to their camp, the men all the time shouting and tearing their hair. His fears for his life diminished when they fed him with a pulpy mixture of gum and water, which he ate greedily, following it up with a couple of fat witchetty grubs. He was further reassured when he realised that they had given him a name — Murrangurk. He later learned that this was the name of a member of their tribe who had recently been killed in battle. It was his spear that Buckley had taken from the mound — the man's burial mound, in fact — and they took this for a sign that their kinsman had returned to them in the form of this tall white man. Buckley wrote:

> They have a belief that when they die, they go to some place or other, and are there made white men, and that they then return to this world

again for another existence ... In cases where they have killed white men, it has generally been because they imagined them to have been originally enemies, or belonging to tribes with whom they were hostile.

The next day Buckley accompanied the group to their main encampment at the mouth of the Barwon River. That night a great fire was lit and he found himself the guest of honour at a corroboree. Relieved that he was not to be roasted in the flames, as he had at first feared, he observed the proceedings with interest.

The women, having seated themselves by the fire, the men joined the assemblage armed with clubs more than two feet long; having painted themselves with pipeclay, which abounds on the banks of the lake. The women kept their rugs rolled tight up, after which, they stretched them between their knees, forming a sort of drum. These they beat with their hands ... Presently the men came up in a kind of close column, they also beating time with their sticks, by knocking them one against the other, making altogether a frightful noise. The man seated in front appeared to be the leader of the orchestra, or master of the band — indeed I may say, the master of the ceremonies generally. He marched the whole mob, men and women, boys and girls, backwards and forwards at his pleasure, directing the singing and dancing, with the greatest decision and air of authority. This scene must have lasted at least three hours, when as a wind-up, they gave three tremendous shouts, at the same time pointing to the sky with their sticks; they each shook me heartily by the hand, again beating their breasts, as a token of friendship.

Several days later Buckley was taken to another camp where he met the brother of the man whose spear he had taken. He was accepted by him and his wife as the dead man returned to life. Over time Buckley became completely identified with this family group. He accompanied them on their seasonal wanderings; he learned how to hunt; he became familiar with their customs; and eventually he mastered their language. Meetings with other tribal groups sometimes ended in fierce fighting, generally over women, but Buckley was never expected to take part and happily remained a noncombatant. For the next 32 years he entered into this new way of life, taking two wives at different times and developing a genuine regard for his Aboriginal companions. He is supposed to have fathered several children but was generally reticent on this point. However, later reports of an exceptionally tall and light-skinned young woman having been seen among the Aborigines inevitably led to the belief that she was his daughter.

On several occasions he heard that white men had landed at Westernport, but he was too afraid of the consequences to give himself up. However, in July 1835 he learned that a group of Aborigines was planning to spear some white men who were living nearby at Indented Head. Buckley later claimed that it was out of concern for their safety that he decided to visit them. They were, in fact, members of a small group who had been left there a few months earlier by John Batman as the advance party of another attempt to establish a colony in Port Phillip. One of their number, the surveyor John Wedge, left an account of Buckley's arrival at the settlement, which at that time consisted of a hut with several Aboriginal families camped nearby:

> On being observed Buckley caused great surprise, and indeed some alarm; his gigantic stature, his height being nearly six feet six inches, enveloped in a kangaroo skin rug; his long beard and hair of thirty-three years growth, together with his spears, shields, and clubs, it may readily be supposed presenting a most extraordinary appearance ... Buckley proceeded at once to the encampments, and seated himself among the natives, taking no notice of the white men, who, however quickly detected, to their great astonishment, the features of a European; and after considerable difficulty, succeeded in learning who he was.[20]

Wedge, who thought that Buckley would be a useful interpreter for the new settlement, obtained a pardon for him. Buckley was thereafter employed at a salary of £50 but was never comfortable in the role of intermediary, sensing that neither the white settlers nor the Aborigines ever fully trusted him. In 1837 he moved to Hobart, where he became a government storekeeper and married a widow with two children.

Meanwhile, far to the north, another wild white man had come in from the bush with a similar story. John Graham, a short, black-haired Irishman transported for seven years for stealing $6^1/_2$ pounds of hemp, had arrived in Sydney in 1825. Assigned to a mill-owner at Parramatta, he became friendly with the local Aborigines, from whom it was later said he learned skills in food-gathering and survival. In 1826 he received a second conviction for theft and was transported to the newly established penal settlement at Moreton Bay for another seven years. There he came under the brutal rule of Captain Patrick Logan, a seasoned veteran of the Peninsular Wars and Quebec, whose reputation for relentless cruelty became legendary. In 1828 alone, 123 convicts took to the bush to escape the incessant floggings and other arbitrary punishments dished out by Logan, often quite illegally. Over half of the escapees were recaptured or returned voluntarily, staggering into the settlement so debilitated they were likened to walking corpses. The remainder were presumed to have died or been killed by Aborigines, who had become extremely aggressive towards the white intruders.

In July 1827, after enduring six months of Logan's regimen, Graham stole away from a working party into the thickly forested country of the interior, where pursuit would be difficult. Most convicts who absconded from Moreton Bay headed south for Port Macquarie or Sydney, but Graham had a different plan — he turned north along the coast hoping to hail a ship that would take him to China. For several months he managed to avoid the Aborigines, living off the land and catching fish. Eventually he strayed into a camp where he was fortunately 'recognised' by an Aboriginal woman named Mamba as the ghost of her dead husband, Moilow, a tribal elder. It is likely that Graham was aware of the widespread

'Convictos en la Nueva Olancia' (Convicts in New Holland). A rare depiction of convicts in the early years of the English settlement at Sydney. Drawn by Juan Ravenet in 1793 during the Spanish Scientific Expedition to Australia and the Pacific (Dixson Galleries).

David Collins, Judge-Advocate of the infant colony at Sydney. He investigated Mary Bryant's escape and had little doubt that she and her companions would reach Timor. Engraved from a miniature by I.T. Barber, 1804 (Mitchell Library).

'A Direct South View of the Town of Sydney taken from the brow of the hill leading to the flagstaff', c. 1794, after Thomas Watling (Mitchell Library).

'A Government Jail Gang, Sydney N.S. Wales', by Augustus Earle, 1830 (Mitchell Library).

Flogging a convict at Moreton Bay, from *The Fell Tyrant or the Suffering Convict* by W. R-S, 1836 (Mitchell Library).

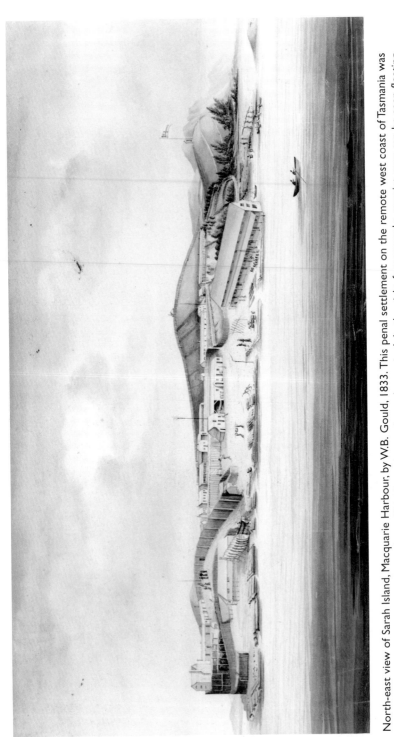

North-east view of Sarah Island, Macquarie Harbour, by W.B. Gould, 1833. This penal settlement on the remote west coast of Tasmania was intended by the government to be a place of 'rigid penal restraint and coercion'. In the right foreground a convict gang can be seen floating a Huon pine log to the shore while another gang carries a log to the saw pit (Mitchell Library).

Kingston settlement, Norfolk Island, by A.M., 1846. In the foreground is the pentagonal prison where William 'Jacky Jacky' Westwood spent the last weeks of his brief life (Dixson Library).

'Our Convicts. What We Do & What Becomes of Them', after S.T. Gill, c. 1851. A hard labour gang in Van Diemen's Land carries heavy bundles of shingles, from *Sketches of Australian Life and Scenery* (Dixson Library).

'Hobart Town, 1826', by Augustus Earle (Dixson Galleries).

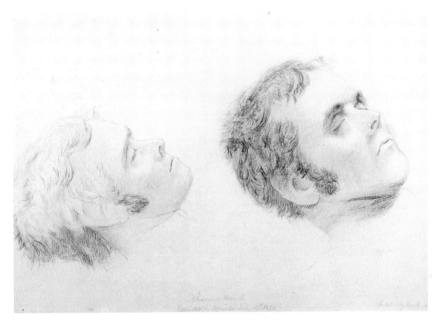

'Alexander Pearce Executed for Murder, July 1824', sketched by Thomas Bock after the execution (Dixson Galleries).

'North View of Eaglehawk Neck', 1842, after Captain Charles Hext. Note the line of guard dogs, the guard house and the semaphore station on the hill, all part of the security system to prevent convicts escaping overland from Port Arthur (Mitchell Library).

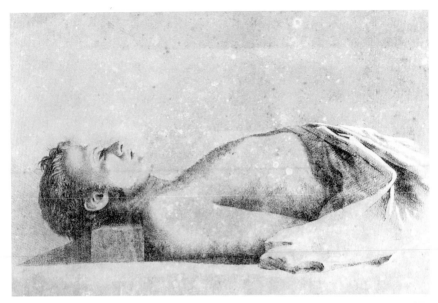

Bold Jack Donahue. Drawn by Sir Thomas Mitchell after the bushranger's death in 1830 (Mitchell Library).

'Bushrangers Waiting for the Mails in New South Wales', after S.T. Gill, c. 1851, from *Sketches of Australian Life and Scenery* (Dixson Library).

belief among Aborigines that all white men were the spirits of their deceased people, and no doubt he was careful not to disillusion his new wife and her two sons. He stayed with them for six years, adapting completely to their way of life, before suddenly returning to Moreton Bay.

During this period there were other escaped convicts living with Aboriginal tribes in the same area, or existing as bushrangers, and Graham seems to have made contact with at least one of them. In his field book, explorer and botanist Allan Cunningham refers to a journey undertaken in 1828 or 1829 by an escapee named George Mitchell, along with his companion, 'a convict named Graham'.[21] Mitchell had been sentenced in Sydney to transportation for life and absconded from Moreton Bay about six months before Graham. Apparently the two men planned to travel overland to the Gulf of Carpentaria, where they hoped to get taken on board one of the Macassan praus which Mitchell was aware regularly visited the north Australian coast in search of bêche-de-mer. After hearing the story from Mitchell, Cunningham calculated that they must have got as far as Broad Sound before turning back, unable to cross the sound or find any 'shell fish or other means of subsistence'.[22]

Details of Graham's years impersonating tribal elder Moilow are shadowy, as, unlike Buckely, he did not produce a lengthy account of his experiences. However, it seems that he took on the responsibilities of an elder and participated in the ritual life of the tribe. When his wife died within a year of his acceptance by her, he did not take another. What is certain is that his return to European society was cleverly planned. He surrendered to Captain James Clunie, Logan's successor, on 1 November 1833, exactly three days after his sentence was due to expire. Somehow, while living in the wilderness, he had managed to keep a record of the passing days and was able to arrive in Moreton Bay in the confident expectation that he was now a free man. How he was able to keep time with such accuracy is not revealed. However, George Mitchell told

Cunningham that he had reckoned time in the bush by observing 'the changes of the moon',[23] and it is likely that Graham adopted the same method. Unfortunately he had no way of knowing that in 1830 the government, by an Act in Council, had decided that time spent on the run would not necessarily be considered as part of a convict's sentence. So, even though his sentence had expired, Graham was now liable to serve the time of his absence. For sixteen days he enjoyed the freedom of the settlement while Captain Clunie considered his case. He had brought back valuable information about unexplored territory, and this was to his credit, but nevertheless Clunie determined that he would have to serve another three-and-a-half years. During Graham's absence, conditions at Moreton Bay had improved, and his subsequent good conduct earned him the position of constable supervising other convicts.

These years were enlivened for him by regular visits from his former Aboriginal companions. Captain Foster Fyans, who had replaced Captain Clunie as commandant in 1835, remarked that a 'party [of Aborigines] annually came to see Graham appearing to love and esteem him. On parting it was distressing to witness their grief, yelling and tearing their skin.'[24] In July 1836 one such party told Graham that a ship had been wrecked off the coast to the north and that some of the survivors, including a woman, were being held by the Aborigines of the Wide Bay region. Further details of the shipwreck reached Moreton Bay a few days later when Lieutenant Charles Otter arrived with two of the castaways, whom he had discovered on Bribie Island. The ship was the brig *Stirling Castle*, under the command of Captain James Fraser, and on 21 May she had foundered on Eliza Reef, east of Bowen. Most of those on board had drowned, died at the hands of Aborigines or later disappeared, and by the time the news reached Moreton Bay there were only four still alive, one of whom was Eliza Fraser, the wife of the captain. Within three days a rescue party set out, led by Lieutenant Otter and with John Graham as guide. His Aboriginal experiences had made him uniquely qualified for the job, especially as he was familiar with the country and by good fortune was known to the people who were holding the castaways captive.

The expedition sailed to the Noosa River estuary, where Otter wisely appears to have sent Graham on ahead. He 'stripped off his clothes, Greased himself up with charcoal and grease',[25] and taking with him only a potato and a piece of bread, crossed the river to the north bank. He quickly picked up tracks and followed them to an encampment, which he reached at nightfall. At first the Aborigines threatened the intruder with their spears and clubs, but after he had identified himself as Moilow and shared his food with them, he was made welcome. When he learned that two 'young ghosts' were being held nearby, he immediately declared them to be his sons and offered tomahawks for their release. The lure of such highly prized items was irresistible, and the two men, one only seventeen years old, were brought to him. They were naked and exhausted, but Graham, who had 'heard some words which I did not like',[26] set out immediately for Otter's camp accompanied by fourteen Aborigines.

The next morning, having been rewarded with tomahawks, fishhooks and food for their services, these same Aborigines treacherously attacked Otter and a small reconnoitering party as they set off northwards along the beach. Appearing suddenly on the cliffs above them, they bombarded them with sticks but were eventually driven off by pistol fire. Fearing that they would return with reinforcements and more efficient weapons, Graham persuaded Otter to move camp to Double Island Point.

The following day, Graham set out again in search of information, 'having nothing on but trousers, and a small bit of bread in the waistband'.[27] After walking about 10 kilometres he came upon two women, who told him that a 'female spirit' had been moved to the corroboree ground near Lake Cootharaba and that a 'male ghost' was on the southern end of Fraser Island. At last he had definite news of the whereabouts of Mrs Fraser and also the second mate, John Baxter. Acting on his own initiative he decided to rescue Baxter first. He crossed over to the island in a bark canoe that he had found abandoned on the shore and repaired with stiff mud. On arrival he was greeted with much suspicion, but after enquiring about his 'brother spirit' he was taken a few kilometres along the beach, where he was shocked to see 'the frame of a Christian man tottering along'.[28] 'What ship, mate, did you belong?' were the emaciated and ailing Baxter's first words. 'I have a ship for you if God prolongs your life,' replied Graham, who was moved to tears.[29] Noticing that the Aborigines' fish bags were empty and that 'their bellys all hollowed in', he had the 'blest Idea' to tell them that the mainland waters were swarming with fish and that further south a whale carcass was lying on the shore. Eagerly they took to their canoes, taking both him and Baxter with them. Pleased with the rich harvest of bream they were able to take, and attracted by a promised reward of tomahawks, they then escorted the two white men to Otter's new base at Double Island Point.

In extracting these three castaways from the midst of their belligerent and unpredictable captors, Graham had covered a lot of ground and was in need of rest. Yet almost immediately this fearless and resourceful man was off again, tracking alone through the bush to Lake Cootharaba, 40 kilometres away, where Mrs Fraser was awaiting deliverance. Among the people holding her were some he counted as relatives, and when he walked into their camp he boldly declared that she was the ghost of his dead wife Mamba. At once much shouting and arguing erupted between two different tribal groups, but, with Mamba's father and his own 'sons' stoutly supporting him, his claim was finally accepted. When she was handed over to him she was in 'the most distress'd state that can be painted' — her feet were shockingly lacerated and the skin on her sunburned shoulders 'hung in scales'.[30]

When Graham left the camp he took four Aborigines with him to help with his crippled and partly deranged charge. 'On her head was a Southwester,' he later recalled, 'the smell of the paint kept the Blacks from taking it. Around her loins were part of the legs and waistband of a pair of Trousers, which covered part of her thighs, wound round with Vines twenty fold as well for delicacy as the preservation of her marriage and Ear rings which she concealed under the Vines, the only articles that were saved from those savage hands.'[31] The speed with which Graham moved was remarkable. Only 40 hours after setting out on his rescue mission he had delivered Mrs Fraser to Lieutenant Otter's care at Double Island Point.

Graham had failed in his first attempt to gain his freedom permanently, but he had high hopes for this second attempt, for there is no doubt that he viewed the rescue of Mrs Fraser as a means of escaping from bondage: she was the great prize that would earn him a pardon. And in thinking this he was certainly not being unrealistic. In concluding his official report of the expedition, Lieutenant Otter could not be faulted in his praise of the 'indefatigable' convict: 'He shunned neither danger nor fatigue, and on the last occasion he was exposed to very imminent risk, by venturing into the large Camp where Mrs Fraser was detained, as had he met there any of the natives who attacked us a few days before it might have been fatal to him.'[32] Captain Fyans readily concurred and wrote to the Colonial Secretary that 'to [Graham] alone are we indebted for the recovery of Mrs Fraser'.[33]

On Fyans's recommendation, Graham was returned to Sydney and on 29 December 1836 he petitioned the governor for his freedom. However, in a letter dated two days earlier, the Colonial Secretary had already directed that he was to receive a ticket-of-leave 'and the sum of ten pounds to provide himself with the means of beginning a new life'.[34] At this point

Graham drops out of sight — there is no further mention of him in the colony's records. How he used his £10, and what became of him, is unknown.

7

The Cruise of the Cyprus

On 5 August 1829 the government brig *Cyprus* sailed from Hobart for the brutal penal settlement of Macquarie Harbour, a destination she would never reach. Confined below decks were 31 convicts, all of whom had been convicted of further serious offences since their arrival in Van Diemen's Land. The most remarkable of these villains was known as William Swallow, a former sailor with a string of daring escape attempts to his credit, including a successful 'home-run' to England.

Swallow was not actually his real name. He was born William Walker at Northshields in the north of England in 1790. At an early age he was apprenticed to the sea and after service in the Royal Navy obtained the temporary command of a coastal trading vessel. By 1815, however, he found that he was competing for work with the thousands of sailors who had been discharged from the navy following the conclusion of the Napoleonic wars. Occasional jobs as a ship's rigger were insufficient to support his wife and three children, and so he turned to thieving, specialising in 'tier-ranging' (plundering the tiers of shipping in the river at night). In 1820 he was caught and sentenced to seven years' transportation. While being shipped from Sunderland to London to join a convict transport ship, he jumped overboard into the freezing North Sea. Rescued by a passing vessel and landed in London, Walker was on the way back to his home town when he was recognised and arrested, despite having grown a beard and calling himself William Brown. His sentence was reaffirmed and he arrived in Hobart on the *Malabar* towards the end of 1821.

As a reward for good behaviour he was permitted to join the crew of the trading vessel *Deveron* on a voyage to Sydney for stores. On the return passage the ship was dismasted in a heavy storm off Bruny Island but was saved from destruction on a lee shore by Walker's initiative in scrambling aloft and cutting the broken spars and stays free. When the *Deveron* limped into Hobart he was given the job of re-rigging her. Some months later she sailed for England, and hidden in the hold by her sympathetic mate were Walker and eight other convicts. They succeeded in reaching Rio de Janeiro, from where Walker made his way back to England in another vessel. He settled down in London, but work was still scarce and once again he fell back to stealing, He was caught but managed to escape by hacking a hole through the police van taking him to Brixton Gaol. At liberty once more he changed his name to William Swallow but not his way of life. In July 1828 he was arrested for housebreaking, tried and sentenced to death. On appeal this was commuted to transportation for life, a lucky stroke for Swallow, for if his true identity as an illegally returned convict had been known he would almost certainly have swung from the gallows. After an unsuccessful attempt to break out of the prison hulk *Dolphin* moored at Chatham, he was drafted on board the convict transport *Georgiana* bound once more for Van Diemen's Land.

During the voyage he made himself useful as a sailmaker with the result that on his arrival in Hobart the ship's surgeon recommended him as 'a very good man'.[1] This earned him the privileged position of coxswain of the guard boat but even so, lifelong exile was not to his taste and he determined to stow away on the *Georgiana* on her return voyage to England. With the connivance of the mate he secreted himself in the hold. Unfortunately the ship's departure was delayed and he was discovered by a zealous constable during a routine search. For attempting to escape he was sentenced to 50 lashes and transportation to Macquarie Harbour. At this time he was 39 years old, tall at 5 feet 9 inches (1.75 metres), with a long nose and a prominent fleshy chin, both bearing small scars. His blue eyes were in striking contrast to his dark complexion and brown hair.[2]

Swallow was placed in the town barracks with 30 other miscreants whose various activities had earned them passage to the colony's most feared penal settlement. It was probably then, while the *Cyprus* was being readied for the voyage, that the idea of seizing her first occurred to him. He would have known that once he reached Macquarie Harbour his chances of escaping would be limited. But recruiting the necessary accomplices to carry out his plan was a risky business, for among the convicts there were always informers willing to betray their fellows to the authorities in exchange for favourable treatment. However, by 16 July, when the convicts were embarked, he had gathered round him a tight group of committed conspirators.

Two days later the *Cyprus* set sail only to be turned back by heavy weather in Storm Bay. A topmast had been lost overboard together with the anchor and cable and it was eighteen days before repairs were completed. During this period the convicts, shackled with leg irons, were kept on board in the cramped, festering hold. The delay was used by Swallow to refine his plan, and when the brig cleared the harbour for the last time he was ready; it was just a matter of waiting for the right moment. At first they had favourable winds and made good progress, but once the sheltering mountains of Bruny Island had been left behind they ran into a westerly gale. All night they battled enormous seas which threatened to engulf the small 80-foot vessel while icy winds, spiked with flinty rain, clawed at the rigging. Their situation was alarming and Swallow with several of his companions were released to help the crew maintain control of the labouring ship. At dawn, the master, Captain Harrison, had had enough. His ship had been badly mauled and he gave orders to change course and run for the safety of Recherche Bay, a land-locked haven about 15 kilometres north of South-East Cape.

For a week the brig lay at anchor in the protected waters of the bay while outside the storm continued to rage. The prisoners were regularly allowed on deck in small groups for exercise, watched over by only two guards. The off-duty soldiers passed the time playing cards or sleeping, while the captain, a noted drinker, remained in his cabin with a supply of grog. Also on board were the surgeon, Dr Walter Williams, and the commander of the military detachment, Lieutenant William Carew, with his wife and two children. Within a day of dropping anchor Swallow was taken ill, apparently with a stricture of the urinary canal. He survived an operation by Dr Williams and was placed in the forecastle to recover. It has been suggested that this was a ruse concocted by Swallow to ensure that he was unfettered and removed from the restrictions of the hold. If so, he must have been horrified when the surgeon produced a scalpel from his medical chest instead of prescribing a less drastic cure.

On the afternoon of 14 August, Lieutenant Carew, Dr Williams and the first mate decided to try a spot of fishing further up the bay. They lowered the jolly-boat and with a convict named John Pobjoy (or Popjoy) at the oars, pulled away from the brig. Pobjoy, a Cockney on a fourteen-year sentence for stealing a horse, had volunteered for service at Macquarie Harbour as coxswain of the settlement's boat. He was to have a decisive role in subsequent events.

With three officers away from the ship and only two sentries on deck in charge of fourteen exercising convicts, in the words of a popular convict ballad:

A better opportunity could never have occurred ...
To capture now the *Cyprus*, or perish every man.[3]

The sentries were distracted and then knocked unconscious with belaying pins. At the same time the hatch over the soldiers' quarters was slammed shut with cries of 'Keep the buggars down, keep them down'. The rest of the crew was easily overpowered while Captain Harrison was woken from a drunken sleep and brought on deck. The convicts then fetched hammers and chisels from the ship's stores and knocked off each other's irons. When they turned to disarming the soldiers trapped below they met with their only serious resistance. As soon as the hatch was cautiously raised, several shots whistled past them, one ball actually whipping between Swallow's arm and his side. However, the soldiers soon realised the hopelessness of their situation, and surrendered. They were relieved of their muskets and sent ashore in the longboat guarded by armed convicts.

Lieutenant Carew, disturbed by the shots, now drew anxiously alongside. When he began to climb on board one of the convicts attempted to shoot him but his musket flashed in the pan. Realising at once what had happened the lieutenant:

> begged of the Prisoners to surrender the ship up to him and he would think no more of the business. The Prisoners said they would not and desired them to shier off if they did not they would fire into her. Lieutenant Carew then begged that they would let him have his sword but they refused to give it to him he then asked for his wife and two children, and they were directly put into the boat. The Prisoners also gave them two Foules, some pieces of Beef, a Sheep and a Bag of Bread, a Cask of Rum.[4]

Finally Captain Harrison was lowered into the boat and it too was escorted to the shore. By nightfall the ship's crew and twelve convicts who wanted no part of the mutiny had also been landed. They were joined by Pobjoy who, having initially decided to throw in his lot with the mutineers (or according to him been press-ganged by them), later repented and 'by Disguising miself got on Shore along with the prisoners and soldiers'.[5]

By midnight all the boats had returned to the brig. A strong south-westerly sprang up, and at about four o'clock in the morning the *Cyprus* spread her sails and slipped quietly out of the bay. The eighteen convicts remaining on board gathered on the poop and, watching the hated coast of Van Diemen's Land drop slowly behind, they gave three cheers for 'glorious liberty'.

A total of 44 men, women and children had been marooned on the bleak, isolated shore of Recherche Bay. Like Lady Franklin, writing nine years later, they would have been 'struck with the dense gloom and blackness of the woods as they rose immediately from the shore upon an outer base of dark-hued rocks'.[6] To reach the nearest settlement, Birches Bay at the mouth of the Derwent River, would entail an 80-kilometre slog through some exceedingly rough country with the possibility of encountering hostile Aborigines along the way. Alternatively they could remain where they were and hope that a passing vessel, seeking shelter from a storm, would put into the bay. With only enough food for about ten days some decisive action was needed and it came not from the officers but from John Pobjoy.

On the day after the mutiny he volunteered to go for help. Rather than march directly overland through the bush he proposed to simply follow the shoreline northwards until he reached Birches Bay. Even so it was a difficult and dangerous route; the wild, serrated coast was cut by a number of rivers, one of which, the Huon, was nearly 5 kilometres wide at its mouth, and all of these he would somehow have to cross or otherwise make extensive detours inland. Taking provisions and one companion he set out on the morning of 16 August leaving the other castaways to settle down and wait. By the third day the two men had made about 40 kilometres, having scrambled over innumerable scrub-covered headlands and swum and waded across three rivers. After crossing the third river, probably the Huon, they sank down cold and exhausted to dry their clothes. They were interrupted in their task by a band of Aborigines, brandishing spears and clubs, 'who compelled us to leave our clothes and everything upon the beach and to swim back'. So, naked and hungry, they began the depressing trek back to Recherche Bay, 'and it was not untill the fifth day that we got back covered with bruises, blood and gore'.[7]

With their meagre supplies dwindling, along with their hopes of rescue, the castaways were plunged further into gloom at the sight of Pobjoy and his mate struggling back into camp. But once again it was Pobjoy who raised their spirits, this time with a plan to construct a boat and paddle it along the coast to Birches Bay. A Welsh seaman named Tom Morgan, drawing on his Celtic heritage, was set to work building a coracle, his only tools being three penknives. He used wattle branches for the frame and covered it with canvas coated with a mixture of boiled soap and rosin. It was about 4 metres long and to everyone's surprise it floated. Pobjoy and Morgan set out at once. It was then Sunday 23 August and the castaways had been reduced to a diet of shellfish and little else. The fragile craft prevailed against the buffeting of the open sea, and two days later the intrepid mariners were picked up off Partridge Island by the barque *Orelia* after a hazardous voyage of over 30 kilometres. Pobjoy and Morgan were dispatched to Hobart while a boat loaded with food set out for Recherche Bay, and within days the castaways were rescued by the government sloop *Opossum*. One week later five convicts, who had set out overland for Hobart shortly after Pobjoy and Morgan, were found exhausted and starving by another ship at the mouth of the Huon River.

Pobjoy's reward for what the *Hobart Town Courier* called his 'gallant and daring conduct'[8] was a stint in the town gaol, 'loaded with chains in a weak state of boddy'.[9] When his story was verified, however, he was given a free pardon which permitted him to return to England. Morgan, a 'lifer' on a ticket-of-

'The Making of the Coracle'. Lieutenant Carew sits in despair while the convicts John Pobjoy and Tom Morgan, encouraged by Mrs Carew, construct a coracle after being marooned at Recherche Bay by the pirates of the brig Cyprus. *Woodcut published in the* Hobart Town Courier, *12 September 1829 (Mitchell Library).*

leave,[10] had to be content with employment in government boats. The remaining convicts, with one exception, were allowed to remain in Hobart as assigned servants. That exception was John Hall (one of the five overland convicts), who had initially joined the mutineers before changing his mind and as punishment was sent to Macquarie Harbour. Lieutenant Carew was court-martialled for 'gross neglect of duty' in allowing the *Cyprus* to be captured, but was acquitted. In his defence he made the interesting claim that Pobjoy was a known informer and that the real purpose of the fishing trip was to 'ascertain from him the character of the prisoners, and to find out if any irregularity existed among them'.[11]

Meanwhile the *Cyprus* had left Van Diemen's Land far behind. Swallow, as an experienced navigator, had been the natural choice for captain. An Irish horse-thief on a life sentence named Leslie Ferguson, who had been prominent in the mutiny, was made lieutenant. To mark his new status he threw off his yellow convict jacket and dressed himself in

Lieutenant Carew's spare uniform. James Jones (alias John Roberts), a former seaman who had come out on the *Georgiana* with Swallow and like him was a second transportee, became first mate. A majority of the convicts voted to head for America but Swallow refused to set such a course until he had done a stocktake of the ship's stores. The result was that the ship certainly held ample food for the voyage (she had been loaded with three months' rations for the settlement at Macquarie Harbour) but only 150 gallons (about 680 litres) of water. He later wrote:

> I remonstrated with the Crew as to the folly of steering for America a Voyage that would in all probability take 9 or 10 weeks sail at least and having so little Water on Board and which would not last half that time however economical we might be. They then asked where I could sail to obtain what water that we wanted. I told them that New Zealand was the nearest and most likely.

Swallow's suggestion was accepted and after a week at sea the snow-capped mountains of New Zealand's South Island were sighted. After following the coast north they entered Cook Strait and on 22 August dropped anchor at Port Underwood in Cloudy Bay where a bay whaling station had recently been established. In his own account of the voyage Swallow wrote that they 'procured about 50 Gallons of water, brackish' and sailed again next day having also taken on board a man named John Wright 'who had been there near two Years'. Additional details of their stay were reported in the *Hobart Town Courier* of 17 October 1829:

> By the arrival of a vessel at Sydney from New Zealand we learn that a brig had put in there for water called the *Friends of Boston*, bound ostensibly from Manilla to South America, but answering in all other respects to the description of the *Cyprus*. She was commanded, the account says, by a man named Walker and the whole crew was in perfect order and discipline. The vessel had been fresh painted black, and had a complete set of ships papers filled up agreeably to their account of themselves. The mate of the Sydney vessel had requested

the favour of some fish hooks from the strange brig, which were wrapped up in a piece of a Hobart town newspaper. There is no doubt but this was the *Cyprus*.

In an earlier edition of the same newspaper it had been confidently stated that 'the villains can scarcely succeed in arriving at a distant port' and that they 'would long before soon murder each other in their quarrels and disorderly attempts at superiority among themselves'.[12] The *Australian* rashly agreed, adding that there was no-one 'on board out of the whole number who joined in the piracy, possessing either talent or address sufficient to pass off the trick dextrously'.[13] In view of the latest report from New Zealand it was only too clear that these predictions had been unjustifiably optimistic.

In the exhilaration of their successful escape the convicts had not neglected practical matters. Apart from repainting and renaming the ship they had cut off her figurehead and gone to the trouble of forging a set of ship's papers including a log of their supposed voyage from Manila. And Swallow had undergone yet another change of identity, this time reverting to his original surname. Yet these efforts had not fooled the crew of the 'Sydney vessel', a schooner named *Elizabeth and Mary* under the command of Captain William Worth. Fortunately for the convicts he was not prepared to take any action, and as he did not reach Sydney until 22 September his information was of little use to the authorities.

With their water tanks filled and in the knowledge that a British warship was cruising in the vicinity, the convicts set sail and stood out of Cloudy Bay on a course for Tahiti, an island with a reputation among sailors for accommodating women and exotic customs, 4000 kilometres to the north-east. On 25 August Swallow recorded that during 'some very rough weather ... we lost one of our men John Brown[14] overboard and he was drowned although I used every means in my power to save him'. As one of the few skilled sailors on board Brown's loss was a major blow. The 'very rough weather' drove them south to the Chatham Islands. They landed at Owenga Bay where they raided a native village and surprised a party of sealers, stripping the latter of their equipment and anything else of value. Seeking more plunder inland they attempted to row up a river but their boats were swamped by surf and they were forced to return to the brig.

The voyage across the Pacific Ocean was long and laborious. At that time of the year the prevailing winds came from the north-east and to make headway the *Cyprus* was continually forced to tack. It was not until the end of September, more than a month after leaving Cloudy Bay, that the desirable coast of Tahiti was sighted 50 kilometres to the south-east. However, they were now under the influence of the south-east trade winds and Swallow was unable to work the brig into Matavai Bay. 'The Prisoners then asked me,' he recorded, 'if there were not some Islands we could go to I replied there were the friendly Islands [Tonga] which were in the same parrellal latitude 18 degrees South and nearly the same Longitude as New Zealand.' With the south-easterly behind them the passage back across the Pacific would take only a week. The concerns of some of the convicts that such a destination would bring them dangerously close to New South Wales were successfully countered by Swallow who explained that if they headed north across the equator, the only other alternative, they 'should in all probability be detained by Calms'.

The favourable winds held and six days after reluctantly turning away from Tahiti they made Niue, a coral island 400 kilometres to the north-east of the main Tongan group. It had been discovered by Dutch navigators in 1616 and visited by Captain Cook in 1774 who named it Savage Island because of the hostility of the natives. During the intervening years they had mellowed and when Swallow and eight others landed they were 'received in a very friendly manner by the King of the Island'. It was Swallow's intention to remain on Niue but there was some determined opposition to this plan. The men became:

incontrollable and mutinous [and] sent letters to the King which were interpreted to him by an American who had been upon the Islands several years. The letters threatened that unless the King immediately sent myself and the other men on Board they would set fire to his Hutts render him all the mischief they could and if he attempted to send any of the Canoes to the Ship they would destroy them all. The King then ordered one of his War Canoes to be manned and myself and Williams[15] went into her leaving the Prisoners Ferguson, Templeman, O'Brien, four others of the crew, and the man named Wright upon the Islands.

It appears that during the six weeks of their stay at Niue two parties had gradually formed: those who wanted to sail on in the *Cyprus* to China or Japan and the remainder who preferred to stay on the island. Swallow, as the only navigator, was crucial to the execution of the first party's plan and hence their desperation to get him back on board. According to him, 'they imprisoned me in the Cabin and kept me eight hours there when they ordered me to come upon Deck and Steer the Ship to Japan'.

The *Cyprus* sailed about the middle of November. The crew had been reduced to ten men, of whom only Swallow and Jones could be considered experienced seamen, although no doubt the rest had at least learned the basics of sailing since leaving Recherche Bay. Swallow shaped his course to the north-west, threading his way carefully among the maze of islands straddling the equator. His account does not mention any landings, only that they did not 'fall in with any ship whatever'. It seems unlikely, however, that they would have passed up the opportunity of replenishing their food and water supplies at one or two of the enticing tropical islands. After leaving the Marshall Islands behind, they moved into open ocean and for three weeks had no sight of land.

Some time towards the end of January 'in North Latitude 38 degrees north [they] made the Coast of Japan being in want of Wood and Water and the Ship being out of repair and having all her sails nearly split to pieces'. As the dilapidated brig stood into the shore looking for a haven several small 'coasting vessels' hove in sight but to Swallow's disappointment they kept well clear. He was probably unaware that for centuries Japan had pursued a policy of self-imposed isolation. Foreigners were forbidden to land on Japanese soil with the sole exception of a small number of Dutch and Chinese traders who were permitted to reside in Nagasaki. This policy had been reinforced as recently as 1825 by an edict stating that any foreign vessel attempting to enter a Japanese port was to be driven away by force.

The *Cyprus* edged cautiously southwards, eventually arriving outside the fishing port of Shimoda on the approaches to Yokohama.[16] Swallow brought her slowly in and dropped anchor in the shadow of an imposing fort. A boat put off from shore and came alongside 'with a Japan Chief in her'. He was unable to speak English but by means of signs he made it clear that he wanted a letter explaining their presence in his port 'and that a Dutchman would interpret the same'. Swallow complied with the request, stating that they were in need of fresh water and firewood and 'would give anything in the vessel in exchange'.[17] The official took the letter ashore. Four hours later he returned and handing the letter to Swallow gave him to understand that unless they departed by sunset they would be fired upon and 'a large ball was shown them as earnest of the intention of the natives'.[18]

However, there was no breeze to disturb the *Cyprus*'s tattered sails and they remained apprehensively at anchor all afternoon unable to move. At sundown, without further warning, the Japanese opened fire from 'about 50 Boats'. The guns in the fort joined in and one shot struck the brig under the counter 'between Wind and Water'. Another one passed so close to Swallow that it knocked his telescope from his hand. At ten o'clock a light breeze sprang up off the land. Frantically the convicts hauled up the anchor and got under way. As the brig slowly cleared the harbour the Japanese ceased firing.

Once at sea it was discovered that there was 20 centimetres of water in the hold, a result of the hit they had taken on the waterline. Swallow ordered the pumps to be manned while temporary repairs were made. At daylight he set a course to the south-west, keeping well away from the coast. The convicts' plight was becoming desperate — the brig was leaking and they were in need of fresh food and water. They dared not risk another landing in Japan, but exactly where they should go was a matter of much argument. Some wanted to head for Canton (present-day Guangzhou), scuttle the brig in the South China Sea 'to get rid of her, to avoid apprehension as pirates' and then make their way ashore in the longboat posing as the sole survivors of a shipwreck. Opposition to this plan came from those who feared 'there was danger of their being discovered and brought to justice in Canton' or that 'they might be discovered by cruisers sent from Botany Bay, in the Chinese Seas'.[19] Swallow himself favoured the Ladrone or Mariana islands to the south as a place where they might replenish their supplies and be safe from pursuit.

In this state of indecision they continued their south-westerly course which brought them to what Swallow called 'the Ten Thousand Islands'. These were in all likelihood the Ryukyu Islands, which lie between Japan and Taiwan in the East China Sea. Here two of the convicts, John Denner and Samuel Thacker, requested to be put ashore, probably in the hope of being picked up by an American whaler or a Dutch trading vessel. Swallow claimed that he 'then sailed towards the Grand Ladrones but after reaching the southern point of Taiwan he turned west instead towards Canton. The *Cyprus* was now near the end of her voyage. It seems that the decision had finally been made to abandon the brig, although later events indicate that Swallow still had hopes of sailing her to a safe port. As they approached the coast of mainland China they fell in with a

Chinese junk. While it was manoeuvring alongside, four of the convicts — George Davis, James Jones, Michael Herring and Matthew Pennell — slipped below and 'cut away the ship's Sealing and two of her Timbers ... nearly thro' to her Copper'. Their intention was to force Swallow's hand by holing the brig and destroying all evidence of their piracy. When they came on deck they told Swallow what they had done and then after some hard bargaining persuaded the master of the junk to land them at the trading port of Whampoa on the north bank of the Pearl River at the price of eight Spanish dollars per man. Swallow was now left with only three crewmen — William Watts, Alexander Stevenson and John Beveridge — none of whom 'could either reef or Steer'.

'It was now blowing very fresh,' Swallow recorded,

and the *Cyprus* was Twenty miles from Land. I stood into the land with the Ship on the Starboard Tack the Wind was Northward and Eastward. I went into the hold and discovered that they had Scuttled the Vessel on the Larboard side nearly three feet below the surface of the water which was rushing in in torrents. I used every possible means to stop the leak but all my efforts proved fruitless. I then tried with some sails which I throwed overboard thinking the leak would suck them in but the quantity of water flowing in defeated every exertion.

It was just past midnight on 2 February when Swallow reluctantly accepted that the brig could not be saved and, fearing that she might founder suddenly, he gave orders for the longboat to be lowered. Watts, Stevenson and Beveridge clambered in and Swallow handed down to them a compass, telescope, quadrant, some beef and biscuits and lastly a writing desk containing the charts and navigational books. The *Cyprus* was wearily settling lower into the water as Swallow, after lashing the helm to leeward, joined the other three convicts in the longboat and pushed off into the darkness.

Sadly he watched the ship, which he had navigated with considerable skill across the broad Pacific Ocean and back, wallow on towards the coast. Presently she disappeared from sight. In Swallow's estimation they were 11 or 12 kilometres from land, and with a following wind they made the mouth of the Pearl River just as the sun was rising. They were worried that the brig may not have foundered and pulled out again to sea to look for her 'but could not find her and concluded that she sank immediately after we left her'. Convinced that the principal evidence against them was now at the bottom of the sea they turned back for the coast. At Lin Tin Island, 70 kilometres downriver from Canton, they hailed a junk whose captain, it luckily turned out, could speak English. They had carefully rehearsed their story and when he asked where they had come from they told him they were survivors from the English brig *Edward*, bound for Manila, which had been lost off the south coast of Taiwan. Swallow introduced himself as Captain Waldron, and the junk-master readily accepted his tale, especially when he was offered 24 Spanish dollars to tow them up the river to Whampoa.

As they swung round the last river bend and Whampoa came into view they anxiously scanned the harbour for any British warships whose captains might have had word of their escape. To their relief there were none, but lying in the roads, loading cargoes of tea and silk, were several sizeable British merchant ships. If they were careful, if they kept their heads, one of these could provide them with passage to England. They tried out their sad tale of shipwreck on Captain Everest, master of the East Indiaman *Charles Grant*, and he, with little reason to doubt them, accepted them at their word. Moreover, he offered to take them on as additional crew. So far so good, but on the following day Swallow was taken upriver to Canton for examination by the Select Committee of Supercargoes. Once again he spun his story and once again he was believed. The four convicts were now officially recognised as shipwrecked mariners and were immediately signed on by Captain Everest. On 5 March 1830 the *Charles Grant* weighed anchor and headed downriver to the open sea, her destination London.

Swallow was later to assert that 'he never heard what became of the four who abandoned the *Cyprus* near Formosa'.[20] In fact they too reached Whampoa and three of them, Jones, Herring and Pennell, found berths on a Danish barque bound for America which sailed on the same tide as the *Charles Grant*. The fourth man, George Davis, now calling himself Huntley, turned up at Canton several days later claiming to be another survivor of the wrecked *Edward*. However, his story was so much at variance with Swallow's account that the Select Committee's suspicions were aroused and he was placed under guard on the East Indiaman *Kellie Castle* for delivery to the authorities in England. With him went the *Cyprus*'s longboat, which had been abandoned by Swallow, and written descriptions of the other seven men.

On the long voyage home the *Kellie Castle* overhauled the *Charles Grant*, reaching England nine days ahead. She berthed at the East India Dock on 1 September and Davis was immediately handed over to the Thames police. When the *Charles Grant* finally arrived, Watts, Stevenson and Beveridge were sent to join Davis in the cells. Swallow was not included for the simple reason that he was no longer on board. With Captain Everest's permission he had left the ship two days earlier at Margate intending to make his own way to London to find his wife and children. Meanwhile the four arrested men were being held on suspicion of having committed a felony — although the exact nature of the felony was not clear to the police. The four had not been recognised as escaped convicts and evidence to support a charge of any sort was distinctly lacking. It looked as though the prisoners would have to be released when by an extraordinary coincidence John Pobjoy appeared on the scene.

After receiving his free pardon Pobjoy had sailed for London, arriving there in July 1830. He now came forward and obligingly identified the four prisoners as pirates of the *Cyprus*. His statement was corroborated by another visitor from Van

Diemen's Land. Thomas Capon, head gaoler at Hobart, had arrived in England on the same ship as Pobjoy and had no hesitation in affirming that the four men were among those who had been embarked on the *Cyprus* as convicts. As a result they were brought before a magistrate charged with being involved in the piratical seizure of the brig. The chief witness was, of course, Pobjoy, but also appearing for the prosecution were several crewmen from the *Charles Grant* who stated 'that Watts, on more than one occasion, had worn woman's stockings during the voyage, and had sold other articles of female wearing apparel to the sailors'.[21] These, in Pobjoy's opinion, had belonged to Mrs Carew, and he also identified the longboat brought home by the *Kellie Castle* as the one carried by the *Cyprus*. After hearing all the evidence the magistrate committed the four convicts for trial at the next sessions of the Admiralty Court. As the men left the court for Clerkenwell Prison, a reporter for *The Times* noted that 'an immense crowd had assembled in the streets, to catch a glimpse of the four men whose lawless and daring exploit was perhaps never equalled'.[22]

Ever since Pobjoy's first sensational identification of the *Cyprus* pirates, the hunt had been on for Swallow. His description had been circulated to all police stations and watch-houses in the city, but he had gone to ground with his family and for five weeks there was no trace of him. And then on the afternoon of 15 October an informer led the police to a squalid boarding house in Lambeth. The surprised occupant, claiming to be a shoemaker named Watson, was arrested. A search of the premises disclosed several pawnbrokers' tickets, one of which was pledged for a quadrant in the name of William Waldron and another for a telescope. By nine o'clock that night the prisoner was standing in the dock of the Thames Police Court. The arresting officers named him as William Swallow and his appearance certainly matched the description of 'Captain Waldron'. When they produced a complete copy of his criminal record he capitulated and offered to make a full statement of his part in the seizure of the *Cyprus*. As a legal tactic this was plump with risk. The magistrate cautioned him that he could expect no advantage from such a course of action and indeed whatever he said now could be used as evidence against him in any future proceedings. Swallow, nevertheless, insisted on going ahead. Presumably his purpose was to get in first with his own version of the mutiny before any witnesses could be called to testify against him. In this way he could make an early bid for mitigation by engaging the court's sympathy.

Wisely he stuck fairly closely to the facts, but — and this was the recurring theme of his statement — claimed that his role in the affair had been entirely involuntary. 'While all this [the seizure of the vessel] was going on,' he told the court,

> I was below, very ill. I was the only man on board among the convicts who understood the navigation of the ship. I was brought on deck and a great-coat belonging to one of the passengers was put on my back. The convicts then told me I must take charge of the vessel, and threatened to kill me if I did not navigate her to safety.[23]

He also stressed the hardships he and the other convicts had endured, adding that 'the cause of their running away with the brig arose from the fear of slavery they would have to undergo at the Government works in Macquarrie Harbour'.[24] It was a clever defence neatly weighted with compelling appeals for compassion but open to doubt in the light of his known history as a persistent and determined escaper. After signing the transcription, when he was observed to be 'much exhausted', he was removed from the bar.

During the course of the hearing the police had made much of the circumstances in which Swallow had been taken. It transpired that after leaving the *Charles Grant* he had made his way to his old home in Lambeth where, to his dismay, he found that his wife had remarried, to a man named Flook. He was able to persuade her to return to him but after three days

Flook discovered their retreat and took her back. Swallow moved to another lodging where his erstwhile wife began paying him regular visits. By then the jealous Flook had had enough and arranged for the police to be informed of his rival's whereabouts.

Four days after Swallow's capture and six days after his own court appearance, Pobjoy found himself in court again but on this occasion in the role of defendant rather than witness for the prosecution. Charged with a violent assault on the father of the girl he was courting, he reminded the magistrate of his initiative, not to mention his bravery, in rescuing the castaways from the *Cyprus* at Recherche Bay. It was not much in the way of a defence but it impressed the magistrate who discharged the self-proclaimed hero with a warning. 'You must not make love to the daughter by beating her father,' he told Pobjoy sternly. 'That can't be allowed.'[25]

On 20 October Swallow was confronted with Pobjoy for the first time when he and the other four convicts appeared at the Thames Police Court for final examination before their trial. Pobjoy made a formal identification of Swallow and swore that he 'was very busy during the mutiny and seizure of the brig [and] appeared to be the director of everything'. Swallow replied by calling Pobjoy 'a base lying villain [who] was in irons himself when the brig was taken', and repudiated his evidence by claiming that 'he was below very ill when the ship was taken, and was forced above to take the command by the convicts'. Almost as an afterthought he added that 'Dr Williams could prove his statement if he came home (from V.D. Land)'.[26] After further evidence was taken from the officers of the *Charles Grant*, the magistrate declared that to his satisfaction:

> The charge of mutiny and piracy, in running away with the brig and cargo, was made out against the prisoners and fully committed them for trial at the Admiralty sessions, which commences on Monday next.[27]

The Justice Hall of the Old Bailey was packed for what was to be the last trial held in England for the crime of piracy.[28] The first witness for the prosecution was John Pobjoy who, in his account of the events at Recherche Bay, stated that he heard Swallow tell Lieutenant Carew that 'he was forced into the mutiny by the convicts, and his conduct not so bad as that of the others'. This was a point for the defence and Swallow must have been further encouraged when Pobjoy added that 'Swallow & Stevenson were unarmed, but the other prisoners held bayonets, pistols and muskets'. The effect of this evidence, as regards Swallow, was somewhat tempered when Pobjoy insisted that:

> Davis and Swallow came and demanded from the Captain the ships's register ... Swallow passed the windlass and ordered a man to stand by with an axe for fear the vessel should shoulder her anchor.

On cross-examination, Pobjoy's evidence took another twist when he admitted that Swallow 'was very ill at the time'. As a witness for the prosecution Pobjoy had not proved entirely satisfactory.

The next witness was something of a surprise. In the earlier hearing Swallow had claimed that Dr Williams, the *Cyprus*'s surgeon, could substantiate his claim that he joined the mutineers under protest. By another amazing coincidence this same Dr Williams had arrived in London only days earlier and now appeared to give evidence on behalf of the Crown. By the time he had finished, however, the prosecuting counsel probably regretted having called him. Dr Williams began by stating that he had overheard Swallow say to the officers of the *Cyprus* as they were being sent ashore: 'You see, gentlemen, I am a pressed man; unarmed, surrounded by armed men.' He added that Swallow had been prevented by Watts from getting some blankets for Mrs Carew. He then went on to confirm that Swallow had indeed 'been affected with a dangerous complaint, but was recovering at the time of the mutiny'. Finally, under cross-examination, he gave a further boost to Swallow's cause by ascribing the leadership of the mutiny to Leslie Ferguson.

When Thomas Capon, the Hobart head gaoler, was called to the witness box he unaccountably retracted his previous testimony by stating that he could no longer 'say whether the prisoners were convicts'. Unexpected as this undoubtedly was, the damage to the Crown's case was only slight. The critical question was whether or not the defendants had pirated the *Cyprus*, not their status as convicts, and on the evidence of the two eyewitnesses there could be little doubt that all five had been on board the brig when she sailed from Recherche Bay. After additional evidence was presented by the Thames Police and officers from the *Charles Grant* and *Kellie Castle*, the prosecution closed its case. No defence was offered by the defendants with the exception of Swallow, who repeated that he had been drafted into the mutiny against his will. The judge summed up and the jury retired. For two-and-a-half hours it deliberated and when it returned the foreman gravely announced its decisions. Davis, Watts, Stevenson and Beveridge were declared guilty, but the latter two were recommended for mercy 'on the ground of their not being so active as others in the mutiny'. As for Swallow the verdict was an improbable not guilty.

As the law required of him, the judge donned the black cap and pronounced sentences of death on the four guilty prisoners. Swallow, despite his acquittal, was not set free. He now faced the charge of illegally returning to England from transportation, another hanging offence. From his cell in Newgate he wasted no time in launching an appeal to the Home Secretary, Sir Robert Peel, for clemency. Capitalising on the fortuitous evidence in his favour presented by Pobjoy and Dr Williams, he reiterated that he had been a 'pressed man' constantly in fear for his life. An inherent weakness of this plea was his inability to produce a convincing explanation for his failure to report his alleged situation to the authorities at Canton, or to Captain Everest, when he had every opportunity to do so. 'I do hope,' he concluded, that when you consider that I was not brought here by any pre-meditated Act of my own, consider also the privations I have already suffered and taking all other circumstances my age being now 45 yrs my Wife and daughter into your humane consideration you will allow me, if not my enlargement, as moderate fine as the case may deserve.[29]

While this petition was under consideration by the Home Secretary, the four condemned men were busy preparing their own appeal. Both documents were examined by the Executive Council and a decision was reached on 8 December. The sentences of Stevenson and Beveridge were commuted to transportation for life, but there was no reprieve for Davis and Watts whose executions were fixed for 16 December. Swallow avoided the noose but he too was to be returned to Van Diemen's land for life.

With only a week to go before Davis and Watts were due to swing, Pobjoy flung himself into the act. Apparently suffering from a fit of conscience over his inconsistent (and seemingly less than truthful) performance at the trial, he produced a flurry of letters and affidavits on behalf of the condemned men, firstly to the King's consort Queen Adelaide and when this was ignored, to the Lord Mayor of London. He now insisted that Swallow had in fact been the ringleader of the mutiny and had concocted the whole operation. Moreover, it was his belief that Swallow's statement to the *Cyprus*'s officers that he was acting under compulsion had been 'intended to cover his original and voluntary design of obtaining possession of the vessel'.[30] As for Davis and Watts, they had been no more actively involved than Stevenson and Beveridge who had been spared. This startling information was conveyed to the foreman of the jury who began to have disturbing doubts about the verdicts. With three other jurymen he urgently petitioned the King to stop the execution and exercise his royal prerogative of mercy.

But it was all too late. The law ground on, blinkered by the need to provide a powerful warning against piracy. Just ten days before Christmas, Davis and Watts were hanged at Execution Dock on the bank of the Thames below Tower Bridge — the last men to be executed in England as pirates. Next month, Swallow, Stevenson and Beveridge were embarked on the convict transport *Argyle* for the long, heart-breaking voyage to Van Diemen's Land. It was the third time for Swallow, and his last. On arrival in Hobart the three convicts were shipped to Macquarie Harbour in chains. Back in England their notoriety lingered on: the story of the seizure of the *Cyprus* was dramatised and performed at a London theatre.

Swallow was returned to Hobart in March 1832 for the trial of John Denner, who with Samuel Thacker, had been arrested by the Chinese authorities on one of the Ryukyu Islands and placed on board a ship bound for Sydney. Thacker managed to escape before the ship sailed, but Denner completed the voyage and was eventually forwarded onto Hobart where he was sentenced to transportation for life. In May he and Swallow were embarked on the colonial brig *Tamar* with sixteen other convicts for Macquarie Harbour. In a nice piece of irony the captain and mate of the *Tamar* had been among the crew of the *Cyprus* when she was seized. This time they made sure that history would not be repeated. The convicts were confined in a purpose-built gaol accessible only from the deck by a small hatchway which was under 24-hour guard.

Of the remaining convicts who had pirated the brig, eight were never officially heard of again — Leslie Ferguson, Patrick Lynch, Thomas Briant, William Templeman and Charles Towers, who had deserted at Niue, and James Jones, Michael Herring and Matthew Pennell, who were last seen on board a Danish barque bound for America. Two others were not so fortunate: James Camm was picked up at Tahiti by the British sloop HMS *Comet*, having somehow made his way there from Niue. Robert McGuire, the only one to remain on Niue, was caught after nearly three years of freedom. Back in Hobart they were both condemned to death but only James Camm was actually hanged. McGuire was reprieved and sent to Norfolk Island.

At Macquarie Harbour, Swallow fell ill and according to one visitor who saw him at the end of May he 'was in a dying state'.[31] However, he was still alive when the settlement was closed down in 1833. He survived his transfer to the new penal settlement at Port Arthur but died there of consumption the following year. According to the prison chaplain 'he expressed a strong desire for salvation and pleaded hard for mercy'.[32] The man who had nearly brought him to the gallows in England, John Pobjoy, failed to outlive him. He was drowned off Boulogne in December 1833 when the ship he had joined was blown onto a sandbank and lost.

8

The Adventures of James Porter

In 1833 the colonial government decided to abandon the penal settlement at Macquarie Harbour. Its distance from Hobart meant that it was difficult to supervise and supply. Moreover, its sheer isolation, its chief advantage, was being threatened by a proposal to open up the west coast of Van Diemen's Land for grazing. As well, the sandbar at the narrow entrance to the harbour was silting up, making what was already a troublesome passage even more dangerous.

On 11 January 1834 the *Frederick*, a locally built brig of about 120 tonnes, embarked the last of the convicts and made ready for the voyage to Hobart. Some years later, one of the convicts, James Porter, wrote an account[1] of his adventurous life, including a description of the *Frederick*'s maiden voyage — a voyage that was to turn out very differently from the routine passage anticipated by her captain. In his memoir Porter also recalled the regrettable series of events which, to his mind, paved the way to his enforced residency at Macquarie Harbour and his eventual escape from that 'place of misery'.

According to his own reckoning he was born in 1807[2] in the neighbourhood of London. In 1815 he was caught stealing a clock, but the affair was hushed up on condition that he left the country. He joined the brig *Sophia* bound for Rio de Janeiro, but once there he deserted after helping himself to a supply of doubloons from the captain's cabin. For over a year he sailed South American waters on a trading schooner before returning to England towards the end of 1817. However, a settled life was not to his liking and after only a few months of domesticity he signed up with the whaler *John Bull* for a three-year voyage to the sperm whale fisheries off the coast of Peru.

Six months cruising the whaling grounds failed to satiate his restless nature and at Valparaiso in Chile he deserted once more, hidden by a local girl until the ship sailed. Presumably having compromised her, and possibly out of gratitude, he promised her marriage, but not right away; at the age of eighteen he considered himself far too inexperienced for such a step. He spent the next fourteen months on the armed schooner *Liberta*, 'sometimes skirmishing ashore and otherwise giving the Spaniards a round turn from the schooner from our two long toms'. At this time Chile was fighting a war of independence against Spain and the Chilean Navy was under the command of the British naval hero Lord Cochrane. Fighting the Spaniards apparently provided the experience Porter lacked, for at the end of this period he 'now considered himself fit for any hardship', including marriage, and returned to Valparaiso to fulfil his promise.

After two years of married life he returned to the sea. Leaving his wife and a young son behind, he shipped on a Chilean brig bound for Lima, Peru. Too late he discovered that she was on a contraband voyage, and on reaching Lima he took his usual course — desertion. However, the ship's mate caught up with him in a grog shop and in the ensuing brawl he fractured the mate's skull with a slingshot. With the military after him and the prospect of death before him if he was taken, he managed to get a berth on the barque *Mermaid*, due to sail for England the next day.

He reached his native land towards the end of 1821, fully resolved to return to his South American family as soon as possible. But money was short and he decided 'to make one push which would make me rich or cost me my life'. With two companions he stole on board a cutter lying at anchor off Northfleet, disabled the crew and removed a quantity of silk and beaver which they planned to sell to the hatters of London. However, one of the thieves was caught in possession of the goods, and to save his own skin betrayed the others. Brought to trial, Porter could offer no defence. He was found guilty and condemned to death.[3]

Reprieved from the gallows in December 1822 he was sentenced to transportation for life. He spent eight months on a prison hulk at Woolwich where in his misery he contemplated suicide. His prison report portrays him as having a 'Very Bad Character' and given to disorderly behaviour.[4] From the hulk he was transferred to the transport ship *Asia* with over 200 other unfortunates, their destination Van Diemen's Land. In the ship's indent his occupation is given as 'boatman' and he is described as being 5 feet 2 inches (1.56 metres) tall with a sallow complexion, brown hair and hazel eyes. This was expanded twelve years later to include scars on his forehead, a dimple on his chin, a mole and scar on his neck and pugilists tattooed on his left arm. At that time he was also said to be blind in his left eye and his occupation had been changed to the unlikely one of 'beer machine maker'.

The *Asia* sailed from the Downs on 9 August 1823. The voyage lasted four months, and early on Porter was released from his irons in order to help work the ship, 'being allowed the same ration and grog as the seamen'. This unexpected good fortune continued when he was landed at Hobart. After service with a blacksmith he was placed behind an oar of the governor's barge and soon afterwards made coxswain of the secretary's gig. It was thus that a few months later he received orders from Lieutenant-Governor Sir George Arthur to take a whaleboat and carry dispatches to the small penal settlement on Maria Island, about 5 kilometres off the coast to the north-east of Hobart. As this would involve crossing East Bay Neck, the home of the 'Stony Creek tribe (the most ferocious and daring blacks on the island)', he and the crew were supplied with firearms and cutlasses.

With a good wind behind them they reached the Neck by dusk. They had succeeded in hauling the boat two-thirds of the way across when the Aborigines were alerted. From the concealing darkness they let fly a shower of spears but were driven off by pistol fire. Porter urged his men on and they struggled to the far side of the Neck before another shower of spears fell among them. The bowman was killed — 'a spear went through his intestines and he never spoke more'. Launching the boat into the surf they scrambled away, leaving their frustrated assailants yelling on the shore. They made Maria Island that night.

On the return journey there was another skirmish but a determined cutlass charge dispersed the enemy without further loss. When they arrived back at Hobart the crew was rewarded with tickets-of-leave and Porter was put in charge of the cutter *Rambler*. His good fortune, however, now deserted him:

> Some evil disposed scoundrel (envying me) gave an information that I was going to take the Cutter away. This caused the first suspicion on my Character and the Cause of my Misery — being not looked upon as a man trustworthy — therefore I was determined to make my escape from the Colony as soon as I could get a Chance.

That chance was not long coming. With another convict, Porter stowed away on the brig *Elizabeth* bound for Macquarie Island 'sea elephanting after the Oil', but lack of a favourable wind delayed her departure and they were discovered. Amazingly Porter was acquitted at his trial on the basis of a good character reference from Captain Welsh, the superintendent of government craft, and given command of a schooner of 25 tonnes. But once again his luck turned around.

A member of the crew, with only ten days of a fourteen-year sentence to serve, was apprehended on board with stolen goods. In an astonishing burst of altruism Porter agreed to take the blame, provided the 'broken hearted' culprit:

> would get a whale boat ready for me should I be sent to a Chain Gang
> — so that I could make my escape to the Straights ... he thanked me
> very heartily and swore upon a Bible he would.

No doubt there was more to this than Porter let on. It is highly likely that he was implicated in the affair and realised that his part would inevitably come out at the trial. After duly making his confession he was sentenced to seven years' transportation and, as anticipated, assigned to a chain gang, 'one of the most dreadful I ever seen — I preferred death to remaining there 3 years and what was worse the Ungrateful Scoundrel that I sacrificed myself for to save deceived me'.

Undeterred, Porter formulated a plan with some of his companions on the chain gang to steal a whaleboat, but at the last moment they let him down. In desperation, and seemingly on impulse, he made a break by himself:

> I was aware of my situation my irons being cut — so I went up to
> the sentinel pushed him off the Bank and ran as quick as possible —
> my pursuers were following. I had just sufficient time to plunge into
> the river.

By this means he eluded the pursuit and made his way to the house of Mr Mansfield, a pilot, who, unaware that he was an escapee, gave him food and shelter for the night.

Next day at dawn he set off for the signal station where he hoped to get help from a friend. But the friend, hopeful of a reward, tried to take him prisoner, whereupon Porter felled him with a musket butt. Resisting the temptation to finish off his would-be betrayer, he fled into the bush and, improvising yet another plan, headed for the limeburners' camp at Oyster Bay about 16 kilometres south of Hobart. There he would wait for an opportunity to seize a dinghy and cross the narrow channel to Bruny Island on the chance of escaping in one of the whaling ships that used it as a base.

The cross-country journey was hard going for someone lacking experience of the bush, and inevitably he became lost. For three days he wandered about without any food and 'felt the horrors of famishing'. On the fourth day he stumbled across a kangaroo freshly killed by dogs and 'took a hearty meal of the raw flesh and drank some of the blood — it was refreshing though insipid repast'. With renewed vigour he set off again, and towards evening reached the outskirts of Oyster Bay. At daylight he crept into the camp and was just launching the limeburners' boat when he was spotted by a party of soldiers who immediately opened fire on him. He eluded them for some time by hiding in a sawyer's hut where he picked up a loaded musket — but when he tried to make his way back to the shore he was seen. As shots hummed past his head he returned the fire and then ran for the beach:

> I sprung into the river keeping under water as long as I could — the tide took me a great distance from my pursuers though not out of range of their muskets. I could hear the bulletts fall into the water very Close to me but did not receive any injury from them.

The soldiers lost sight of him when he drifted into a raft of kelp and he was eventually washed up on Bruny Island 'exhausted, cold, wet and Hungry'.

He spent a week on the island sheltered by an assigned convict of his acquaintance whose master, Richard Pybuss, was away. On the ninth day he heard of a vessel which had anchored in Blubber Bay to take on oil before sailing for London, but an attempt to stow away failed. 'I several times endeavoured to swim on Board and was as often repulsed by the surf.' His disappointment was compounded when Pybuss returned unexpectedly and recognised him as a runaway. He managed to get away and cross over to the other side of the island where he went to ground for the night, covering himself with sheets of bark.

Early in the morning he was woken by the splash of oars:

> I considered this my time to escape off the Island but to my surprise who should it be but Mr Pybuss and two boys in his Gig going with the news to Mr Folly concerning my being on the Island. I suggested a plan for my escape. I hailed him and gave myself up to him, I went

and sat in the Bow of the Boat — when all of a sudden I snatched the Boathook off the thwart and requested him in a menacing attitude to land me at the Bluff ... He remonstrated with me, saying he should lose all his Government men if I compelled him to land me.

Porter, according to his own account, felt sorry for Pybuss. A cutter was getting under way nearby and he told the distraught Pybuss to hand him over to the crew and he would take his chances of being able to escape from her instead. Pybuss agreed and in a short time Porter was a prisoner on the cutter:

All went on very well until we came opposite 7 Mile Point (from Hobart Town) when I watched my opportunity, and at the moment they were putting her about, I jumped over the stern, and in the confusion they did not miss me until I was on the point of Landing.

The rush of exhilaration he felt on once more being at liberty was short-lived. He sought out a friend he thought he could trust, but instead of bringing help the friend brought two constables 'for the sake of the reward of 50 pounds'.

Back in Hobart he was tried in January 1830 for 'being illegally at large under a second conviction', found guilty and sentenced to death. Again Captain Welsh interceded for him at the last moment, 'pinioned and going out to execution'. As a result, his sentence was commuted to transportation to Macquarie Harbour for seven years.

Towards the end of May 1830 after a rough voyage beating against the prevailing winds, the brig *Tamar*, with Porter on board, passed through Hell's Gates, the appropriately named entrance to the bleak, tortured outpost of the British Empire that was Macquarie Harbour. Immediately on landing he was brought before the commandant, Captain James Briggs. 'I found him everything but a Gentleman,' lamented Porter.

A complete Tyrant, he ordered a good suit of clothing I had on to be burned and gave me a suit of yellow and sent [me] to work and at night to be sent on an island in the centre of the river where there was 200 miserable beings, men that he considered would hazard their lives to make their escape. It was an awful, wretched place for the most common necessaries or comfort — hours before day we were roused and a pint of miserable thin gruel was allowed each man — into the Boat was the word — and there we had to remain (in a bleak wind hailing and freezing) until day light when we were mustered sent to our work having nothing whatever to eat until we returned again to the island which would be dark, wet through and not a spark of fire to dry our Clothing — if a man should chance to save a small portion of his bread at night to eat with his gruel in the morning it was ten to one but he would lose his life, for the said small bit of bread — so horrible was the hunger there that I knew 2 men to be executed for knocking a man's brains out (on this very island in question) for the sake of the bit of bread he had concealed under his head when in bed, and divided it between them with the blood of their Victim on it (this my gentle reader will give you a faint idea of the acute sufferings of an unhappy captive) nothing but misery flogging and starvation.

Porter's undesirable new home was Grummet Island — not much more than a rocky outcrop supporting a few huts — where absconders and other incorrigibles were confined. New arrivals were also sent there until they proved by their good behaviour that they were eligible for transfer to the main settlement on nearby Sarah Island.

For nearly two years Porter endured 'this dreadful state of things', all the time looking for a chance to escape. In December 1832 an opportunity finally came when a group of convicts including Porter was ordered to take a launch to Kellys Basin at the head of the harbour to collect a load of logs. He and two other desperates made careful plans to 'rush the launch (i.e. take her by force) and walk overland to headquarters [Hobart Town]'. The moment they reached the shore they secured the axes and then threw the oars overboard to prevent the other convicts from returning to Sarah Island to give the alarm. They took what they needed from the boat and headed off into the mountains. From the summit of Sugarloaf Mountain, however, they were dismayed to see a boat already coming to the rescue of the launch.

Pushing on, they made for the sawyers' camp at Phillips Creek on the north shore where they managed to steal some provisions. That night they swam out to Phillips Island where a few convicts were employed in growing potatoes.

> [They] made the three men there get up out of their beds and show us where there canoe was. They did so — for it was concealed as it was prohibited (they had it expressly for fishing).

Returning to the mainland with the canoe, Porter and his companions lay up for the day among long grass at the water's edge. Some time during the morning three boats appeared and to their horror landed nearby. The commandant was in charge and passed very near to where the fugitives lay trembling. Frantically hugging the damp, pungent earth they heard him giving orders that they were to be shot on sight; luckily the search party moved on without discovering them.

At nightfall they slipped warily from their hiding place, launched the canoe and paddled across the harbour to the mouth of the Gordon River. Their idea was to navigate the river to its source which they believed, erroneously, to be close to Hobart, a town which offered greater possibilities of escape from the colony. It was daylight by the time they entered the river, but they pushed on, battling the turbulent current until night fell once more, when they collapsed exhausted on the bank near Guy Fawkes Creek. At dawn they were on their way again, but in negotiating a wide bay they were seen by the members of a timber-cutting party who gave chase in a launch. Forced into shore, the fugitives abandoned their canoe and provisions and took to the mountains.

Without food and having nothing but their shirts and trousers they were 'in a most wretched condition'. Their only shelter from the hostile weather was the frail canopy of fern growing on the otherwise bare mountain slopes.

> We lay down on some wet ferns (it was raining incessantly) keeping as close as we could to each other for warmth and what with despair and meditation we fell into a sleep (as it were of death) and knew nothing

of what passed until we were roused by the firing of musketry over our heads by the Military.

It was too late to run and besides, their condition was such that they were unable to walk and had to be carried by the soldiers to their boat. Back at the settlement they automatically received the standard punishment for absconding — 100 lashes and six months in irons, plus two months sleeping in a dark cell.

Earlier in the year, Captain Briggs had been replaced as commandant by an Irish officer, Major Pery Baylee, a far more humane man, according to Porter, than his predecessor. This opinion was shared by the Quaker missionary James Backhouse, who visited Macquarie Harbour in 1832. He wrote that under the new regime living conditions were much improved, the convicts reasonably well fed and corporal punishment greatly reduced with the result that the commandant 'could go about the settlement, unattended, with perfect confidence'.[5] Porter appears to have made a favourable impression on Major Baylee, for within twelve months he had been made coxswain of the pilot boat. (This was in line with Baylee's policy of offering positions of responsibility to convicts of good behaviour.) The commandant also had a small cutter which he used for recreational sailing, and when the weather was rough he generally took Porter with him. On one of these occasions Porter conceived a novel way of gaining his freedom, far easier and simpler than attempting another crossing of the mountains. As he recalled, 'I had tried all the schemes to obtain my liberty in a manly manner and this was the only one I could pick on to save me.'[6]

His plan was to 'accidentally' capsize the boat and save Baylee from drowning. The grateful major would then reward his heroic rescuer by recommending him for a pardon. He made careful preparations, 'adjusting the lanyards of the Water Breakers which were used for ballast so that when the boat gave a surge they would brak and fall to leeward and assist in capsizing us'. Everything went smoothly. The boat was caught on the beam by a sudden squall and heeled right over. 'But she turned out stiff as a crutch — she righted — the Major eased off the main sheet, jib sheet to windward hove her round on her heel, and we returned home.' To Porter it appeared that after so many unsuccessful attempts to escape 'he was certainly born under an unlucky star'.

Something about the incident must have aroused Major Baylee's suspicions, because a few days later he sent for Porter at a time when he was entertaining guests. After singing a few shanties he suddenly turned to Porter and asked him if he could swim. When Porter admitted that he could, the major accused him of deliberately upsetting the boat and added that if he would admit this in the presence of witnesses he could have 'a good dram of grog'. Realising that denial was useless, Porter confessed which 'caused a smile among the company'. Clearly the commandant was in a jovial mood, helped no doubt by a few drinks and the convivial company. He forgave Porter and told him that if his scheme had succeeded 'his pardon was sure'.

In October 1833 two vessels, the *Charlotte* and the *Tamar*, arrived at Macquarie Harbour for the purpose of evacuating the settlement. At that time the brig *Frederick* was still on the slipway under construction, so it was decided that thirteen convicts would remain behind under guard to complete the work and then return with her to Hobart. Porter was very pleased when he was chosen among the thirteen, for at least nine of the others were 'determined to take the brig and once more chance our lives for our liberty'.

Major Baylee departed with the bulk of the convicts on 25 November and those remaining behind commenced their work 'with good heart'. By early January the *Frederick* was completely fitted out and ready to begin her maiden voyage. In command was the pilot, Charles Taw, together with the master shipwright, David Hoy, a corporal and three soldiers. The thirteen convicts were to form the crew. Of necessity they were treated as ordinary sailors with freedom to move about the vessel under minimal supervision.

They sailed from Sarah Island on 12 January 1834 under a light south-westerly wind. When they reached Hell's Gates they anchored so that a party under David Hoy could go ashore to collect some potatoes from Captain Taw's garden. This delay was to prove very costly. By the time they were ready to sail again the wind had changed to a nor'westerly, bringing a heavy surf boiling over the sandbar at the entrance. It was considered too hazardous to proceed, so the captain turned back for the safety of Wellington Bay, about 5 kilometres inside the harbour, where they anchored for the night.

Next morning the convicts were allowed to go ashore, ostensibly to wash their clothes, but their real purpose was to prepare and distribute weapons for they expected 'a bit of a round turn with their being 9 of them and 10 of us'. They armed themselves with tomahawks and pistols which had been secretly made by life transportee John Barker, a former gunsmith and watchmaker who had been 'overseer of smiths and a most injinious man at anything'. On returning to the brig, they all went down into the forecastle. It was still too dangerous to attempt a crossing of the bar, so to pass the time the corporal, a private and one of the convicts not in the conspiracy took the whaleboat to go fishing. This suited the conspirators very well as it reduced their opposition by a third.

They now put their plan into operation. One of the soldiers was enticed into the forecastle to hear some singing. Porter began with a solo, but he was so nervous that William Shires had to help him out. Benjamin Russen, who, with several others, had slipped out while the soldier was distracted, gave the signal by stamping on the deck. At once Shires, a highwayman in his former life, pulled out his pistol and held it to the soldier's head. While Charles Lyon and John Jones held the soldier down, Porter and Shires rushed on deck securing the hatch behind them with a kedge anchor. Meanwhile the other soldier had been noiselessly seized. He was quickly bundled into the forecastle which was again secured. The convicts then crept cat-footed and wary-eyed down the aft deck to the armoury where they took possession of the ship's muskets and ammunition.

Captain Taw, Hoy and his convict servant were in the cabin drinking, oblivious of the action taking place elsewhere on the ship until Shires burst in and attempted to subdue them by himself. They were not too drunk to defend themselves; Shires, who had been briefly joined by James Leslie, was forced to retreat to the deck. The captain, bleeding from a tomahawk gash on his head, refused to surrender and eventually the convicts 'determined to frighten them'. Two muskets were poked through the skylight and 'the word was given to fire down upon them (with no intention of so doing)'. It is unlikely that such a transparent ruse by itself would have suceeded, but as one of the muskets went off accidentally and shot a bunch of keys from Hoy's hand, it had the desired effect. The beleaguered men 'cried out for quarter' and came apprehensively up on deck. They were rapidly bound but received no other ill treatment.

A musket was then fired as a signal to recall the whaleboat. No doubt the soldiers were stunned when they came alongside and were confronted by their former prisoners, armed and triumphant. They were quickly relieved of their guns and ordered into the jolly-boat under guard. The captain and Hoy were permitted to take spare clothing from the cabin before joining the soldiers and the three convicts who had not been part of the mutiny, in the boat. Their request for a pistol, for protection against the Aborigines 'as they wished to make us believe', was rejected with the wry comment — 'we begged to be excused'.

The jolly-boat was swung over the side and the soldiers were directed to row for the shore escorted by six convicts in the whaleboat — 'we guarded them ashore, we then requested them to launch the Boat into deep water again to prevent them from rushing on to the whaleboat. We then returned to the brig.' That night a strict watch was to be kept to prevent any attempt by Captain Taw to recover his ship.

At daybreak, flour, oatmeal, salt beef and other provisions were loaded into the whaleboat and taken to the shore where they were gratefully received by Hoy. He was also supplied with bandages and plaster for a painful back, as well as two bottles of wine and four of porter. In this atmosphere of cordiality Hoy attempted to persuade the convicts to give up the brig, promising to swear on the Bible not to report their actions to the authorities. When they declined he gave them his blessing:

> Since I find you will not give her up — I thank you all for your kindness to the whole of us, myself in particular. I know you have but little provisions to cross the expanding ocean and likewise a brig that is not seaworthy for such a voyage and may God prosper you in all your perilous undertaking.

It was a remarkable gesture for the convicts to give away a considerable portion of their supplies when faced with a hazardous voyage across the Pacific to their objective, South America. This charity, their friendliness towards their former oppressors and the care they took not to shed blood unnecessarily during the mutiny may have been a response to Major Baylee's own generosity. Before departing from Macquarie Harbour he had given orders that the thirteen convicts were to be put 'on marine rations and a gill of rum per diem' and that if they behaved well he would recommend them for tickets-of-leave. Perhaps, too, a bond of comradeship had developed between gaolers and prisoners as they worked together during those last six weeks to complete the *Frederick*. In fact David Hoy was later to say that he had a good opinion of the convicts, and Captain Taw stated that he did not regard them as convicts at all but as recommended men.[7]

It appears to have been a somewhat emotional farewell. As the convicts pulled back to the brig, those on shore cheered them and Hoy was observed to wipe his eyes.[8] Once on board they made preparations to get under way. The anchor was weighed and the laborious task of warping the vessel the 5 kilometres to the harbour entrance began. Eventually, after some anxious moments crossing the bar, the brig reached the open sea with sails set.

The wind freshened and they set their course east-south-east, cutting crisply through the ocean swell. Porter noted that it was 14 January when 'we took our final farewell of Macquarie Harbour heads with light hearts'. Only four of the convicts — Lyon, Jones, Porter and John Fare — had experience of the sea, but Barker, who alone had some knowledge of navigation, was made captain. It was soon evident that Hoy's warning of the brig's unseaworthiness was only too true — the brig leaked to an alarming degree. The pumps were manned and it was found necessary to keep them operating throughout the voyage.

The weather deteriorated during the night; by next morning it was blowing a full gale. They ran before the wind under a single reefed main topsail for nine days, harried by the long, muscular rollers of the Southern Ocean. So violent was the sea that at times it required two men to hold the helm. On 24 January the gale abated and they 'carried a stiff Topgallant Quarterly breeze for 4 weeks with a heavy range of a sea after us', passing well to the south of New Zealand away from the normal shipping lanes.

Despite this precaution they did sight one ship. Barker at once gave orders to bring the arms and ammunition on deck, for should she bear down on them they were determined to 'run on board of them capture them or die in the attempt, for we knew if we were brought back Governor Arthur would hang us to a dead certainty'. However, the stranger proved to be a French whaler, not the British warship they feared, and passed by without challenging them.

As expected, their supplies were insufficient for such a

lengthy voyage and for some time strict rationing had been necessary. They 'still continued on their way with prosperous gales' and on 27 February they sighted the coast of Chile, 'after six weeks and one day of a passage, and proud we were of it as the Brig was getting the upper hand of us in the leakage'. It was decided after some debate to abandon the *Frederick* and make their landfall in the longboat, a large seaworthy vessel of seven tonnes, which the carpenters among them, Shires, Leslie and Russen, had improved by raising it a plank higher and adding decking. Weakened though they were by the strain and hardship of the voyage they immediately got to work. With difficulty, they swung the longboat over the side and loaded her with firearms, ammunition, the remains of the provisions (about 2 kilograms of bread and meat) and other necessities, notably the ship's cat, a large tom which had shared their fate.

The sun was setting by the time they were ready to leave. They dropped astern, hoisted the sail and headed for the unknown shore. Ever since land had been sighted they had neglected pumping and as they moved away into the darkness the *Frederick* was already low in the water. 'I never left my Parents with more regret,' lamented Porter,

> nor was my feelings harrowed up to such a pitch as when I took a last farewell of the smart little *Frederick* ... the Brig stood to seaward, and in the state she was in water logged and so much dead weight in her for ballast she soon went down.

When dawn broke they were close ashore, drenched and shivering after a long night during which they had struggled against a boisterous sea to prevent the boat from being swamped. Cheered by the warmth of the sun they followed the coast north for most of the day, searching for a suitable landing place. At three o'clock in the afternoon they entered a large bay and found a sheltered anchorage in the lee of a reef. There they discovered shellfish in abundance and ate their fill. With darkness falling they set up camp. During the night the cat, no doubt as pleased as its masters to be on land, deserted.

He reappeared briefly in the morning but then disappeared into the forest for good. Before they left the bay they managed to kill a seal and left some of the flesh for the cat in case he returned.

For five days they continued coasting, moving from bay to bay in search of friendly inhabitants from whom they might get information as to their exact whereabouts. They had a narrow escape one night when they were caught by 'a smart breeze' on a lee shore and it was only by the most strenuous exertions that they kept the boat from foundering. On the sixth day they weathered a bluff projecting a long way out to sea. According to their chart it was named Tweedale Point. Just before dark they finally rounded it and steered for the beach in the hope of finding a secure anchorage. Suddenly they heard a noise on shore 'like a bullock or a cow'. Peering into the gloom they made out a fire around which a number of people were standing. Porter hailed them and they responded with 'a kind of yell', but as there was no apparent landing place the convicts stood offshore and let the anchor go in 22 fathoms (40 metres) of water, determined to wait until dawn to renew contact.

At first light they rowed in towards the shore where a group of Indians was waiting 'each with a scalping knife in his belt'. Porter and four of his companions, each armed with a brace of pistols, nervously leapt ashore. The other five immediately pushed off and moored the boat to some seaweed a short distance away, for as Porter commented 'it were far better for 5 of us to lose our lives than 10 of us'. Meanwhile the landing party was taken to the Indians' village, which Porter found to be remarkably clean and neat. He observed that they 'understood Agriculture' but when he asked for food they either would not or could not understand him. When he mentioned the town of Valdivia, however, they understood perfectly and made signs that it was only three leagues away. Overjoyed with this information, they rewarded the Indians with a few trinkets, returned to the beach and embarked.

At three o'clock that afternoon they passed beneath the twelve-gun battery of Fort San Carlos which dominated the entrance to the port of Valdivia, an almost landlocked anchorage into which flowed the Valdivia River. They were greeted in a friendly manner by the inhabitants who took them for shipwrecked sailors. 'We found them a very humane race of people,' wrote Porter, 'yet some of the lower Class shewed a great disposition for thieving which made us keep a strict watch on their actions.' It was probably for this reason that they chose to remain on the boat that night. Next morning it was agreed that the tradesmen among them — Barker, Shires, Leslie, Russen and William Cheshire — would set out that day for the town, about 15 kilometres upriver, in the hope of obtaining work in the local shipyards. The rest would sail north to Valparaiso where Porter hoped to find his wife and child 'and remain in Comfort during my life and return thanks to God that I did not founder on the rocks of despair'.

They spent the night of 6 March carousing with the locals, 'dancing and singing to the guitar'. They were still sleeping off the effects late the following morning when a party of soldiers hauled them from their beds and ordered them to row up the river to the town. On arrival they were thrown into a prison called the Quartell. No explanations were offered, but they did learn that Barker and the others had also been detained. They remained in prison for a week, during which time Porter managed to bribe a guard who told him that one of their number, probably Cheshire, 'had been drinking with a man called Cockney Tom and that he believed he had been saying too much to him about our circumstances and that was the cause of our confinement'.

Finally they were brought before the governor, Don Fernando Martell. With the aid of an interpreter by the name of Captain Lawson (a smuggler, according to Porter) he interrogated them closely, calling Cockney Tom as a witness against them. Unconvinced by their story of being shipwrecked sailors and suspecting them of piracy, he threatened to have them shot the next day unless they told the truth. At this point Porter, who had assumed the name of James O'Connor, boldly took the offensive with a stirring speech:

> Avast there — a word with you upon the subject — we as sailors shipwrecked and in distress expected when we made this port to be treated in a Christian like manner not as though we were dogs, — Is this the way you would have treated us in 1818 when the british Tars were fighting for your independence and bleeding in your cause against the old Spaniards — and if we were pirates do you suppose we should be so weak as to cringe to your Tyranny, Never! I also wish you to understand that if we are shot england will know of it and will be revenged. You will find us in the same mind tomorrow we are in now, and should you put your threat into execution tomorrow we will teach you Spaniards how to die.

Porter's effrontery was undoubtedly risky, but the governor seems to have been impressed. He sent for a Lieutenant Day, who had apparently fought with Lord Cochrane when he captured Valdivia from the Spaniards in a daring attack in 1820. When asked if he remembered Porter from that time he stated that he did indeed have some recollection of him — 'that he was only a Boy when on board ship with Lord Cochrane'. This seemed to satisfy the governor. Even so, the convicts were all returned to the Quartell with the exception of Cheshire and they 'soon heard for a fact, that he had turned approver and stated the whole facts of the case fearful of what would follow'. In these circumstances it was agreed that a full confession was now their only hope.

When they were brought before the governor next morning, Porter, who seems to have been elected spokesman (probably because he had some lingering knowledge of Spanish), 'told the whole of the circumstances' and asked for sanctuary. The fact that they had committed no offences against Chilean subjects was clearly in their favour, and Governor Martell ordered their discharge on condition they gave their parole not to escape. In the meantime he would seek confirmation of his decision from the federal government in Santiago. The convicts' shipbuilding experience appears to have been a consideration in his decision as he added that there was plenty of work for them in the shipyards.

At this point the 'traitor' Cheshire, who had hoped to save himself from the firing squad at the expense of his companions, realised the game was up. He threw himself before the governor pleading for protection, especially from Porter who, he claimed, had threatened to kill him. The governor reassured the wretched informer and then warned the others:

> This man Cheshire is afraid of his life — therefore I am in duty bound to protect him as well as the rest of you, therefore as he represents himself as a carpenter he shall reside near me and when he wants to go abroad one of my orderlies shall go with him and I hope none of you will molest him.

Turning to Cheshire he added: 'Had you been a South American instead of what you are all the forces I command could not have kept the rabble from tearing you to pieces.'[9]

After their release they all found lodgings in the town. Porter was taken in by a merchant, Don Fernando Lopez, and his family, who 'were soon very fond' of him. Two days later they all assisted in the launching of a vessel which had been three years on the stocks. The owner was so pleased with their efforts that he employed them to fit her out at the rate of sixteen Spanish dollars per month. Now followed a period of stability for the fugitives. Conscious of their good fortune they settled down to honest work and a quiet life, the height of their excitement being the gossip of the marketplace and the nightly dances with the dark-eyed local girls. In due course Barker, Leslie, Shires, Russen and Cheshire were married. Presumably Barker and Leslie omitted to inform their brides that they already had wives back in England.

By May 1834 their presence in Chile had been brought to the attention of the British Consul General, John Walpole, in

Santiago. A brief account of their escape had been published in a local newspaper, the *Araucano*, on 9 May, and Walpole dispatched copies to London and Hobart. Lieutenant-Governor Arthur replied on 10 November asking for Walpole's assistance in bringing the convicts to trial for piracy as soon as possible. In the meantime an English frigate, HMS *Blonde*, had arrived at Valdivia, presumably under orders from the Consul General. The commander, Commodore Mason, requested that all Englishmen residing there be sent on board to give an account of themselves. The governor refused the request and when a cutter from the frigate attempted to pass the outer battery, the Chileans fired a 32-pounder across her bows, causing her to put about promptly. Mason, 'being aware he could not get them on Board by fair means or foul, he up helm and bore away for Valparaiso'.

After this alarm, life continued pleasantly enough for the convicts. It is possible that some of them met the scientist Charles Darwin, who visited Valdivia at this time during his famous voyage on HMS *Beagle*. His journal entry for 5 February 1835 mentions that among the Englishmen living there were some:

> run-away convicts from Van Diemen's Land. They stole (or made) a vessel & ran straight for this coast, when some distance from the land they sunk her & took to their boats. They all took wives in about a week's time, & the fact of their being such notorious rogues appears to have weighed nothing in the Governor's opinion, in comparison with the advantage of having some good workmen.

He went on to describe Valdivia as:

> a quiet little town ... seated on the low banks of the river: it is completely hidden in a wood of Apple trees; the streets are merely paths in an orchard. I never saw this fruit in such abundance. There are but few houses, even I think less than in S. Carlos; they are entirely built of Alerce planks.[10]

Meanwhile a new governor arrived to relieve the convicts' 'warm-hearted friend', Governor Martell. Within days they were called to Government House where their situation was made known to the new incumbent. He promised to treat them well and keep them under his protection. However, when Governor Martell departed two weeks later, he left the convicts 'at the disposal of a tyrant' who had 'meant in his black heart' to keep his promise 'only while our friend remained a witness to his conduct'. The new governor gave orders that the convicts were to present themselves at the guardhouse every evening at six o'clock, a routine which exposed them to public humiliation. And when Porter went to work on a barque which was anchored 11 kilometres downriver, the governor set two soldiers to watch over him. 'This looked so much like Macquarie Harbour Discipline,' he bitterly complained, 'that we were determined the first opportunity we had to escape we would embrace it and sail clear of him.'

To this purpose Barker offered to build a whaleboat for the governor, his real object, of course, being to use it as a means of escape. (Their own whaleboat had been sold by Governor Martell for 40 dollars.) While he and the two carpenters, Russen and Leslie, were working on the new boat, another opportunity for escape arose. A brig named *Ocean* put into the port. When it was found by the authorities that she was carrying contraband goods she was seized and put up for sale. The commander, Captain West, was convinced that he had been betrayed, and, hearing of Barker's skills as a gunsmith, brought a brace of pistols to him for repair so that he could 'blow the informer's brains out'. The belligerent captain, who was facing ruin, calmed down when Barker suggested a more profitable course of action. He and eight of his companions would help him 'take the brig from under the Battery or perish in the attempt'. Captain West approved the plan, provided that his negotiations for the return of his vessel were unfruitful. Two days of tension followed but the convicts' high hopes were dashed when they learned that the captain had succeeded in getting two merchants to act as bondsmen at 1000 Spanish dollars each so that he was free to sail when he pleased.

Nevertheless, as Porter related, they were still determined to be on board the *Ocean* when she departed:

> On the Sunday night, as she was to sail on the Monday 6 of us took a small dinghy to go down in the middle of the night and get on board of her ready to sail in the morning, but cruel fate had decreed it otherwise, we got to the bar among a foaming surf and had to pull before it for our bare lives which was the means of our not being able to get on board the Brig and at daylight (to our grief) we saw her get underweigh.

Three of the convicts — Fare, Jones and John Dady — who had had the same idea were more fortunate. They had been working on a cutter moored in the harbour and when the *Ocean* sailed past they swam out to her and got clean away. They were last heard of in Callao, the principal seaport of Peru.

Fatigued and vexed, the others slipped back into town. Their absence had not been noticed and they returned to their usual work in the shipyards with no questions asked. Nourished by their disappointment, Barker, Russen and Leslie completed the whaleboat in only a few weeks and fitted her out with sails and provisions, all at the governor's expense. They planned to leave on a Sunday (probably 4 July 1835) after nightfall and warned Porter to be ready. On the Saturday evening he turned into his bunk confidently expecting it to be his last night in Valdivia. It was not to be. He was woken next morning at nine o'clock, not by his companions, but by a squad of soldiers who marched him off to the Quartell. There he was joined by Cheshire, Lyon and Shires; the four of them were chained together in pairs. It was not long before they learned the reason for their imprisonment. Barker, Russen, Leslie and another man, 'the second mate of the brig *Liberta*', had decamped in the whaleboat during the night, one day earlier than planned. Dropping quietly down the river they had got clear out to sea before being missed. A pursuit was ordered by the furious governor but the fugitives had too great a lead and were not even sighted. Strangely Porter did not display any bitterness towards them for their apparent treachery. His only comment concerning their premature departure was simply that it was 'owing to some circumstance or other'. They are known to have reached Talcahuano, about halfway between Valdivia and Valparaiso, but their ultimate fate is a mystery.

For seven months Porter and his luckless companions languished in prison. He had surrendered all hope of regaining his liberty when he received a note from Don Fernando Lopez warning him that an English ship was on its way to take them back to Van Diemen's Land. This horrifying news spurred him from his lethargy and he 'determined to make a bold push for it'. He persuaded Shires, to whom he was chained, to feign sickness so that they would be separated.

> This had the desired effect, they put me on a pair of Bar Irons, the Bar placed across my insteps so that I could not stride a step more than 4 or 6 inches at a time, this I endured for 7 weeks until I found an opportunity.

The opportunity was provided by a female admirer who brought him a file and a small knife, which she had concealed in her waist-length black hair. After three-quarters of an hour's work with these, he was able to take his irons off at will. That night he sat down by the fire with his guards and as a diversion regaled them with tales of the Royal Navy. At eight o'clock he stood up, and after squeezing Shires's hand, shuffled out into the backyard. For the last fortnight he had made it a regular practice to go out at this time every evening in order to establish a routine and allay any suspicion. As usual, when the guard stopped him and he said he had the sergeant's permission, he was allowed to pass. Looking around to check that he was not observed, he shook off his irons. Then picking up a plank, he carefully leaned it against the wall. He moved back about 20 metres, took a deep breath and launched himself.

> I made a spring and ran to the top of the plank and with a sudden spring caught hold of the top of the wall; hauled myself up, ran down a verandah on the other side and jumped off, being 12 feet from

the ground, strange to say I only stunned my feet, picked myself up and made all the headway I could.

It was vital not to panic, not to run. Although it was a moonless night, he was dressed all in white and he craved invisibility. As he strolled round a corner he came upon a woman carrying a lantern which lit up the road for metres around. Afraid that he would be recognised, and unable to avoid her, he walked straight up and kicked it out of her hand. The terrified woman screamed in alarm but to him it was worth it to be cloaked in darkness once more. Speed was now everything. He fled past a side street, then doubled back and dashed down it in an effort to confuse any pursuit. Blundering into a swamp on the edge of town he took the opportunity to camouflage his white clothes with black mud before hastening on. He crossed a few farms and pulled up short at a road. It was a wise precaution, for at that moment a patrol of mounted soldiers clattered past. As soon as they were out of sight he sped across the road and faded into the forest on the other side. The river, the last barrier to his freedom, was now not far away.

He emerged from the forest at the river's edge close to a fisherman's hut. A canoe was lying on the beach and he wasted no time in launching it:

> I then crossed the river in a dismal fog, my Clothing covered with mud, from which the cold was almost insupportable, and I thought catched with the cramp as I was all my troubles was coming to a close, and I should never again see the rising sun. I could then hear the soldiers bawling out Sentinels Alert, this aroused me from my reverie. I struggled with all the strength I had which Circulated my blood and I soon reached the opposite shore. I then launched the Canoe adrift, to prevent them knowing for a certainty where I landed. I then made the best of my way into the interior.

In his account Porter does not reveal where he was heading nor how he meant to retain his newly won freedom. Perhaps his intention was to strike north to Valparaiso and take refuge with his wife and family. Whatever his plan, he was in desperate straits, for he was without food or drink. All he had with him was a knife, twenty grams of tobacco, and five dollars. Cold and miserable, he pushed on through the darkness, and when night lurched into day he found, to his surprise, that he was on a farm. Approaching the farmhouse gingerly, alert for danger, he was greeted at the door by an old woman. Showing no fear of this ragged, mud-streaked figure from the forest, she ushered him in and sat him down with some boiled milk, bread and butter. She watched him with shrewd eyes while he ate. When he had finished she asked him bluntly where he had escaped from. He had his story ready which was that he had run away from a French whaler anchored in Valdivia Harbour. At this glib reply she smiled knowingly:

> and made answer, you cannot deceive me Santiago,[11] do you not know Carmaletta Rey, I replied yes, That is my daughter, she is married to an englishman called Cockney Tom. She saw me start at the name, when she said, do not be alarmed, for I do not allow him near my premises, and it is my wish for you to stop here and I will wash your Clothing for you, and you can start early in the morning clean and Comfortable.

Porter had little choice but to trust to the woman's kindness. He slept deeply and woke next morning still free. His hostess refused his grateful offer of money and he departed in good spirits. He walked solidly all day. When darkness fell he threw himself down numb with fatigue and was instantly asleep. Waking at midnight, chilled and drenched with dew, he got stiffly to his feet, shook himself, and set off again. When the sun rose he was walking through a field of corn, about 40 hectares of it, and even in its raw state he found the corn delicious. At the far end of the field was a large farmhouse, which yielded to his cautious assault, and he came away with a much-needed poncho.

Hugging his prize, he struck back into the mountains, but after walking all day was devastated to find himself back where he started. Too weary to start again and not bothering to conceal himself, he huddled down under the poncho and slept. A little after daylight he was woken by something tugging at the poncho. He sprang to his feet in alarm. Standing before him was a young man brandishing a knife and demanding the poncho, claiming it to be his father's. Porter handed it over but this was apparently not enough. The young man then tried to take him prisoner. Porter distracted him with talk and when the opportunity arose grabbed a branch to defend himself. The young man lunged at him with his knife but Porter dropped him with a dazzling blow to the head. Before the man could recover, Porter had disarmed him and retrieved the poncho. Lost as he was, to have a native of the region in his power was luck of the first order. When the stunned young man was able to walk, Porter, with the advantage of the knife, forced him to guide him over the mountains as far as the road, which led to the coastal village of Concepcíon, about 440 kilometres north of Valdivia.

Porter's luck was now nearly at an end. As he topped a hill, five horse soldiers surprised him. He had no time to run and with rough efficiency they bundled him onto a horse, lashing his feet beneath its belly. As it was late in the afternoon he was taken to the nearest village. Being in a weakened state from dysentery, Porter was allowed to sleep in a bed closely watched by his captors who relieved each other every two hours. They rode on next day and at four o'clock came to a river where a canoe was waiting to take them across. In the confusion of getting everyone on board and urging the horses into the water, Porter realised that a chance of escape was on offer:

> I was standing on the Bank about seven feet above the canoe when I was ordered to come into the canoe. I jumped from the bank of the river on the gunwale with the reviving hope of capsizing her, not caring if we all perished together, or have a chance of escape by swimming, but all was in vain, nor did any of them have the slightest suspicion of my design, we very soon reached the opposite shore, and mounted again.

That night they stayed at a farmhouse. After supper Porter was confined in a pair of stocks and, as he wrote, 'sleep was an entire stranger to me that night'. Deciding to have a little fun with him to relieve their boredom his guards lit a fire close to his feet. When the pain became too much, Porter:

> took the stone from under my head and threw it with all the violence I could among the three of them, and knocked one of them down, the alarm was given, they rushed in upon me and confined as I was entirely helpless, they belaboured me with the broad part of their sabres until I was black and blue. The cruelty did not cease here, they fastened a cord above the ankle of each leg, and then hauled them as far through the stocks as they could get them, passed the cord over a beam above their heads, making them fast, leaving me in the most excruciating agony, I remained in this torture until daylight.

His injuries were serious enough to prevent him travelling the following day, and even then he could not have been fully recovered as it was decided that only one guard was needed to accompany him. If they considered he was now incapable of escaping they had misjudged his resourcefulness. To reach Valdivia it was necessary to negotiate a mountain pass only a metre wide with a drop of 90 vertiginous metres on one side. As they entered this pass, Porter perceived at once the possibilities for escape.

> The thoughts of their cruelty to me came fresh in my memory, I was resolved to be revenged and get my liberty if I could at the same time. I then went to the tail of his horse catched hold of it and as I thought with a sudden jerk hurl him and horse down the precipice. I did my best by suddenly snatching the quarter of his horse towards the precipice, one of the horse's hoofs I got over the brink, by the sudden twist I gave him, no sooner did the Choler find his horse giving way than he drove the rowel of his spur that was on the right heel into the side of his horse with such violence that he fairly lifted him clean out of the imminent danger he was in, nor could he account for it in any other way than he thought his horse slip't, no suspicion fell upon me as I thought for it was never hinted to me as such.[12]

No further opportunities for escape occurred and as they came down into the plain they fell in with a lieutenant and five soldiers who had been on the lookout for the escapee. It was evening by the time Porter and his escort rode into Valdivia but he was taken at once to Government House. His old enemy the governor was lolling and gloating in an easy chair surrounded by his officers when Porter was ushered into his presence. When the governor asked him why he had run away, he rashly answered: 'Two reasons I had for so doing, first, the cruel treatment and oppression of a Tyrant, secondly the reviving hope of regaining my Liberty.' The governor's response was predictably ferocious. He gave orders for a blacksmith to weld iron bars onto his legs and that preparations be made for him to be shot in the public square the next day. 'I was quite indifferent as to his putting his threat into execution,' Porter confessed, 'for (for to speak Candid) I was tired of my wretched life.'

At the blacksmith's shop irons were clamped on his legs and 'a piece of red hot iron hissing from the fire was placed in the end of the bar and actually welded in to prevent the bar from slipping through'. Hobbled in this grim manner he was led to the Quartell where he spent an uncomfortable night unaware that friends were working anxiously to secure him a pardon. In the morning a priest, Padre Rosa, came to his cell with the news that:

> himself and several of his Brotherhood and also several females of distinction had been to the Governor pleading on my behalf, and they found him a long time inflexible, when at last by their earnest solicitations he consented to spare your life.

Porter was suitably grateful to the priest who promised to send him meals regularly from his own table. Shortly after Padre Rosa had left, the governor made an appearance, anticipating the delight, it may be presumed, of accepting the prisoner's abject gratitude. Far from grovelling, Porter surprised his visitor with another of his defiant outbursts. 'I have nothing to thank you, nor could I thank you under any Circumstances, yourself being the Chief Cause of my heartfelt misery by your cruel oppression and Tyranny.' The governor contented himself with 'a fierce glance' and stalked out leaving Porter to himself.

Months rolled past until one day in autumn 1836 the four convicts received orders that they were to be transferred to the English schooner *Basilisk*, the tender to HMS *Blonde*. There must have still been considerable public sympathy for their plight because the governor specially arranged for them to be removed from the Quartell during the afternoon when the populace was enjoying its siesta and the risk of protest was minimal. For the last time they rowed down the familiar river winding through the dense crush of forest, unbroken save for a few hovels and the occasional cleared patch of ground, until they emerged into the harbour where the *Basilisk* lay waiting. Also waiting for them was the governor, the first person Porter saw as he stepped on board. Without pausing he snatched up a copper belaying pin and swung it at his oppressor. 'The blow glided from his head and struck him on the collar bone which caused him to shriek.' As Porter raised his arm again he was seized by the quartermaster and hurried below before he could be 'dispatched there and then by the Spanish Guard'.

At sunrise the schooner got under way, and after calling at Valparaiso eventually caught up with the *Blonde* in Callao. There they were drafted onto the frigate, ordered between decks, and ironed. Porter soon earned the enmity of the first lieutenant but was fortunate enough to find two bluejackets among the crew with whom he had once sailed — '(fulfilling the old proverb that a sailor's heart is always open to a shipmate in distress), they relieved me in every sense of the word'. They remained in Callao a few days before putting to sea for the return voyage to Valparaiso. On the way, they put into the small harbour of Concepcíon. There Porter hatched yet another escape plan, which he discussed with the trusted Shires. In his unending determination to renounce his convict state Porter must have been an emblem of freedom to his friend.

Although Lyon's and Cheshire's reliability was questionable, Shires's advice was that these two would have to be included as the escape could not be made without their knowledge. When the appointed time came, Porter slipped his shackles, but to his dismay Shires, who was unable to swim and was fearful of the water, was having second thoughts. 'I should be sorry Jimmy to be the means of preventing you of getting your liberty,' he whispered.

> I care not for the other two as I am aware they are villains of the worst
> cast, yet you could not do it without their knowledge, therefore there
> being no dependence to be placed in them when I am overboard they
> may swim away and desert us, and I should be too heavy for you
> which would endanger our lives and liberty and they would get clear
> off. Therefore I will remain where I am, my only request is should you
> be fortunate, you will not forget to see my wife and little son Bernardo
> and be a friend to them for I shall never see them more.

The logic of Shires's argument was unavoidable and Porter did not attempt to talk him round. To his surprise Lyon and Cheshire had also changed their minds and declined to make the attempt with him. This sudden unexplained volte-face should have raised his suspicions, but he was anxious to be away and was probably relieved not to have their company. After stuffing his bed with his pea jacket (they were sleeping on the deck) to make it appear that he was lying with his head under the blankets, he shook hands with Shires for what he thought was the last time. Then noticing that the marine on sentry duty was momentarily obscured by one of the ship's guns, he quickly crawled into the main chains.[13] From there he snaked along the side of the vessel to the mizzen chains as he wanted to get out of the sentry's hearing before he entered the water. He had scarcely got his foot onto the mizzen chains, however, when the marine appeared out of the shadows, presented a pistol to his head and ordered him to climb back on board. He thought about breaking away and plunging into the harbour but with a full moon spreading its dangerous light he realised he would either be shot or swiftly overtaken. Dejectedly he allowed himself to be led back to his bed. Later a sailor woke him up to tell him that he had been betrayed by one of his companions who had rattled his irons to attract the sentry's attention.

In the morning the convicts were interrogated by the first lieutenant one at a time. Cheshire and Lyon pleaded ignorance of the escape attempt. Not so Shires, who admitted his complicity and swore that 'the two scringing villains that denied any knowledge of it, also knew about it, and said they would go, but their cowardly hearts would not allow them'. When Porter was asked why he had tried to escape, he replied that he thought he had been prisoner long enough and had an undoubted right to try to escape. In his usual defiant manner he also gave warning that if he caught the sentinel off his guard again he would repeat the attempt. Commodore Mason's response was unexpectedly mild. He ordered Porter below, commenting that:

> It is natural the man would endeavour to make his escape, and it is our duty to prevent him if we can. If they are guilty of the offence they are charged with they are to be treated as men and if innocent their case is very hard and aggravating to them.

With the four convicts safely back in irons the *Blonde* set sail for Valparaiso where they were transferred to the 28-gun ship *North Star* bound for England. On 10 June 1836 they left their home of two years for good. They soon ran into foul weather and spent seven weeks attempting to round Cape Horn, all the time having to negotiate towering packs of icebergs. It was not until late October that they were landed at Portsmouth.

There was little time to experience their native land before they were removed to the hulk *Leviathan* and reintroduced to the English penal system. The next day they were forwarded to the guard ship *Britannia* where Porter's reputation for slipperiness was well catered for. 'We were handcuffed from friday afternoon to monday morning,' he noted,

> two and two, upon two gratings, with two marines over each grating and a man for the express purpose of cutting our provisions in small pieces for they would not trust us with a knife on any consideration, not one of us were allowed to the head of the vessel without a marine being handcuffed to us.

On Monday they were examined by the commander, Captain Dundas. Several former convicts and a number of hulk captains were brought on board but failed to recognise them, with the result that Captain Dundas was inclined to order their release, but as he explained this was beyond his power. Instead they were returned to the *Leviathan* where they 'went through a complete change with regard to our clothing, shaving and hair cutting'. Their fate was determined by the Home Secretary, Lord John Russell, who decided that they should be returned to Van Diemen's Land without delay to stand trial. On 23 December they were transferred to the barque *Sarah*, which sailed the following day for Hobart with a total of 254 convicts in her hold. Unusually the four escapees are not noted on the ship's indent, although their names do appear on the assignment list where Porter is listed as James Connor, clearly a variation of his Chilean alias of James O'Connor.

At first the voyage went well for Porter. He made himself useful by nursing the sick prisoners and keeping their quarters clean. In this manner he earned the trust of the ship's doctor, Surgeon Superintendent James McTernan, and the captain, who ordered his irons to be struck off so that he could go aloft and help in the working of the ship. This happy state of affairs ended abruptly one morning about a month later when Porter and 60 other convicts were ordered onto the quarterdeck and accused of conspiring to take over the ship. William Shires was the first called out for punishment and received four dozen lashes 'with a log line which nearly killed him'. Porter was next, led out loudly protesting his innocence. At this point Lyon and

Cheshire stepped forward declaring that he was lying and had been 'going to head 12 Canadians to rush the quarter deck and slaughter all before him'. Porter was astounded. 'Knowing my innocence,' he wrote,

> I stood almost petrified and before I could recover myself, I was seized by the soldiers and lashed to the grating and a powefull black fellow flogged me across the back, lines and every other part of the body until my head sank on my breast with exhaustion, as for the quantity of lashes I received I cannot say for I would not give them the satisfaction to scringe to their cruel torture, until nature gave way and I was senseless.

The flogging of the remaining accused continued for more than three hideous hours after which they were chained below, bleeding profusely, their hands manacled behind their backs, in a space scarcely big enough to contain them. For three weeks they endured these appalling conditions until they presented 'more the appearance of skeletons than living beings'. In his misery Porter managed to beg a scrap of paper from the surgeon on which he jotted the following deeply felt lines:

How wretched is an Exile's state of mind
When not one gleam of hope on earth remain
By grief worn down, with servile chains confined;
And not one friend to soothe his heartfelt pain.

Too true I know that man was made to mourn
A heavy portion's fallen to my lot
With anguish full my aching heart is torn
Far from my friends by all the world forgot.

The feathered race with splendid plumage gay
Extend their throats with a discordant sound
With Liberty they spring from spray to spray
While I a wretched exile gaze around.

Farewell my Sister, Aged parents dear
Ere long my sand of life will cease to run
In silence drop a sympathetic tear

For your Unhappy Exiled long lost son.

  O cease my troubled aching heart to beat
Since happiness so far from thee has fled
Haste, haste unto your silent cold retreat
In clay cold earth to mingle with the dead.

Just as he was writing down the last few mournful words, an officer accompanied by two marines burst through the door shouting, 'I have got you at last', and snatched the paper from his hand. On reading the poem the officer relaxed and explained that Cheshire and Lyon had informed the surgeon that he, Porter, was writing messages inciting his friends to mutiny. When Porter asked the officer his opinion of the two men he answered, 'I believe them to be two perjured villains and on that account I will stand your friend'. After this episode Porter was allowed a little more freedom on the ship and his and Shires's names were removed from McTernan's final list of suspected conspirators. However, they were still closely watched.

When the *Sarah* was a week out from Hobart, Porter had the satisfaction of seeing Cheshire ensnared in his own machinations. He was accused by two other convicts of endeavouring to persuade them to swear with him that another mutiny was being plotted, presumably in the hope of gaining the captain's favour. 'The promoter of all evil' lost all credibility and was placed in solitary confinement under constant guard to prevent him communicating with anyone, 'To exhult in a fellow prisoner's downfall is quite foreign to my nature,' Porter piously stated, 'but pardon me on such an occasion as this, I could not avoid it.'

On 28 March 1837 the *Sarah* arrived at Hobart. For most of the convicts this merely meant exchanging a floating prison for one on land, but to the irrepressible Porter it represented an opportunity for escape, 'as I knew every Creek and Corner in the town'. But when the Police Magistrate, Captain Matthew Forster, came on board he recognised the supposed James

Connor as the noted escapee James Porter and immediately placed him under close guard. As he was led ashore the press of the crowd thrust Cheshire forward, offering Porter a chance of revenge which he gratefully accepted. 'I seized him by the throat and hurled him over my hip and would have throttled him but was prevented by the police.'

On 26 April Porter, Shires, Cheshire and Lyon were tried before Chief Justice John Pedder for the piracy of Her Majesty's Ship *Frederick* on the high seas. The *Hobart Town Courier* followed the trial closely, describing Porter and Lyon as 'intelligent — and what may be termed "smart men"; Shires apparently a quiet man, and Cheshire a weak lad'. The reporter went on to remark that 'Porter was busily occupied in taking notes, of which he availed himself in his cross-examinations, which were conducted with considerable acuteness'.[14] In his defence Porter put forward an ingenious argument. As the *Frederick* had not been formally commissioned or registered she was not a ship in the legal sense but a mere bundle of materials in the form of a ship. Therefore the crime was robbery and not the more serious one of piracy. In addition he pointed out that the seizure had not taken place on the high seas, as the crime of piracy required, but in a virtually landlocked harbour. The jury was not swayed by such subtleties and after deliberating for half an hour found all four guilty as charged.

For more than two years they were confined in Hobart Town Gaol in irons without any sentence being passed, owing to Chief Justice Pedder's doubts as to the correctness of the verdict. (Unlike the jury he had been impressed by Porter's defence.) It was not until May 1839 that Lieutenant-Governor Sir John Franklin finally came to the decision that the four of them should be transferred to Norfolk Island for life. They left Hobart on 13 July in the *Marian Watson*. At Sydney they were transferred to the *Governor Phillip* and arrived at Norfolk Island on 26 August. At that time the island's commandant was

Major Thomas Bunbury, described by Porter as 'a second Nero', a man who believed fervently in the efficacy of the lash. Porter recorded an example of his methods which he observed soon after he landed: 'a man was being dragged before him with irons on he could scarce crawl in, and before he could reach the office he ordered him 50 lashes without even enquiring into the case'.[15]

Conditions improved rapidly in 1840 when Captain Alexander Maconochie arrived to take command. It was his firm opinion that reform rather than punishment should be the focus of the prison system, a vision quite alien to Norfolk Island practices. One of his first acts, much to Porter's satisfaction, was to have the gallows cut down and burned, and it was also under his enlightened regime that Porter was encouraged to set down his story. In this account, with nothing now to lose, Porter presented himself as one of the main protagonists in the seizure of the *Frederick* whereas in an earlier memoir, written in Hobart Gaol in 1837 when he was writing to save his neck, he downplayed his role and suggested that he had been led astray by his companions. In the intervening years he had lost none of his canniness and concluded this new version of his story with some unashamed flattery of Maconochie and his novel methods:

I speak for myself and six more young men that would rush upon Bayonetts to obtain our liberty previous to the arrival of Capt. Maconochie, we have given our words neither to abscond with a boat or allow one to be taken under any circumstances and we have proved to him and all the officers on the island that our Commandant's Humanity has brought us to a sense of our Duty, never to lose the only thing an unfortunate exile doth possess — His Word — where harsh treatment and Tyranny would drive a man to Despair and compel him to break a thousand words to get away from it — thus you find my gentle reader after all my trials and troubles I am now on Norfolk Island and live in hopes by my good conduct to become once more a member of good Society.

Porter remained on Norfolk Island for only four years. He was reported to be 'much worn out but steady and well conducted'.[16] Within a short time he was made signalman and then promoted to the boat crew, eventually being given responsibility as an overseer and policeman. In May 1841 his colonial life sentence was reduced to fourteen years for his part in rescuing some officers of the settlement when their boat capsized. The following year he was rewarded with a further reduction of seven years for his part in taking the boat out in heavy seas to supply water to a brig in distress 19 kilometres off the island.

In May 1843 he was returned to Sydney. He spent a year in Newcastle where he served time in the cells on three occasions for absenting, disobedience and assault. While working in Customs he gave information which led to the seizure of an illicit still, but he was refused a reward on account of his previous history. However, hope was held out that as soon as his behaviour improved he might be in line for a conditional pardon or some other indulgence. By June 1845 he was back in Sydney as a wardsman at the Hyde Park Barracks. On 22 January 1846 he received a ticket-of-leave, only to have it cancelled three months later when he was convicted of theft. He was sent to Newcastle again, and there he makes his final appearance in the records of the colony. On 18 May 1847 he is noted as having absconded from the district, supposedly on the brig *Sir John Byng* bound for Wellington, New Zealand. He was never heard of again. As far as the colonial government was concerned he had made his last and most successful escape.

9

The Gentleman Bushranger

From the earliest days of settlement, many of those convicts who escaped into the interior managed to survive by turning to banditry. In December 1791 Captain Watkin Tench noted in his journal that 'there are at this time not less than thirty-eight convict men missing, who live in the woods by day, and at night enter the different farms and plunder for subsistence'.[1] Six years later the problem had become serious enough for a shipment of arms to be ordered from England for the use and defence of settlers in remote regions.[2] By about 1810 a new word was being used to describe these marauders — 'bushrangers'.

In Van Diemen's Land, the repository for some of the most hardened types, the bushranger problem was particularly grave. The first settlement there had been established at Hobart in 1803 and only four years later Governor William Bligh was expressing dismay at the number of escaped convicts infesting the interior. He hoped that 'by vigilance and Bribes they may be laid hold of'.[3] However, by 1814 the situation had failed to improve. A worried Lachlan Macquarie (Bligh's successor) reported that in the vicinity of Port Dalrymple and elsewhere 'some very violent excesses have been lately committed by bands of run-away Convicts [who] support themselves by plundering Houses, and driving off the cattle of the unfortunate settlers'.[4] His solution was to offer an amnesty to all those 'prolifigate and disorderly persons' who surrendered before 1 December that year. An unforeseen effect was that not only did it offer a pardon for past crimes but also granted a licence to ravage the colony until the expiry date. In the end, few bushrangers surrendered, and in desperation Lieutenant-Governor Thomas Davey, against Macquarie's wishes, proclaimed martial law. But with insufficient troops to enforce it, this measure proved almost as ineffective. Among the crags and shadowy gorges of the Tasmanian wilderness the bushrangers were secure. Their sympathisers, with whom they traded kangaroo meat for grain and sugar, provided them with shelter and gave early warning of the thinly stretched patrols of redcoats.

In time the convict-turned-bushranger was elevated in popular sentiment to the status of folk hero and celebrated in ballads as the victim of injustice and the cowardly police. The model for this figure of romance was a freckle-faced, blue-eyed Irish killer named John Donahue. He arrived in Sydney in 1825 on a life sentence. He was soon at large embracing a career of highway robbery and murder. His luck ran out in 1830 when he was tracked to his lair at Bringelly (outside Sydney) and shot dead. It was not long before a sanitised version of his short, violent life was being sung around lonely campfires and in the teeming public houses of the towns. 'Bold Jack Donahue', as he was now known, had been transformed by the balladeer into one of those:

> gallant bushrangers who gallop on the plain
>
> Who scorn to live in slavery and wear the iron chain.

As a promotion for the bushranging way of life the ballad was considered potent enough for Governor Sir Ralph Darling to prohibit the singing of it in any public house on the pain of the loss of licence.

Rivalling Donahue as a figure of bushranging legend was another transported convict named William Westwood, better known as Jacky Jacky. He was a veteran of numerous escape attempts and during an energetic career on the road gained a reputation for gallantry towards his victims, especially the ladies. In 1846 he wrote a memoir of his short life while awaiting execution on Norfolk Island. It is a fast-paced narrative crammed with dramatic incident most of which can be verified in official records and other contemporary sources. He was born in 1820 in the village of Manuden, Essex, but despite the advantages of kind parents and a good education fell foul of the law at an early age. A conviction for highway robbery was followed by another for stealing a coat, and at the age of sixteen he was put on board the transport *Mangles* bound for New South Wales under a fourteen-year sentence. In the ship's indent his occupation was given as errand boy and he was described as being 5 feet 5 inches (1.65 metres) in height with a ruddy complexion, brown hair and dark grey eyes.[5]

On arrival in Sydney in July 1837 he was assigned to Captain Phillip Parker King, the former governor's son, who forwarded him to Gidleigh Station, his property near Lake George. According to Westwood the overseer there was 'a very hard and severe man' who 'did not allow me a sufficiency of food, and only a scanty supply of clothing'.[6] Finding his situation impossible to endure, he fled into the bush after eighteen months, but having only a limited knowledge of bushcraft was soon picked up by a detachment of mounted police. As punishment he was given 50 lashes which only increased his resolve to escape. Once more he absconded but was again quickly recaptured and received another 50 stripes.

Conditions at Gidleigh failed to improve and Westwood 'did not fancy stopping [there] to be starved to death in a land of plenty'. One night he stole a fowling piece and with two companions 'went out and committed a robbery with arms in order to supply our wants and things went on in this way for some considerable time'. Working for their master by day and themselves by night was an exhausting business and eventually they slipped up. In December 1840 they were taken on suspicion of robbery and brought before the magistrate at

Queanbeyan. Westwood was discharged for lack of evidence but three days later he heard that one of his mates had turned Queen's evidence. Faced with the prospect of transportation for life, if not hanging, he made a fast decision:

That night I bolted, with the intention of taking arms, and the first place I made for was one of my master's sheep stations, to see one of my old farm mates. I had not been there long when I heard the noise of a horse's feet come galloping up to the hut. I ran to the door to see who it was, and who should it be but a man I knew very well, who had been in the bush 18 months. He was a terror to the settlers in that part of the country, and was well mounted and armed. He dismounted and came into the hut. I liked his appearance very much. I got into a yarn with him and told him how I was situated, and that I liked his line of life and would serve with him as his companion if he was willing.

Westwood's new acquaintance was Patrick Curran, a brutal character who had been transported for life for assaulting a soldier with a knife. Since arriving in the colony he had moved on to arson, murder and rape as well as robbery. He liked Westwood well enough and the two rode off together into the bush.

Within days Westwood was launched on his new career. The two men bailed up a traveller near Queanbeyan, relieved him of £7 and a watch, stripped him and left him stranded without clothes or horse. They did, however, leave him with the sound advice not to move his hands if he was ever stopped again because other 'gentlemen' of their kind would most likely shoot him. Drawing confidence from this easy success they then paid an uninvited visit to a settler's homestead. Taking the owner and his servants by surprise they disabled the men and ordered one of the women to get them some refreshment. After 'a good snack, and drinking a couple of bottles of wine', Westwood went outside to see to the horses. He had not been long gone when a scream brought him running back into the hut where he saw, as he delicately put it, Curran 'attempting some liberties with the mistress of the house'. When he intervened on behalf of the unfortunate woman, Curran, outraged at being deprived of his pleasure, drew a pistol on him. Furiously Westwood swept it from his hand:

> This led to a row between us, and I resolved to part from such a hot-tempered companion, as two of the same sort were better asunder. I left him there, and mounting my horse went off by myself.

It turned out to be a wise decision. Six months later Curran's uncontrollable nature led to his undoing. He was cornered near Bathurst, brought to Sydney by mounted escort, found guilty of murdering an overseer, and promptly hanged.

Meanwhile Westwood 'was now left alone trying', as he wrote, 'to manage a trade which I did not much understand, but my heart was good to learn'. And he wasted no time in doing so. Next day, coming out onto a road after a long ride he determined to stick up the first person to come along. He did not have long to wait. A solitary rider came into view, whereupon the novice bushranger rushed out from hiding shouting to him to stand or be shot. The man was too astonished to resist and Westwood had no difficulty in making off with his saddlebags. These, to his delight, turned out to be mailbags containing upwards of £70 in cash and £200 in cheques and orders. As he later commented drily, 'After this I was always very partial to mailmen'.

Over the following few weeks Westwood ranged the bush, robbing settlers and travellers in the southern districts around Goulburn and Yass. On at least one occasion he had a narrow escape. Shortly after robbing a man and then impudently sitting down with him for a smoke and 'a yarn about the affairs of the country', he was spotted by three mounted policemen. Fortunately he was well mounted on a horse 'as lively as a bag of fleas' and took off 'like the wind'. The further they chased him the further they fell behind and he quickly 'gave them the go-by'. Reports of his exploits began to appear in the local press and he soon found himself famous. It was at about this time that he acquired his nickname of Jacky Jacky. Its origin is obscure but a likely explanation is that as he was in the habit of disguising himself by blackening his face with charcoal, he was thought by some to be an Aborigine.

His early success may have bred overconfidence, for on 20 January 1841 the *Sydney Herald* reported that 'the notorious Jack Jacky' had been captured without a fight near Bungendore:

> On Wednesday, the 13th instant, a man came running to this place and said that Jacky Jacky, the bushranger, who recently robbed the mail, and committed numerous other daring robberies, was following him to shoot him. A few minutes after, Jacky hove in sight, on the Plains, mounted on a splendid mare, belonging to one of the Messrs. Macarthur, continuing to ride up and down for half an hour in the line of a quarter of a mile, dressed in a handsome suit, of which he had robbed a store at Boro a day or two previously. He rode up to Egleton's and continued for some time in conversation with parties there.

At this point William Balcomb, a local landholder, and Father McGrath of Queanbeyan nervously approached the group. 'This seemed to act happily,' the article went on to say with a tantalising lack of detail, 'and Jacky was secured, expressing his regret that his two muskets were in bad condition.' The bushranger's own explanation for his ignominious capture was that he was drunk. He was taken to a public house at Bungendore and confined in the parlour under the charge of two armed ticket-of-leave men. About seven o'clock that evening, by which time he had no doubt sobered up, he made a desperate effort to escape. He knocked one of his guards down, seized his pistol and lit off across the plain. Frank Powell, the local magistrate's brother, who happened to be standing nearby, sent a bullet whistling past his head and then, snatching up another gun, set off in pursuit. A kilometre into the bush he caught up with his quarry and, with the aid of a mailman who was providentially riding past, secured him and brought him back. This time he was 'tied up like a faggot' with 'as many ropes and cords round me as a man could well carry'.

Several days later he was transferred under police escort to Goulburn and thence to Berrima to stand trial at the next Assizes. On 15 April he was found guilty on various charges of armed robbery and sentenced to transportation for life. The authorities, well aware of his record for escaping, packed him off to Sydney for safekeeping, with a sergeant and three troopers for company.

They halted for the night at Picton, then called Stonequarry, where Westwood was lodged for safety in the inner room of the local lockup, a fairly primitive affair of wooden slabs. At about three o'clock in the morning, when he reckoned the guards were likely to be at their least vigilant, he made his move. With another prisoner he managed to clamber over a partition into an adjoining room where they found the gaoler fast asleep. They grabbed his carbine and then after removing some loose shingles escaped through the roof. To have broken out of the gaol without raising the alarm, laden with irons as they were, was an impressive feat, but as Westwood himself related, they were not yet clear of the police:

> Before I could get well into the bush daylight made its appearance. I was surrounded by constables in all directions searching for me. I expected to be taken every minute. The thought came into my head to get up a tree. I picked out a good one, and scrambling up, there I remained all day. At night I came down, but dare not proceed any further, as the constables would be lying in wait all round me. I remained in this way for four days, up in the tree in the daytime, and down at night.

On the fourth night he dropped down from his perch as usual. He hobbled off into the darkness and this time made it safely to a homestead whose lights he could see in the distance. The occupants gave him food for his empty belly, a knife and a file to cut off his chains and were no doubt immensely relieved when he 'bid them good night'. The rest of the night he spent lying up in the bush. Morning found him concealed under a bridge waiting to stop the first person to come along. Within an hour a gentleman on horseback made his appearance. He was taken completely by surprise when a wild-looking man, shockhaired and filthy, suddenly rose up in front of him roaring out, 'Stand or I'll blow your head off'. At the bushranger's command he hastily tumbled from his horse. 'I then ordered him to turn out his pockets,' Westwood recalled.

> Then I mounted his horse and marched him in front of me a mile into the bush. I made him take off everything but his shirt. Then I put on his clothes and gave him my trousers, his own mother would hardly have known him, I told him I was going up the country. After I had got out of sight I turned my horse's head right round, and took down the country. I came onto the road and held gently along until I met two gentlemen going up the country. I stopped them, and took all their money and their watches. This job over I put spur to my horse, and went full gallop along, robbing everyone I met until came to the Cow Pasture.

Following this fresh series of outrages, the government plastered the countryside with reward notices offering £30 or a conditional pardon for his apprehension and speedy lodgement in one of Her Majesty's gaols. But there were no takers. The stolen thoroughbreds he rode could generally be relied on to outrun the mounted troopers' nags and if the hunt did get too close there were friends and sympathisers among the shepherds and stockkeepers of the outlying districts only too ready to hide him.

Some time in May 1841 Westwood moved further north and began operating on the West End Road near Parramatta. The first person he stuck up was a parson. In keeping with his gentlemanly reputation, he forbore to rob him but he did detain him for an hour of conversation. He declined the parson's invitation to accompany him to church, preferring instead to rob the driver of a horse and chaise whom he accosted shortly after.

A few days later the tollkeeper on the Parramatta road was roused by a well-dressed man on a thoroughbred who asked him for a pipe of tobacco. The old man invited him in and after he had taken a few puffs the stranger asked him if he had ever heard of Jacky Jacky, the notorious bushranger. 'Yes,' replied the tollkeeper, 'but there was no fear of him coming to Sydney, as he was sure to be nabbed.' 'Not at all,' said the other, 'I am Jacky Jacky.' And raising the skirts of his coat he displayed a brace of pistols. He then gave the tollkeeper some money and asked if he would get him some grog. When he refused to leave his post, Westwood went himself to a nearby inn and brought back a flagon of spirits which he divided with his host.[7]

The Parramatta district, however, proved not to his liking, probably because it was unfamiliar and the police were too much in evidence. Before long he retired to his old haunts in the south among the steep ravines and thickly timbered hills of the Jingera Range. There, while he continued to baffle police efforts to track him down, his progress was carefully plotted by the newspapers. On 12 June 1841 the *Sydney Gazette* noted that 'he was said to be levying contributions between Bungendore and Manaroo Plains'. A few weeks later, on 29 June, he was reported by the *Australian* to be in the Yass district:

> dressed in the most fashionable style with a Newmarket-cut riding coat, white cord breeches and top boots. On Friday week he stopped a gentleman between Carey's public house at Mudbilli and Gunning, and robbed him of his horse, saddle, bridle, coat, spurs and sixteen shillings in silver, but did not otherwise molest him.

On 15 July he featured again in the *Sydney Gazette*. After describing Westwood's most recent hold-up the correspondent echoed general opinion that the outlaw's 'headquarters are among the notorious horse and cattle stealers of the Jingberry Mountains'. He then went on to suggest that 'if some of the foot police were to pay some of these gentlemen a visit, it is more than likely a clue to his retreats would be speedily obtained'.

However, this advice was not needed, for by the time the report had been filed Westwood was already a prisoner. He had been taken on the evening of 13 July after bailing up an inn on the Berrima road. He had been walking out the door with £40 in silver coin and an armful of guns when the landlord leapt on his back and one of the inn servants bashed him senseless with a hammer. When he came to, he found himself in the tap room secured to a dray wheel by a bullock chain padlocked round his neck. Next day he was conveyed to Berrima and thence to Sydney, where he was confined in the new Darlinghurst Gaol.

Within three weeks Westwood was testing the gaol's escape-proof reputation. He managed to cut through his irons with an old knife but his preparations were discovered at the last moment. Brought before a magistrate the next day he was sentenced to a flogging but, unusually, the sentence was not completed. His health had suffered during his imprisonment and after only seventeen lashes the medical officer in attendance ordered the punishment to be stopped.

It was clear that Westwood would never submit tamely to captivity and he was removed to Cockatoo Island in Sydney Harbour, the home of several hundred hardheads and recidivists. No one had ever made a successful escape from the island and Westwood would be no exception. He is said to have made one attempt, however, but the details are not known other than that he planned to swim across the harbour to the north shore with 25 other convicts. Following this latest example of defiance he was put on board the brig *Marian Watson* bound for the penal settlement of Port Arthur in south-eastern Van Diemen's Land. Another unsubstantiated story claims that during the voyage he and his fellow transportees managed to break free of their chains and were only narrowly prevented from taking over the brig. The *Marian Watson* had an otherwise uneventful passage and Westwood was disembarked at Port Arthur in March 1842.

Established in 1830, the main settlement was situated on the Tasman Peninsula, a broad stretch of land joined to Forestier Peninsula and the mainland by a narrow land-bridge only 150 metres wide. Called Eaglehawk Neck, it was the gateway to Port Arthur and as such was guarded with considerable care. Stretching from Pirates Bay in the east to Norfolk Bay in the west, a line of eleven ferocious dogs was chained in such a way that any man attempting to pass between them would be shredded. Convict lore said that these dogs, whose names included such descriptive gems as Ugly Mug, Muzzl'em and Tear'em, were provoked daily to maintain their savage dispositions. Near these sentinels a row of oil lamps on posts flooded the approaches with sufficient light to detect any attempts to escape at night. To prevent convicts trying to skirt these defences by wading through the surf, additional dogs were kennelled on floating platforms. Guardhouses, regular patrols and a line of signal stations completed the system.

To escape overland from the peninsula appeared impossible, but this did not deter convicts from trying. One attempt in the early years of the settlement displayed considerable ingenuity. A convict named William Hunt, a former actor, dressed himself in the skin of a huge forest kangaroo and began hopping across Eaglehawk Neck. He was spotted by two guards, who, taken in by his disguise, levelled their muskets at what they anticipated would be that night's meal. To their amazement the kangaroo threw up its arms and called out, 'Don't shoot, I am only poor Billy Hunt'.[8] Other convicts tried to bypass the guards at Eaglehawk Neck by building rafts and boats or drifting past under clumps of seaweed. The fact was, however, that very few convicts successfully escaped from Port Arthur.

One notable exception was an Irish convict from County Wexford named Martin Cash. He had been transported for seven years for housebreaking (in his version it was for the more romantic crime of shooting his mistress's lover), and then

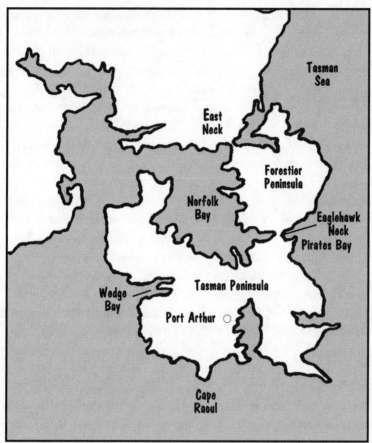

Tasman Peninsula

re-transported to Port Arthur for larceny. Undeterred by one unsuccessful breakout, when he had remained at large for five days but failed to reach the mainland, he gave much thought to his next escape attempt. On Boxing Day 1842 he and two other convicts disappeared into the bush from a timber-cutting gang. They headed south away from Eaglehawk Neck. For three days they holed up in thick scrub at the foot of Mount Arthur, reasoning that by then the hunt for them would have been called off or at least relaxed. On the night of the third day they emerged from their hiding place and, doubling back, made their way north to Norfolk Bay. At times they were forced to crawl long distances through the undergrowth to avoid military patrols. They reached the shore safely and piling their clothes on their heads swam across the bay without alerting the dogs or their keepers, or indeed the sharks which were believed to infest these waters, a belief assiduously cultivated by the guards. Once on the mainland they took up bushranging, descending from their mountain fastness north-west of Hobart to rob inns and homesteads with seeming impunity. Over the next few years Westwood's life would follow a similar pattern to Cash's and the two men would eventually meet up on the grim territory of Norfolk Island. A fortnight after his arrival at Port Arthur, Westwood's name was added to the settlement's long list of failed escape attempts. With ten other convicts from Sydney he absconded from a working party and took to the bush. After wandering around the unfamiliar countryside for three days they were discovered by a detachment of soldiers fast asleep near Wedge Bay on the western shore of the peninsula. While they were being rounded up a musket was accidentally fired, killing one of the convicts. The remainder were herded back to Port Arthur and summarily awarded 100 lashes each by the commandant, Captain Charles O'Hara Booth, a man with an unwavering belief in discipline rather than rehabilitation. In his report to the Chief Police Magistrate he noted that the flogging 'was severely administered and I trust will have a beneficial effect. Westwood alias Jackey Jackey made great resistance during his punishment and aggravated his sufferings much'.[9] Westwood wrote:

> I was also put in irons and my daily work was to carry a log of wood one hundredweight up and down the settlement road. This continued nine weeks, when one day the commandant released me and sent me to gang with the other men.

In August he absconded again, this time with the idea of making a canoe and paddling to the mainland. With three companions he struck out for Cape Raoul, the southernmost point of the Tasman Peninsula, but after several days of bush bashing they were running short of food and beginning to struggle. 'One morning,' said Westwood,

> I smelt a great smell, like the smell of meat roasting. We were more like hounds put on a scent, and seeking the hare. At last we got to the sea, and there on the beach we saw a large whale, dead, I should say, several days. It had been harpooned at sea, and washed in by the tide.

With an assured food supply at hand, they began building their canoe. It was almost finished when they were found by a party of constables. They scattered and ran for it. His comrades were quickly run down but Westwood managed to elude his pursuers for two days before he too was captured. After receiving another flogging he was ironed and set to work breaking stone. By day he was chained to a ringbolt, the nights he spent locked in a cell.

Nearly a year passed before he was released and returned to an ordinary working gang. For four months he kept his head down and then in November a rumour surfaced that he and two other convicts had perished during an attempted escape. The rumour was partly true. There had certainly been an escape but only two men were dead. The third man was Westwood and he was very much alive, although languishing in solitary confinement. In his memoir he explained how he alone had survived:

> I took to the bush with two men who knew it well. We got to the place agreed on, and there I could see the mainland at about two miles distance. We must get across to it and had no boat. I was a very bad swimmer, and two miles is a long pull for a new beginner, But my two companions did not hesitate, but pulled off their trousers, and plunged into the water with me after them, with my trousers thrown over my neck, for I was determined to get over to the mainland. After swimming about a mile, one of my companions, and very soon the other — was seized, and drawn down by the sharks. I was left alone to the mercy of the waves, expecting the same fate every minute. At last, after a desperate struggle I got to the land, but had lost my trousers

and shirt, and scrambled ashore quite naked. I made a bed in the long grass and picked up some shell fish that kept me alive for three days. On the fourth day the constables saw me and I was brought back to Port Arthur once more.

This time he was sentenced to twelve months' hard labour in chains, 90 days of which was to be served in solitary confinement. He spent the 90 days locked in a dark, fetid cell where he ate all his meals and where silence was imposed at all times. The only concession he received was to be let out each day for a short period of exercise. When he emerged from his cell for the last time he found that Captain Booth had been replaced by William Champ. According to Westwood the new commandant 'treated me with great kindness. He took off my leg irons, and removed me from the chain gang, and soon placed me as a servant to Mr. Laidley, the commissariat officer.' He, too, apparently was a sympathetic character and eventually Westwood was rewarded for good behaviour with promotion into the commandant's boat crew. He now had a stroke of luck. One day two visitors were sailing in the harbour when their boat capsized. They were rescued by the commandant's boat and as a result, in May 1845, Westwood and his fellow crew members were transferred to the probation station at Glenorchy near Hobart, a far more congenial situation.

After several months Westwood was overcome with 'a longing desire to see Sydney again'. In August accompanied by Thomas Gilling and George Allom, who claimed to know the country, he took to the bush once more. They broke into a settler's homestead and came away with single- and double-barrelled guns and a brace of pistols, as well as a bundle of clothes. Next day they were intercepted by a party of constables. Shots were exchanged but no-one was hit and both sides withdrew. The three convicts now struck out for Browns River in the hope of finding a boat there and sailing it to Sydney; they were disappointed and turned towards New Norfolk. After raiding another farmhouse they took refuge on the slopes of Mount Dromedary, where two years earlier Martin Cash and his gang had hidden out. 'From the top of this hill,' Westwood wrote,

> we could see for miles round the country. Among the rocks we made up a fire, and with melted snow made tea and had our supper, for we were hungry, tired and cold. Next day Allom again took the lead. But I saw very soon that he did not know the country, and I had some sharp words with him for deceiving us before we bolted by bragging of his acquaintance with it.

Westwood now took over leadership of the band but as they straggled through the damp, heavily wooded country, first Gilling and then Allom became separated from him. 'I was left to myself,' he continued,

> ignorant of the country, hungry and tired, constables on the alert in all the townships, my comrades lost, and no hope of getting to the coast and escape. I spent a very miserable night after Allom's departure, and next day pushed on by myself to the Lovely Banks, where I was seen and challenged by a constable, who called on me to surrender. This roused me and levelling my gun at him I ordered him to throw down his piece, or I'd blow his head off. To my astonishment, he threw it down at the first word. I bid him stand back, and then I took up his gun and fired it off and rifled him of his ammunition. I was going to break his gun, but he begged hard of me to give it back to him and I did so and let him go.

The constable's version of this incident, as it appeared in the *Australian* on 23 August, put a rather more heroic slant on his actions:

> In pursuing his course, Jackey fell in on Monday with a Bothwell constable, between whom and himself a running fight ensued, until Her Majesty's petty officer having expended his ammunition he was made prisoner by Jackey, who, after spiking his musket in a manner peculiar to himself, took his unfortunate captive to assist him in robbing a neighbouring settler's establishment. Here the constable, in the midst of his compulsory task of tying the servants' hands, contrived to escape and give the alarm at Bothwell.

Westwood was outraged by the constable's story and denied it firmly, stating that 'this cowardly fellow swore in court that I fired five shots at him, when I never fired at him at all'.

Whatever the truth of it, the alarm was raised and the fugitive was tracked to a public house called the Cape of Good Hope and from there to the outskirts of Oatlands. He helped himself to a large slice of damper from a settler's hut and this being communicated to the police the hunt began to close in. At sundown, exhausted and dejected, he turned off the road and made camp for the night beside Blackmans River. A stockman spotted him and rode with the news to the nearest farm. When Westwood woke next morning he found four well-armed men standing over him. Resistance was useless. He was handcuffed and taken to the Oatlands lockup. From there he was escorted to Hobart to stand trial for 'robbery, being armed while illegally at large'. The judge sentenced him to death but added that as 'no violence had been used on the part of the prisoner' he would recommend him 'to the merciful consideration of the Executive Government'.[10] The recommendation was accepted and for the second time Westwood was sentenced to transportation for life, this time with the additional punishment of ten years' detention on Norfolk Island.

Westwood was landed on the island just before Christmas 1845. No doubt he quickly realised that escape from this isolated speck in the Pacific Ocean would not be easy. True, it was not uncommon for convicts to slip away from labour gangs into the bush, but to get right off the island was another matter altogether. Just three years before his arrival twelve convicts unloading the brig *Governor Phillip* had turned on their guards and hurled them overboard. They managed to hold the deck for half an hour before they were overcome by a determined charge from the soldiers and crew below. Five of the mutineers were killed and two wounded. A few years earlier a party of officers hauling in their nets on the beach after a day's fishing were surprised by a bunch of convicts who suddenly sprinted past them, dashed through the shore-break and climbed into their boat which was lying offshore. The convicts tipped out the crew, took over the oars and were away before the officers could recover. Two fast boats were sent in pursuit and soon closed on the runaways who, realising they had no chance of outrunning them, gave themselves up.

Instead of stealing a boat some convicts preferred to build their own. In 1839 Thomas Cook, serving an indefinite sentence on the island for forgery, determined on building a boat even though he calculated the odds of a successful getaway at three to one against. In partnership with four other prisoners 'operations commenced in a spot selected as the most retired for constructing and the most convenient for launching our frail vessel'.[11] For three weeks they laboured, mostly at night, but 'when the day of Freedom was at hand' they were betrayed and the boat impounded. In an earlier attempt one inventive convict put to sea on a door through which he had bored two holes for his legs. He was eight hours in the water before being spotted by the brig *Union* about 3 kilometres off shore. When brought on board 'almost exhausted' he declared that nearly the whole time he had been surrounded by sharks 'although he did escape their voracity.'[12]

Disheartening though such stories were, escape attempts were common and occasionally successful. In 1841 nine convicts snatched a small boat belonging to a government brig and sailed it to New Zealand. In 1843 six convicts in concert with three renegade soldiers made off in a whaleboat and foiled their pursuers by steering into a sea mist. Less fortunate were the six convicts who succeeded in building a boat in a cave — they probably drowned when they ran into a gale shortly after leaving the island.

Conditions for the convicts were mostly unbearable, and escape, even the temporary refuge of a bolthole in the bush, afforded the only respite. The commandant at the time of Westwood's arrival on Norfolk Island was Major Joseph

Childs, an officer of marines with the reputation of being a stern disciplinarian. He had succeeded Alexander Maconochie in 1844 and with the government's blessing had replaced Maconochie's benevolent regime with a system based on repression, hard labour and brutality. Incessant flogging according to Westwood — 'upwards of 2000 lashes were served out in one day' — was supplemented by other sadistic forms of punishment devised unofficially by the overseers and turnkeys. Chief among these was the 'tube-gag', a small cylinder of ironwood which was forced into the victim's mouth, generally with the loss of a few teeth, and held in place by a tight leather strap. Breathing was only possible through a tiny hole in the gag. Then there was the 'scavenger's daughter', which consisted of leaving an offender on the floor of his cell for hours with his head trussed between his knees. Another favourite was the 'water-pit'. This was an underground cell where a man was stripped and left for days at a time standing in waist-deep salt water.

Living conditions for the convicts were also deplorable as evidenced by the report of Robert Pringle Stuart, a magistrate sent from Van Diemen's Land in May 1846 to investigate the administration of the island. 'The buildings are generally filthy,' he observed, 'the accommodation and general arrangements defective and wretched in the extreme.'[13] In particular he was appalled by the mess-shed which was situated next to a large uncovered privy. The gaol also attracted his displeasure: it 'is generally crowded, is badly ventilated, low, and damp; the prisoners have each a thick straw mat, and a blanket, which forms a bed on the stone floor'.[14] Dysentery and other diseases were endemic. Food was deliberately rationed and of such poor quality that at times it was inedible.

Despite the relentless sadism and violence, Stuart was shocked to discover that 'instances of the most gross insubordination and resistance to authority are also permitted to pass altogether unpunished'.[15] On five occasions in January, he was told, convicts had refused to go out to work until their food and housing had improved. Yet not one man had been brought to trial. Stuart also noticed that swearing at officers was habitual, to which a deaf ear was usually turned. Even more astonishing, several officers had actually been assaulted. With his own eyes he saw an officer, who attempted to prevent a prisoner smoking, struck two violent blows in the face. The fellow was backed up by a threatening crowd of mates, there was a glint of knives and the officer hastily withdrew.

The centre of disobedience and rebellion was the lumberyard in which the convicts messed. It was dominated by the 'Ring', a vicious confederacy of old hands who lorded it over the other convicts and openly defied the guards. For a constable to enter the lumberyard to arrest one of their number was to risk serious injury and informers could count on very short lives. The disembowelled body of one such fool was left in the bush, his own guts replaced by those of a sheep. When it came to their own punishment, the men of the Ring accepted the lash, as their brotherhood expected, without flinching or crying out. It was just another way of showing their contempt for authority.

And authority, as represented by the inept and vacillating Major Childs, was unable to correct this slide towards anarchy. 'He is totally unfitted for the peculiar situation in which he is placed,' wrote the Comptroller-General of Convicts after reading Stuart's report. 'It is impossible to conceive that an officer endued with sufficient degree of firmness would have tolerated ... the insolent insubordination of the convicts, and allowed it to pass uninquired and unpunished.'[16] He concluded by recommending that the commandant be replaced. But it was too late. By the time the report had been read by the Executive Council, the island had boiled over into mutiny, and among the foremost mutineers was William Westwood.

On the night of 30 June, after the convicts had been locked

in the barracks, Major Childs sent the superintendent and chief constable into the lumberyard to remove the convicts' personal cooking utensils. They carried off a load of pots, pans and kettles as well as a hoard of maize-meal and secured it all in the barracks store. Next morning, while being mustered for breakfast, the convicts discovered that their precious cooking equipment, most of it fashioned by themselves, was missing. They crowded round the muster officer, yelling and gesticulating. Things were beginning to look ugly for him when 200 of them suddenly rushed out of the lumberyard gate and headed for the store. They cracked open the lock and retrieved their belongings without being troubled by the guards. Back at the lumberyard they settled down and began to cook their breakfast as usual.

For fifteen minutes all was peaceful. Then, without warning, a wild cry was raised and, headed by Westwood, a horde of men swarmed through the gate brandishing lumps of wood, staves and other improvised weapons. They charged into the cookhouse, where Westwood dispatched an overseer with a single blow of his cudgel. Without pausing, the maddened mob moved on, spattering a gatekeeper's brains against a wall before turning towards the constables' huts near the lime-kiln. They stormed inside and Westwood, now armed with an axe, split open the skull of one constable while he was still in bed. 'Mind, I saw who did that,' called out another constable.[17] They were his last words. Westwood smashed him to the ground and pulped his face with a torrent of blows.

Meanwhile the military had been alerted and as the convicts swept towards the stipendiary magistrate's cottage they were met by a wall of soldiers advancing towards them with fixed bayonets. At the first sight of cold steel they broke, stumbled over each other and fled pell-mell back to the lumberyard. But this time the Ring had gone too far and there was no sanctuary for the mutineers there. The chief constable marched in and arrested six convicts, whose blood-stained clothes proclaimed their guilt, and another 45 as accessories in the murders. About half of them were summarily tried for unlawful riot and sentenced to twelve months' hard labour in chains. The remainder, including Westwood, were locked in the Old Gaol to await the arrival of a judge from Hobart to try them.

What the mutineers had hoped to achieve was not entirely clear. The chief constable believed that they had intended to take to the bush and attack the free settlers. Martin Cash, who had been a prisoner on the island since 1844 but had not taken part in the mutiny, had this to say:

> The men who followed Westwood had not the slightest conception that their leader meditated anything further than the chastisement of a few of the 'old dogs', as they termed the prisoners who were placed over them as flagellators, constables and watchmen. But it was not so with Westwood. He contemplated murder from the first, although he did not state his intentions to his followers, who, from their being in his company at the time, were placed in the same position as the ringleader. Jacky Jacky was, generally speaking, a quiet inoffensive man ... All his acquaintances believed him to be tired of his life, and the terrible circumstances just narrated prove not only that fact but that he had been flogged, goaded, and tantalised till he was reduced to a lunatic and a savage.[18]

Westwood himself wrote that at first he thought:

> We might have a chance of taking the Island or at least the boats but this I found could not be done [and] seeing myself foiled in these things I was determined as I could not reach the tyrant I would kill some of his tutors.[19]

During the weeks leading up to the trial Westwood made several last-ditch attempts to escape from his cell. On 3 September he was found to have two spring-saws and the lead from the night tub concealed in his belt, the latter apparently to be used as a weapon. He was transferred to the additional security of the new pentagonal gaol. On 12 September he was detected in the act of cutting a hole in the wooden ceiling of his cell. While balanced on his cell-mate's neck he had been patiently working away for days when he was betrayed by the prisoner next door who, hearing the ragged sound of sawing, had alerted the gaoler. According to Aaron Price, the principal overseer of public works, Westwood's plan had been to set fire to Price's house and in the ensuing confusion release as many prisoners as possible and lead them into the bush. He was removed to another cell where his wrists were ringbolted to the wall and his legs chained to the floor. The next day three spring-saws were discovered beneath the stone flagging of his former cell. Following this further revelation of his ingenuity and determination it was decided to take the additional precaution of leaving his cell door open with a police man on duty watching him night and day.

On 23 September Westwood and thirteen others, the presumed ringleaders, appeared in court charged with the murder of the gatekeeper, John Morris, and aiding and abetting in murder. Although they all pleaded not guilty, their petition for a lawyer to assist them in presenting their defence was refused. Twelve witnesses were produced for the prosecution, but none of the prisoners had the skills to cross-examine them effectively. As the Anglican chaplain, Reverend Thomas Rogers, complained bitterly:

> [They were] compelled to go through a cruel mockery of trial; perplexed by the legal technicalities of the crown prosecutor, and often-times disheartened by an array of prisoner witnesses ready to swear anything, in the hope of gaining a government indulgence ... Hence the unbecoming behaviour of many of them at the bar. They resembled a number of schoolboys engaged in a holiday frolic more than men occupied by an awful enquiry on which their lives depended.

There was no surprise when the jury, which consisted of five army officers, found twelve of the fourteen guilty. On 5 October the judge sentenced them to death.

While awaiting execution they were visited every day by Reverend Rogers and the Roman Catholic chaplain, Father Bond. According to Martin Cash, Rogers was known to have smuggled them provisions in the crown of his hat and it was suspected that he may even have slipped Westwood a steel file. It was Rogers, too, who encouraged Westwood to set down his life story. The bushranger also wrote a letter to his former chaplain at Port Arthur in which he laid ultimate responsibility for 'the affair of the first of July' at the feet of Major Childs and his subordinates. In trying to explain his sudden orgy of killing, which was altogether at odds with his bloodless career as a bushranger, he said:

> I have been treated more like a beast than a man, until nature could bear no more. I was like many others, driven to despair by the oppressive and tyrannical conduct of those whose duty it was to prevent us from being reared in this way.[21]

Reverend Rogers appears to have been particularly taken by Westwood, and some years later remembered him in striking detail as being:

> a young man of good stature, broad-chested, and muscular in limb, though not of brawny build, but lithe and agile as a leopard. He was of fair complexion, regular features, and a good-humoured expression of countenance, to which a broad forehead gave an air of intelligence. This broad forehead was overhung with a profusion of straw-coloured hair of a dark shade. He had a pleasant smile, which disclosed two rows of small white teeth, so small and white as to give him a somewhat feminine appearance, which was made more feminine by thin red lips, small mouth, and well-shaped chin. But most noticeable of all his features were his eyes, which were deep-set and of a rich violet blue.[22]

As for his demeanour, the chaplain agreed with Martin Cash that he was quite inoffensive. He 'was not of a peevish or quarrelsome temper, nor did he mix himself up with the common squabbles of the Lumber-yard'. In short his role in the July riot was totally out of character.

Instead of making the traditional speeches from the scaffold and 'indulging in tedious and excited oratorical display',[23] Rogers convinced the condemned men to put their last thoughts down on paper. In his statement Westwood confessed his own guilt but asserted the innocence of four of the others:

> I, William Westwood, wish to die in the communion of Christ's holy church, seeking mercy of God through Jesus Christ our Lord, amen; I acknowledge the justice of my sentence; but as a dying man I wish to say that I believe four men now going to suffer are innocent of the crime laid to their charge, namely, Lawrence Cavenagh, Henry Whiting, William Pickthorne, and William Scrimshaw. I believe that I never spoke to Cavenagh on the morning of the riots; and those other men had no part in the killing of John Morris, as far as I know of. I die in charity with all men, and I ask your prayers for my soul.
>
> William Westwood, aged 26 years.[24]

On the morning of 13 October the chaplain's wife and some other ladies delivered a basket of cold meat, eggs, bread and coffee for the prisoners' last breakfast. 'What a pity it is,' remarked one of the condemned men, 'that we aren't to be hanged every morning, if the ladies would only send us such jolly fine breakfasts.'[25] As soon as they had finished their meal the first six men were led out to the gallows, which had been specially erected in the gaol yard during the previous week. Their irons were struck off so they could climb the ladder to the scaffold but their arms remained pinioned. The nooses were adjusted around their necks by the two executioners. The ministers each read a prayer and then the voices of the condemned men rose in a hymn above the dull booming of the surf breaking on the coral reef in the bay below the gaol. At a quarter past eight the trapdoors dropped open and 'they were no longer part of the dwellers upon earth'.[26] The bodies were cut down and the next six were brought out to suffer the same fate. When it was all over, the twelve corpses were bundled into coffins and hauled by bullock dray to an abandoned sawpit outside the cemetery. There, in unconsecrated ground, they were buried unceremoniously in an unmarked mass grave. It was all done in such haste that Reverend Rogers arrived too late to conduct the funeral service.

10

The Last of Norfolk Island

While visiting Norfolk Island in 1844, the journalist and traveller David Burn was the excited witness of an attempted escape by 'fourteen athletic convicts'.[1] He had been inspecting the agricultural station at Longridge when news was brought that the crew of a launch rowing out to unload the barque *Agincourt* had surprised the guards, thrown them overboard, and was pulling out to sea. Burn wrote in his journal:

> Mounting our steeds we instantly retraced our steps towards the settlement at a much more rapid pace than that at which we quitted it — Gaining the hill whereon the signal staff is fixed, the scene of action was spread map like before us — The soldiery were lining the beach towards Windmill point, betwixt which and Nepean Island we descried one of the launches pulling to the E[ast], a whale boat being in full chace and coming up rapidly. The *Agincourt* being well to windward and under a press of sail was rapidly closing and in such manner as to cut off the fugitives whose attempt it was evident had been entirely frustrated — At this moment a musket was discharged from the Whale boat, a preconcerted signal to warn those on shore that the guard had been rescued from a watery grave — The Whale boat drew rapidly ahead, the *Agincourt* held steadily on her way — the dream of liberty was gone, so, there was but one alternative, surrender — which they did accordingly to the ship.[2]

It was some time later, after the drama was over and he had ridden down from his panoramic vantage point, that Burn learnt the full story. The launch had been manned by fourteen convicts and a free coxswain under the control of a sergeant and three privates. Accompanying them was a police constable. When they had got about half a kilometre clear of the Kingston bar, one of the forward oars was lost overboard, no doubt the first step in a preconceived plan. After some bustle and debate among the convicts, one of them volunteered to jump in after it, but instead the coxswain ordered them to back water. As he and the soldiers all turned to watch the drifting oar, they were rushed by the convicts. The coxswain was grabbed by the throat and nearly throttled before being thrown into the bottom of the boat. The ring-leader, John Fletcher, grappled with the sergeant, disarmed him and knocked him down. Two of the privates managed to snap off a couple of pistol shots without effect before being overpowered and dumped unceremoniously over the side, along with the third private. Three of the convicts who declined to join in threw their oars away and lay down.

Richard Ellam, 'a notorious burglar and ruffian' who had only just arrived on the *Agincourt* from England, took control of the steering oar, and Fletcher, 'a tall muscular fellow', gave orders to head for Windmill Point.[3] The convicts gave a cheer and bent to their oars. At the same time another group of convicts stormed the mill and began pillaging it of maize and meat, while others dug up caches of knives, buckets, masts, sails and water casks from the beach and began carrying them down to the water's edge. By now the alarm had been raised and a party of soldiers under Lieutenant Lloyd of the marines had launched a whaleboat in pursuit. Also, the *Agincourt* had been telegraphed to bear down on the runaways. Lloyd soon had the whaleboat flying through the foam, stopping only to rescue the three privates struggling to get ashore. Meanwhile another party of soldiers was pouring onto the beach. On seeing them, the convicts there rapidly dispersed, and the launch, which had been backing in to pick them up with the supplies, pulled out to sea. The soldiers opened up a rapid fire, and all the convicts except Richard Ellam and George Head flung themselves into the bottom of the boat. A pistol was clapped to the sergeant's chest and he was forced to stand up beside Ellam in the hope that the sight of his red jacket might induce his comrades to stop firing. However, the ploy failed, for the soldiers did not falter in their rate of fire. Perhaps there were some old scores to pay off, or perhaps they simply did not recognise their sergeant. In any case, he obviously had a low opinion of their marksmanship and was not too concerned at being made a target, for he would later say that he believed 'that he was less likely to be shot by his comrades than by the felons under whose control he found himself'.[4]

It was at this moment that the convicts, realising their escape route had been cut off, stopped rowing and surrendered. The coxswain resumed the steering oar, signalled the soldiers to cease firing and brought the launch alongside the *Agincourt*. Although over 200 shots had been fired and several had struck the boat, no-one was hit, confirming the sergeant's assessment of his men's ability with their muskets. When the convicts were landed, heavily ironed and led off to the cells, Burn observed that 'there was abundant ill suppressed passion on both sides'.[5] The soldiers wanted summary vengeance for what they believed was an attempt to drown their three comrades, while the convicts were smarting, their carefully thought-out plan involving the coordination of two converging groups having come to nothing.

Nine years later, in March 1853, there was another attempt to get off the island in an open boat. In essence the plan was a simpler version of the earlier one. There was no shore party involved, and this probably made the difference, for this time the convicts got clear away. It was to be the last successful escape from Norfolk Island.

The commandant at the time was Captain Rupert Deering of the 99th Regiment, who had replaced John Price, the most notorious of Norfolk Island's commandants, at the beginning of the year. Price had come to the island in August 1846 and immediately flagged his intentions by overseeing the kangaroo-court trial and execution of William Westwood and his eleven fellow mutineers. He followed this up with five more executions three weeks later. From this beginning he instituted a rule of legitimised violence. In particular he promoted the practice of arbitrary and capricious punishment. One prisoner, who was in hospital recovering from a beating he had received on a chain gang, was gagged and chained to the floor for getting up to the window for air. A cart driver who had found a young bird in the bush was brought before Price charged with 'having a tamed bird' and awarded 36 lashes. Another man, charged by a constable with 'pushing a tree with his foot', received a total of 72 lashes on his back and buttocks. Six days later he was flogged again for possession of tobacco. When a man named Launder tried to defend himself before Price for having improperly obtained some government paper, the commandant ordered him to be gagged. The gaoler carried out his task with such enthusiasm that the poor fellow, who was nearly blind with a severe eye disease, had two teeth smashed and his jaw nearly dislocated.[6] On the few occasions that Price's methods were challenged by officialdom, he justified them as being necessary to prevent insurrection. He continued in the same way, with increasing harshness, to the end of his administration. Twenty years later he achieved literary immortality as the infamous commandant Maurice Frere in Marcus Clarke's novel *For the Term of His Natural Life*.

In the months after Price's departure the number of floggings decreased. It was in this more restrained atmosphere, under Captain Deering's command, that a small group of convicts plotted their escape. The ringleader was Joseph Davis, a 41-year-old labourer who had originally been transported to Van Diemen's Land from New Zealand for fifteen years after being convicted of assault and robbery. He was marked down as 'a desperate character exhibiting indications of having been a convict'[7] and for an act of piracy was subsequently sent to Norfolk Island for life. He was a solidly built man, 5 feet $6^{1}/_{2}$ inches tall with a high forehead, long ears and a large Roman nose. His convict description also refers to 'several dots and marks about the left hand',[8] which suggests that he belonged to a secret criminal society known as 'The Forty Thieves' whose members had an arrangement of dots tattooed between their thumb and forefinger. Davis's accomplices included James Merry, who had received a ten-year sentence in London for burglary, which had been extended in Van Diemen's Land by another ten years for absconding while on a ticket-of-leave, and Dennis Griffiths, also a twice-convicted felon. This trio were members of a boat crew and they were joined in the plot by their fellow crewmen — Robert Mitchell, Joseph Cooper, Thomas Clayton, James Clegg, John Meek, John Sullivan and Edward Witt — who all said they 'would be glad to get away also'.[9]

On 11 March a launch manned by these ten convicts and a free coxswain named John Forsyth was engaged in unloading the *Lord Auckland*, which lay about 4 kilometres offshore. They were guarded by three soldiers armed with pistols and bayonets, supported by three unarmed constables. It was eight o'clock in the evening and a dark twilight had settled over the island. The launch had just brought a load to the landing place and was returning to the ship so that the men could sleep on board in order to begin work first thing in the morning. However, when they came to haul up the anchor they found that it was fouled and the coxswain ordered everyone to come aft until the swell came in to drag the anchor free. The convicts eagerly obeyed. Dropping their oars they crowded around the guards in the stern. There was a scuffle, a few choked shouts and the soldiers were overpowered and disarmed. Davis and Merry stood over them, each with a pistol in his hand. 'Not a word,' Davis warned them, 'or you will get it very severely.'[10] Griffiths grabbed a third pistol and took station amidships while the other convicts went forward to try and free the anchor. It was firmly snagged and, unwilling to waste any more time, they paid the cable overboard.

Having carried the launch, the convicts now took up their oars again and pulled away with Davis at the tiller. When they had gone along the coast for about 6 kilometres, Davis steered in towards the rock-infested shore and ordered the guards and Coxswain Forsyth over the side. The soldiers, two of the constables and the coxswain were already in the water and kicking through the dark, tumbling surf when someone called out that he could see a boat. It was probably just the sea washing across a rock, but the alarmed convicts immediately began heading out to sea. The coxswain was caught across the chest by an oar and, finding himself sinking, grabbed hold of it. To save time he was hauled in again and joined the remaining constable in the bottom of the boat. The convicts kept at the oars all night, heading to the south-west. An hour after daylight they glimpsed what they hoped was their last sight of Norfolk Island. They set the sail and pushed on for the mainland. The launch had only limited supplies — some biscuits, potatoes and a little water — so Davis put them on a daily allowance.

Meanwhile, Captain Deering with a crew of six had launched a whaleboat and set off in pursuit of the fugitives, but as Principal Overseer Aaron Price recorded in his diary, 'at 4 pm [a] very much exhausted Commandant arrived — no intelligence of the launch, 6 pm and nothing heard of Coxswain Forsythe and [Constable] Bordmore who it is supposed are drowned'.[11] However, Deering did have one small success. Convict Edward Witt had somehow been left behind and was discovered at the landing place feigning sleep. He was sentenced to nine months' labour in chains and taken back to the cells for 'being accessory to the fact of the launch being intended to be seized and not giving information of the same to the Police'.[12]

On Friday 25 March the convicts sighted Moreton Bay, having been at sea for fourteen days, six of them in a dead calm.

They nosed in through the south passage at about seven in the evening, but in attempting to land at Amity Point on Stradbroke Island to replenish their water supply, the launch was thrown up on the beach by the surf and damaged. While the convicts were unloading the sails, rations and equipment, two Aborigines came down to the beach and offered to take them to a white man. Leaving Mitchell to watch over Forsyth and Constable Bordmore, Davis and the others followed the Aborigines inland to the camp of a 'Manila man' named Fernando Burnan, who was fishing in the bay.[13] Representing themselves as the survivors of a wrecked schooner, they asked him for his boat to salvage the cargo from the wreck. He refused, but agreed to talk to Mitchell, who they said was their captain. Meanwhile, Mitchell, who had avoided taking an active part in seizing the launch, had told Forsyth that he was willing to give himself up. At this point Burnan arrived and, on learning the truth, he and Forsyth hurried back to his camp. There they found that the convicts had put off in his boat with all his rations and ammunition and were waiting about 500 metres offshore, having left two of their number, Griffiths and Clegg, behind to bring off Mitchell. Forsyth managed to secure Clegg and then dissuade Griffiths from swimming out to the boat by warning him that the bay was swarming with sharks. In their frustration at this turn of events, the convicts in the boat fired several shots at the coxswain before pulling away. Forsyth and the others remained on the island until Monday, when they were rescued by a bay fisherman who took them to Brisbane. After examination by Captain John Wickham, the police magistrate, the convicts Griffiths, Clegg and Mitchell were ordered to Sydney in irons to be dealt with there.

For the last ten years, Brisbane had been the centre of a growing pastoral economy, a town populated by free settlers striving to forget its origins as an isolated penal settlement. The news that there was a gang of Norfolk Island incorrigibles loose in Moreton Bay sent currents of alarm and excitement through this newly respectable northern metropolis. The *Moreton Bay Courier* carried the headline 'Piracy and Robbery — Escape of Nine Convicts from Norfolk Island' and warned its readers that these desperadoes 'would attempt any outrage'.[14] The customs boat with an armed crew of constables was dispatched in pursuit, and Chief Constable Sneyd himself inspected the settlements on the other side of the river and then proceeded to scour the country around Cleveland Point.

For some time there was no sign of the six runaways and it appeared that the broad reaches of Moreton Bay had swallowed them up, but then reports of possible sightings began to drift in. The steamer *Brothers* was dropping downriver when the master noticed a strange sailing boat in the distance. That night he became aware that a boat full of men was lying astern. When the captain hailed them they immediately pulled off without answering. A boat with muffled oars was also reported to have rowed around the *Agricola* during the night. The next contact with the convicts occurred on Wednesday morning when they boarded the outgoing barque *Acacia* near the river bar. They were wearing their clothes inside out to conceal the broad arrows on them, and the captain readily believed their story that they had lost their ship near Wide Bay. He was sympathetic enough to invite them to have breakfast with him and the harbourmaster's crew who were acting as pilots. After asking where the entrance to the Brisbane River was, they left the barque and pulled over to the river, disappearing behind Luggage Point.

Several hours later the harbourmaster's boat set out to return to Brisbane. As it rounded Luggage Point the convicts suddenly surged out from the river bank, where they had been lying in wait, and on coming alongside seized the painter and secured it to their own. Levelling their pistols at the astonished crewmen, they ordered them to strip. They then swapped clothes and also boats, their own boat being in very poor condition. As they got dressed the convicts casually mentioned that they intended to seize the *Acacia* after first paying a visit to the Pilot's Station on Moreton Island. They asked for someone to show them the way but, not surprisingly, there were no volunteers. They were about to press-gang one of the men but then changed their minds and pulled away, curving around Fisherman Islands. When the harbourmaster's crew reached Brisbane that afternoon and told their story to Captain Wickham, it was generally agreed that in talking of the Pilot's Station the convicts had been laying a false trail and that they were really heading south for Cleveland Point. 'The poor men cut rather an extraordinary figure in convicts clothing,' observed a reporter, 'and several seemed anxious to get home and get rid of their unmerited branding.'[15]

However, either the convicts had pulled a very clever bluff or they were simply careless in their talk, for on Thursday morning the pilot, Mr Watson, arrived in Brisbane and reported that they had turned up at his station the previous evening and robbed him of 'everything portable'.[16] It seems that after passing around Fisherman Islands they had turned eastward and landed on Moreton Island at Cowan Cowan, where they were found by Watson. No doubt with tongue firmly in cheek and smiling inwardly, Davis told him that he and his men belonged to a vessel in the bay and that some men had come alongside in a boat, boarded it and robbed him of £200. He was determined, he said grimly, to pursue them until he overtook them. Not to be outdone, the gullible pilot responded with his own story of how he himself had seen a strange boat the day before and, having some suspicion of it, had pursued it for some distance but without success. Davis must have been enjoying the situation immensely, especially when Watson invited them all to his home to 'partake of some refreshments before they proceeded any further'.[17] Instantly they stepped inside, Watson realised he had been duped. Davis shoved him down hard on a sofa and, clapping a pistol to his head, ordered him to 'remain there on peril of his life'. He was kept in that position under guard while the convicts rifled the premises, taking away all his clothes and provisions, £40 and anything else useful to them that they could lay their hands on. They were very pleased to come across several bottles of rum, 'and indulged in a slight carouse' during which Watson overheard them talking about how they were planning to seize the *Acacia*. At one point some of Mr Watson's children, accompanied by one of his men, were observed coming towards the house. The convicts opened fire on them, fortunately without effect, and they retreated into the bush. Eventually the convicts went away, but not before taking care to stave in the pilot's boat. However, Watson was able to patch it up temporarily, and after gathering his men together sailed forthwith for Brisbane to report the outrage.

On receipt of this information Captain Wickham immediately chartered the steamer *Swallow*, which had just been loaded for a voyage upriver to Ipswich. The cargo was taken out of the hold and replaced with a supply of coals, and a little before dark she started for the bay under Wickham's command. As a seaman of considerable experience — he had sailed with Charles Darwin on the *Beagle* and then commanded the same vessel on a surveying voyage of the north-western coast of Australia — it was felt that he had every chance of finding the convicts. Mr Sheridan of the Customs Department also set out with a crew of Aborigines, hoping to fall in with the customs boat, of which nothing had been heard, and warn its crew that the fugitives had increased their stock of arms and were well supplied with ammunition. On Friday morning Captain Wickham returned for the hearing of an insolvency case. He had nothing to report and sent the *Swallow* across the bay towards Moreton Island in case the convicts had doubled back. In the afternoon the chief constable also returned without having found any trace of the runaways.

Over the next five days the search for the convicts continued, but once again they seemed to have vanished. Ever since their encounter with Mr Watson, a heavy sea had been rolling in from the south-east, and it was thought by many that they had gone north. But then a report reached Brisbane that they had been seen at the south end of Stradbroke Island with their boat, hidden among the mangroves, presumably waiting for the sea to calm so they could escape by the south passage. The customs boat, which had only just returned, was sent out again to investigate but found no evidence of a boat having been dragged ashore. Meanwhile Mr Watson had remembered that the convicts had mentioned going south to the Tweed and Richmond rivers for a vessel if their attempt on the *Acacia* failed. To cover this possibility, two mounted constables were sent racing overland to put the people of those districts on their guard. In the absence of any confirmed sightings, the *Moreton Bay Courier* kept the story alive by filling a column with theories as to the fugitives' whereabouts:

> Various opinions are afloat respecting the pirates, some being that they were lost at sea; others that they would run to the northward, and secrete themselves, having plenty of provisions until the southerly winds ceased and they could get to the southward; and others again think that they at once made their way to one of the Islands to the eastward, although one might suppose that they would not desire to return in that direction. At all events, supposing them to have escaped destruction, they seem to have managed their escape in a very business like manner throughout, and proved themselves to be no novices.[18]

Then, on Thursday 12 May, eighteen days after they first entered Moreton Bay, a fisherman arrived in Brisbane with the convicts' boat, the one they had taken from the harbour-master's crew. From far out in the bay he had watched them land and drag the boat in amongst the mangroves near the mouth of the river on the south side, and then set off into the interior. As soon as they were out of sight, he and his Aboriginal crewmen had come ashore, refloated the boat and brought it upriver. On receipt of this news Mr Sheridan and

Chief Constable Sneyd marshalled a party of volunteers and constables under the command of William Duncan, the water police magistrate, and proceeded downriver to the spot where the boat had been abandoned. From there they used Aboriginal trackers to follow the trail of the runaways through the scrub until darkness forced them to make camp. Early next morning they picked up the trail again and followed it until noon, when they came upon the six runaways about 13 kilometres short of Brisbane. They immediately rushed in and ordered them to lay down their arms. The surprised convicts, who had only two guns and two pistols among them, surrendered without putting up a fight. They were handcuffed and escorted to Brisbane.

On examination next morning they stated that after robbing the pilot's station they had run to the northward for Wide Bay, which one of them knew well, but their attempts to land there were frustrated by hostile Aborigines and so they had made their way back to Moreton Bay, intending to go up-country to replenish their supplies and then separate. They were brought before the Circuit Court on 17 May and each man was sentenced to fifteen years' transportation beyond the sea. 'Too much praise cannot be given to those who have assisted in the capture of these daring men,' effused the *Moreton Bay Courier*. 'They have set at rest the fears naturally excited by their being at large in this neighbourhood.'[19]

However, this was not end of the story. In June the first three to be apprehended, Mitchell, Griffiths and Clegg, were forwarded to Hobart from Sydney on the brig *Emma*. As administrative control of Norfolk Island had passed from New South Wales to Van Diemen's Land in 1844, it was deemed more appropriate for their trial to take place there. The *Emma* called in at the whaling port of Twofold Bay, and while she was lying at anchor Clegg slipped his irons and jumped overboard, taking his chances with the sharks that patrolled the bay. Luck was with him, for he got ashore safely, and meeting up with some whalers was able to convince them that he was a shipwrecked sailor. They supplied him with provisions and clothes, and next morning he 'bade them an affecting farewell'.[20]

At their trial in Hobart, Griffiths and Mitchell both pleaded not guilty to charges of 'piratically and feloniously assaulting John Forsyth on board a certain launch belonging to Her Majesty at Norfolk Island and with putting him in danger of his life'.[21] They were also charged with 'piratically, feloniously and violently' stealing the launch. The principal witness was Forsyth, who downplayed Mitchell's role, saying he took no part in disarming the soldiers and merely did what he was told. Griffiths, however, did not receive the same indulgent testimony from the coxswain, who had no hesitation in identifying him as a principal in the affair. The jury took only half an hour to find Mitchell not guilty and Griffiths guilty.

They were both embarked on the government barque *Lady Franklin* with twenty other convicts, to be returned to Norfolk Island for completion of their sentences. To their astonishment they discovered that among their fellow travellers were Davis, Merry, Cooper, Clayton, Meek and Sullivan, who had been transferred from Brisbane, and also Clegg, whose spell of freedom had been all too brief. After sailing from Hobart on 16 December, the *Lady Franklin* touched at Port Arthur. Everything was 'peaceable and orderly',[22] and the master, Captain William Willett, shaped a course for Norfolk Island, happily unaware that below decks a group of convicts (not Davis and Co.) was planning to take over his ship. During the next few days, using the handle of a tin pannikin, they cut a hole in the 2-inch gumwood bulkhead of their prison. On the night of 28 December they broke through into the hold, where they armed themselves with some old guns. They freed the other convicts, who, bereft of hope, joined them to a man. Emerging suddenly onto the main deck, they overpowered the watch and guard and then ordered the rest of the military detachment, who were off duty in their cabin, to surrender their weapons or be fired upon. Convinced by his men that resistance was useless, the sergeant consented, and the soldiers handed up their muskets, butt first, together with a quantity of ball-cartridge and percussion caps.

At this point Captain Willett appeared on deck. Seeing convicts, crewmen and soldiers milling around, he realised what had happened. Unlike the sergeant, who was later condemned for not having 'behaved very gallantly upon the occasion',[23] Willett was unwilling to give up the ship without a fight. With a vain cry of, 'Soldiers, to your arms!' he fell upon the nearest convicts. It was a short but ferocious fight, and when he was finally overwhelmed he had a broken collarbone, several teeth knocked out and nine assorted wounds on his body. His wounds were dressed by Davis, and according to Willett 'it was principally through him the lives of the crew were saved otherwise they would have been murdered'.[24]

The convicts locked the crew and soldiers in their quarters, with the exception of three seamen who were compelled to help work the vessel. Captain Willett was brought up to take observations, and knowing that water was getting short he told them they had better make up their minds quickly where they were going. After some argument the convicts agreed on Fiji. At this time the Fijian archipelago was an ideal refuge for escaped convicts and all manner of deserters. For many years there had been almost continual fighting between the various islands, but by the early 1850s warfare had been replaced by trade. The population had been converted to Christianity by Wesleyan missionaries and was friendly towards Europeans.

On 8 January the outlying Fijian islands were just below the horizon. The convicts launched the longboat and cutter, both of which were fully laden with provisions, arms and ammunition. Before embarking they confined everyone below, save for a boy whom they sent aloft, telling him to remain there until they signalled, whereupon he could come down and release the captain and crew. They also cut the barque's sails and part of the rigging to prevent an effective pursuit. After cruising around for three days they landed on the island of Matuku. There they dispersed, joining the other convict flotsam that over the years had been washed up on island beaches across the Pacific.

After a vain attempt to reach Norfolk Island, Captain Willett made sail for Van Diemen's Land and the *Lady Franklin* limped into Spring Bay 35 days after the mutiny. The Police Department responded to the outrage by issuing circulars to the various authorities along the coast to keep a watch for the mutineers and, if possible to intercept them, but of course to no avail.

For almost a year nothing was heard of the convicts. Then on 16 October James Merry was detained on Ovalau by an officer of HMS *Herald* on suspicion of being a runaway. The *Herald*, under the command of Captain Henry Mangles Denham, was on a long voyage to explore and chart the islands between Sydney and Valparaiso. On arriving in Fiji, Captain Denham had heard stories of a group of Europeans who had mysteriously arrived in the islands in open boats, and he decided to investigate. He recovered one of the *Lady Franklin*'s boats, which had been sold to a missionary, and then set about tracking down the convicts. Merry was brought on board the *Herald*, where he made a full confession, although denying that he had taken an active part in the seizure of the *Lady Franklin*. Among the crimes he claimed that some of the other convicts had subsequently committed was the capture of a Dutch barque, which they sank after murdering the officers and crew.

Captain Denham was next put on the trail of Davis (now calling himself Murphy) and Griffiths (who was known as Dan). A few weeks earlier they had attempted to seize a small trading vessel. According to a crewman named Dyer, Davis had threatened him with a gun, and when he tried to grab hold of it one of the barrels went off, the bullet grazing his arm. Griffiths was armed with an American musket which he then fired, without hitting anyone. At the same time another member of the crew struck Davis on the head with a tiller, and before Griffiths could reload, Dyer wrenched the musket from him and threw it overboard. During the struggle the boat ran ashore and Davis and Griffiths got away. With the help of two Fijian women they managed to steal another boat, whereupon they fled to the main island of Vitu Levu. Midshipman Andrew Nugent and a party of bluejackets tracked them there and ransomed them from the Fijians for five muskets and a barrel of gunpowder. He escorted them to the *Herald*, where they joined Merry in irons. However, on the voyage back to Sydney through the Solomon Islands, Griffiths escaped to Guadalcanal. Davis and Merry were handed over to the Sydney police and committed to Darlinghurst Gaol before being returned to Van Diemen's Land and further years of imprisonment.

Even if the *Lady Franklin* had made an uninterrupted passage to Norfolk Island, Davis and his companions would not have been there long enough to complete their sentences. In 1852 Lieutenant-Governor Sir William Denison had recommended that the penal station be abandoned, and under Captain Deering's successor, Captain Day, it was gradually wound down as batches of convicts were transferred to Port Arthur by the *Lady Franklin*, still under the command of Captain Willett. In January 1856 the captain made his last run, carrying away the few remaining convicts. Only the buildings remained as memorials to nearly 70 years of human degradation and suffering.

11

By Land and Sea

Transportation to New South Wales officially ceased in 1840 although there was a short-lived revival in 1849. The last convict arrived in Van Diemen's Land in 1853. During this period, from 1788 to 1853, the relatively small but steadily increasing drain of convicts from the colonies was never satisfactorily countered. In 1823 Commissioner Bigge reported that no reliable record had been kept of escapes from the colony but that it was the superintendant of convicts' belief that many more were successful than had become known to him. Between 1803 and 1820 he thought that about 255 convicts had attempted to escape 'either by concealing themselves on board vessels, or by attempting to seize them by violence'. Of these 194 had been re-taken and 9 had died.[1] The remainder were never seen again. In the six years between 1825 and 1830 another 132 convicts were believed to have escaped from New South Wales, a considerable rise in numbers from previous years.[2] New security measures were regularly introduced by the colonial government to prevent this exodus and as regularly circumvented, prompting the imposition of more stringent regulations designed to lock up the colonies even more securely.

By 1800 masters of all incoming ships were required to post a bond of £200 not to carry any convicts away without the governor's written authority. Before departing every ship was invaded by constables with unassailable orders to winkle out any concealed absconders. Where suspicion fell upon a vessel that 'she had such ballast' the hatches were fastened down and the ship was smoked with brimstone, an effective method of either suffocating stowaways or forcing them, half blinded and choking, into the open. Governor King's suggestion that patrol boats also be provided to guard harbour entrances was, however, rejected by the parsimonious home government as too expensive. By the 1820s masters of all vessels in Sydney Harbour clearing out for foreign ports were required to give written notice of their departure at least ten days before sailing together with an accurate muster of all passengers and crew. This allowed the muster to be compared with the convict indents and thus identify any runaways that might be on board.

From time to time the standard port regulations were intensified to meet special circumstances. After the sloop *Norfolk* was captured by a party of convicts in the quiet reaches of the Hawkesbury River in 1800, boats and decked vessels were only permitted to sail there from Sydney in company with two or three other vessels and not before giving three days' notice to the governor. In 1802 during the visit to Sydney of the French navigator Nicholas Baudin, it was arranged for shifts of guard boats, each containing three privates, to row continuously around his two ships until their departure. Despite this precaution eight convicts somehow managed to get themselves on board. They were later discovered by Baudin and marooned on King Island in Bass Strait.

Reinforcing the port regulations and other security measures were the various kinds of punishment directed at deterring would-be escapers. Chief among these was flogging. The usual penalty for running away was 50 lashes but it could be higher depending on the circumstances. While attending Bathurst Court House to identify an absconder from his farm Alexander Harris was witness to the destructive effect of a cat-o'-nine-tails. 'I had to go past the triangles,' he wrote, where they had been flogging incessantly for hours. I saw a man walk across the yard with the blood that had run from his lacerated flesh squashing out of his shoes at every step he took. A dog was licking the blood off the triangles, and the ants were carrying away great pieces of human flesh that the lash had scattered about the ground. The scourger's foot had worn a deep hole in the ground by the violence with which he whirled himself round on it to strike the quivering and wealed back, out of which stuck the sinews, white, ragged and swollen.[3]

Equally dreaded by convicts was the iron gang, a common punishment for persistent absconders. Shackled on each ankle with irons or chains weighing 10 pounds or more they were employed in the backbreaking work of making new roads — cutting through mountains, blasting rocks and felling trees. By day they were supervised by a military guard assisted by brutalised convict overseers and at night were locked up in small wooden huts behind stockades. Their rations were poor in quality and quantity and they were liable to be flogged for trifling offences such as insolence and obstinacy.

The penalties for aiding and abetting escaping convicts were also harsh. Any convict caught harbouring another convict on the run faced a flogging or one year in an iron gang. If the harbourer proved to be a free man he was liable to pay a fine of between £5 and £10 and if he gave assistance to an absconder knowing him to have committed some additional offence, such as robbery or housebreaking, he could expect to be executed as an accessory.[4]

Despite their fairly low success rate and the dreadful results of failure, convicts never ceased trying to escape. Their motives varied. Freedom from bondage was always a powerful incentive but it was the threat of starvation hanging over Sydney during its first few years that provided the impetus for Mary Bryant's escape while Thomas Cook, author of *The Exile's Lamentation*, was driven to abscond from Port Macquarie by the determination of seeing his parents again. On Norfolk Island a timid fellow named John Williams, fearful of reprisals, fled into the bush after losing the weekly allowance of provisions for his mess in a card game. According to the penal reformer Edward Gibbon Wakefield, who gave evidence before the Select Committee on Secondary Punishments in 1831, 'in a majority of cases the motive for returning is to resume a connection with some woman in England'.[5] This was certainly the case with William Swallow. So desperate was he to be reunited with his wife and children that he made it back to England twice. Wakefield mentioned another convict (whose name he withheld) who outdid Swallow by escaping to England three times, on each occasion paying a ship's captain to take him on board as a stowaway. He stated that 'his motive for returning was a connection with a woman who would not leave [England]'. He was described as 'a very clever, determined man' who had once been smoked out but had 'borne the fumigation till he was nearly suffocated'.[6]

For convicts incarcerated in brutal penal settlements like Moreton Bay, Macquarie Harbour and Norfolk Island, escape from the incessant floggings and unremitting hard labour became an obsession even though their isolated situations made survival beyond their boundaries extremely doubtful. At Macquarie Harbour the hope of making a successful escape was kept alive by rumours brought in by fresh batches of convicts that 'such and such a party of men who had left the settlement at such a time, had made their escape from Launceston or Hobart Town, or some place that ships visit'.[7] But the reality was very different. Of 116 convicts who absconded from Macquarie Harbour between 1822 and 1827, 75 were reported to have perished in the bush. The skeletons of some were found on the shore where they had died of starvation, sometimes only a few kilometres from the settlement. Only a handful were thought to have reached the settled districts, the remainder being recaptured, shot by the military, drowned or eaten by their companions.[8] In their desperation to get away from the horrendous conditions some convicts were willing to make the 'final escape'. On Norfolk Island they would murder an overseer or a fellow prisoner 'in order to be sent to Sydney to be tried', and almost certainly executed, 'rather than drag on a miserable existence on the island'.[9]

Some convicts displayed considerable ingenuity in their efforts to escape, such as the particularly neat scheme uncovered by Governor King in 1800. For a price, generally money, a watch or some other valuable, corrupt government clerks would alter a convict's term of transportation in the official registers from life or fourteen years to a lesser period, thus enabling a certificate of freedom to be issued before time. This practice was surprisingly widespread as King grumbled to the Home Secretary the following year.

> It appears that at least 200 prisoners have had their terms thus changed, which introduced such confusion into the indents and Orders in Council by which these convicts were transported, that there is great difficulty in tracing any convict's term of transportation but by secret means and secondary enquiries.[10]

A remarkable instance of this was revealed in September 1801. Shortly after Captain John Hunter returned to England he was called as a witness in the trial of a convict appearing in England after being transported for life. The fellow had actually been brought home by Hunter as his servant and the embarrassed captain assured the court that according to the registers in Sydney the convict had been transported for only seven years and this term had already expired. However, the prosecution was able to produce the original court records which showed that he had indeed received a life sentence.

Another clever way of escaping without the physical demands and dangers of travelling overland or stealing a boat was devised by two Irish brothers, Patrick and Owen Flanagan. Their plan depended on the fact that they bore a striking resemblance to each other, both having a fair complexion, brown hair and grey eyes, although Patrick was the taller by one inch. In 1825 they had been convicted of burglary and sentenced to seven years' transportation to New South Wales. Three years later Patrick was transferred to Moreton Bay for three years on a charge of absconding. On board the same boat was his younger brother, Owen, who had received a seven-year sentence for stealing pigs. After arriving at the settlement they exchanged Christian names, each assuming the other's identity. Three years later when Patrick's sentence expired Owen obtained a certificate of freedom in his brother's name. As soon as he had sailed for Sydney the real Patrick came forward and demanded his freedom. The commandant, Captain Clunie, declined to release him and instead sent a report of the deception to Sydney where Owen was quickly rounded up. At an enquiry held by the Superintendent of Police his real identity was firmly established and he was sent back to Moreton Bay to complete his sentence. At the same time the Attorney General decided that, despite his role in the affair, Patrick was still entitled to his certificate of freedom.[11]

Yet another enterprising escape plan, but of a very different kind, was hatched by a group of convicts being transported to Norfolk Island on the brig *Governor Phillip* in 1832. Among the ringleaders was a prisoner of birth and position named John Knatchbull. The younger son of a baronet, he had served in the Royal Navy during the Napoleonic Wars and risen to the rank of commander. However, his naval career was cut short when he was dismissed for failing to pay a gambling debt. His fortunes took a more serious dive in 1824 when he was caught picking a pocket in Vauxhall Gardens and transported to Sydney for fourteen years. A further conviction in 1832, this time for forging a money order, saw him sentenced to a term of seven years on Norfolk Island. During the voyage there he plotted with his confederates to poison the crew and guard and take over the brig which he would then navigate to South America. Five days after leaving Sydney the conspirators were ready. They had filed through their irons with a serrated knife and persuaded a volunteer servant to lace next morning's breakfast with arsenic. At the last moment the conspiracy was betrayed by one of their number who slipped a warning note to a guard during the night. Knatchbull and his mates were duly landed on Norfolk Island where their failed exploit earned them notoriety among their peers as the 'tea sweeteners'. In 1834 Knatchbull was involved in an unsuccessful mutiny on the island but managed to evade the gallows by turning King's evidence. This respite was only temporary for ten years later the downward spiral of his life was completed when he was hanged in Sydney for the brutal murder of a widow for her savings.

It was unusual for convicts to receive help in organising an escape attempt, especially from outside the colony. Whether they took off into the bush or left the colony on a ship they generally made their own preparations, wisely relying on as few people as possible for assistance. One exception was the Irish political prisoner John Mitchel, a leading member of the militant Young Ireland movement and editor of the radical newspaper the *United Irishman*. In 1848 he was convicted of treason and sentenced to fourteen years' transportation. After spending time on the hulks in Bermuda he was transferred to Van Diemen's Land, arriving in Hobart in April 1850. Upon giving his parole not to escape he was granted a ticket-of-leave and allowed to live at Bothwell. A year later he was joined by his wife and children. Meanwhile members of a secret organisation in the United States called the Irish Directory were working to procure his escape.

Early in 1853 a representative of the Irish Directory, Pat 'Nicaragua' Smyth, arrived in Hobart from New York. Posing as a correspondent for the *New York Tribune* he met Mitchel at Bridgewater a few miles north of Hobart where they discussed ways of getting him off the island. A first attempt was abandoned in April when the details became known to the governor and 'the plot blown to the moon'.[12] By June they were ready to try again. Accompanied by Smyth, Mitchel walked into the Bothwell police magistrate's office and handed over a letter withdrawing his parole and resigning his passport. The magistrate read the note but surprisingly made no move. The two men bade him good morning and turned to go. 'The hand of Nicaragua was playing with the handle of the revolver in his coat,' Mitchel recalled. 'I had a ponderous riding-whip in my hand, besides pistols in my breast pocket. The moment I said, "Good morning," Mr Davis [the magistrate] shouted "No, no — stay here! Rainsford! Constables!"'[13] But Smyth and Mitchel were already out the door and heading into the street. They passed two constables who made no attempt to stop them, mounted their horses and lit off into the bush where they split up. Smyth had arranged for Mitchel to be picked up by the brigantine *Don Juan* off Badger Head on the east coast but the plan unravelled when the vessel failed to show up on the agreed day. Another scheme to get Mitchel on a steamer sailing from Launceston to Melbourne also failed. Disguised as a priest he then made his way by coach back to Hobart where a fourth plan was put into operation. The captain of the *Emma*, a passenger brig bound for Sydney, agreed to pick him up 3 or four 4 miles downriver provided he remained in disguise throughout the voyage and avoided his family who were sailing legally as passengers. On the night of 16 July, with his wife watching anxiously from the poop deck, he was taken on board and formally introduced to the other passengers, including Smyth, as 'Mr Wright'. The voyage passed uneventfully and after arriving in Sydney he transferred to another vessel. By November he was in New York receiving a hero's welcome.

Many convicts of course made no effort to escape and were content to quietly serve out their time. Colonial records show that new arrivals were the most likely to abscond. Thrust forcibly into a strange new world their instinct was to try and regain their former lives, to return to what was familiar. However, once they overcame their longing for home and adapted to colonial life they tended to accept their lot.

Moreover, in many cases they enjoyed a better standard of living than they had left behind and this, of course, was a powerful incentive against escape. Writing to friends in England one convict was able to reassure them that he was perfectly satisfied with his situation. 'I did expect to be in servile bondage,' he wrote, 'and to be badly used but I am better off this day than half the people in England, and I would not go back to England if anyone would pay my passage.'[14] Richard Dillingham, who had been transported to Van Diemen's Land in 1832 and assigned to a market gardener, wrote to his parents with a similar tale.

> As to my living I find it better than ever I expected thank God. I want for nothing in that respect. As for tea and sugar I could almost swim in it. I am allowed 2 pound of sugar and ¼ pound of tea per week and plenty of tobacco and good white bread and sometimes beef sometimes mutton sometimes pork. This I have every day. Plenty of fruit puddings in the season of all sorts and I have two suits of Cloths a year and three pairs of shoes a year and I want for nothing but my liberty.[15]

Of course not all convicts had the same good fortune as Dillingham as he himself pointed out.

> Though I am thus situated it is not the case with all that come as prisoners. It is owing to a persons good conduct that they get good situations for some through their misconduct get into road partys and some into chain gangs and live a miserable life.[16]

Nevertheless the lesson was there. For men and women of industry, honesty and initiative opportunities for advancement existed as evidenced by the business empires developed by transportees such as Mary Reiby and Simeon Lord.

Such rewards offered no temptation to the inveterate escapers who continued to bolt, no matter the odds, until they either succeeded or were claimed by the hangman. To them imprisonment was a constant provocation and freedom a passion. Their attitude was encapsulated by a one-eyed Irishman named Dennis Doherty. A former soldier who had been transported for mutiny, his subsequent career included robbery, bushranging and piracy. When asked by visiting English writer Anthony Trollope why he had repeatedly attempted to escape over a period of 42 years he replied: 'I have tried to escape; always to escape as a bird does out of a cage. Is that unnatural; is that a great crime?'[17]

Appendix

'Seizure of the *Cyprus* Brig in Recherche Bay'
Within a few years of William Swallow's return to Van Diemen's Land, the capture of the *Cyprus* was being celebrated in a popular ballad written by Frank Goddard or Macnamara, known as 'Frank the Poet', himself a convict transported in the 1820s for forgery. Titled 'Seizure of the *Cyprus* Brig in Recherche Bay', it exalted the convicts' exploit as a noble attempt to break free from the chains of oppression.

Come all you sons of Freedom, a chorus join with me,
I'll sing a song of heros, and glorious liberty.
Some lads condemn'd from England sail'd to Van Diemen's Shore,
Their Country, friends and parents, perhaps never to see more.
When landed in this Colony to different Masters went,
For trifling offences, t' Hobart Town gaol were sent,
A second sentence being incurr'd we were order'd for to be
Sent to Macquarie Harbour, that place of Tyranny.
The hardships we'd to undergo, are matters of record,
But who believes the convict, or who regards his word?
For starv'd and flogg'd and punish'd, depriv'd of all redress,
The Bush our only refuge, with death to end distress.
Hundreds of us were shot down, for daring to be free,
Numbers caught and banished, to lifelong slavery,
Brave Swallow, Watt and Davis, were in our noble band
Determin'd at the first slant, to quit Van Diemen's Land.
March'd down in chains and guarded, on the *Cyprus* Brig convey'd
The topsails being hoisted, the anchor being weighed,
The wind it blew Sou' Sou' West and on we went straightway,
Till we found ourselves Wind-bound, in gloomy Recherche Bay.
'Twas August eighteen twenty nine, with thirty one on board,
Lieutenant Carew left the Brig, and soon we passed the word
The Doctor too was absent, the soldiers off their guard,

A better opportunity could never have occurr'd.
Confin'd within a dismal hole, we soon contriv'd a plan,
To capture now the *Cyprus*, or perish every man.
But thirteen turn'd faint-hearted and begg'd to go ashore,
So eighteen boys rush'd daring, and took the Brig and store.
We first address'd the soldiers 'for liberty we crave,
Give up your arms this instant, or the sea will be your grave,
By tyranny we've been oppress'd, by your Colonial laws,
But we'll bid adieu to slavery, or die in freedom's cause.'
We next drove off the Skipper, who came to help his crew,
Then gave three cheers for liberty, 'twas answered cheerly too.
We brought the sailors from below, and row'd them to the land
Likewise the wife and children of Carew in command.
Supplies of food and water, we gave the vanquish'd crew,
Returning good for evil, as we'd been taught to do.
We mounted guard with Watch and Ward, then haul'd the boat aboard,
We elected William Swallow, and obey'd our Captain's word.
The Morn broke bright, the Wind was fair, we headed for the sea
With one cheer more for those on shore and glorious liberty.
For Navigating smartly Bill Swallow was the man,
Who laid a course out neatly to take us to Japan.
Then sound your golden trumpets, play on your tuneful notes,
The *Cyprus* Brig is sailing, how proudly now she floats.
May fortune help th' Noble lads, and keep them ever free
From Gags, and Cats, and Chains, and Traps, and Cruel Tyranny.

Notes

ABBREVIATIONS

AONSW Archives Office of New South Wales

AOT Archives Office of Tasmania

BT Bonwick Transcripts, Mitchell Library

CO Colonial Office Records

CON Colonial Department Records, Van Diemen's Land

CSO Chief Secretary's Office Records, Van Diemen's Land

DL Dixson Library, State Library of New South Wales

FO Foreign Office Records

HO Home Office Records

HRA Historical Records of Australia

HRNSW Historical Records of New South Wales

ML Mitchell Library, State Library of New South Wales

NLA National Library of Australia

PCOM Prison Commission Records

PRO Public Record Office, London

INTRODUCTION

1. Young, Heads of Plan, HRNSW 1/2, p. 17.

2. Collins, vol. 2, p. 57.

3. Phillip to Nepean, 18 November 1791, HRNSW 1/2, p. 557.

4. Cunningham, pp. 282-3.

5. Noah, DL MSQ 49, p. 79.

6. Hunter to Portland, 15 February 1798, HRNSW 3, p. 359.

7. Cunningham, p. 284.

8. Collins, vol. 1, pp. 271-3.

9. Ibid., p. 13.

1. THE GIRL FROM BOTANY BAY

1. White, p. 772.

2. Collins, vol. 1, pp. 44-5.

3. Ibid., p. 45.

4. Tench, p. 162.

5. Ibid., p. 165.

6. Ibid., pp. 191-2.

7. Collins, vol. 1, p. 126.

8. Ibid.

9. Easty, p. 127.

10. Tench, p. 145.

11. Easty, p. 127.

12. Collins, vol. 1, p. 132.

13. Ibid., p. 129.

14. Ibid.

15. Scott, p. 62.

16. Collins, vol. 1, p. 129.

17. Ibid.

18. Ibid.

19. Ibid.

20. Easty, p. 127.

21. Bligh, pp. 149-51.

22. Ibid., p. 151.

23. Martin, p. 19. Except where otherwise indicated all further quotations concerning the voyage to Timor are from Martin's
Memorandoms.

24. Bligh, p 151.

25. Ibid., p. 273.

26. Ibid., p. 149.

27. Ibid.

28. Collins, vol. 1, p. 182.

29. Tench, p. 219.

30. Yet another version was recounted by George Hamilton (p. 162):
The captain of a Dutch East Indiaman, who spoke English, hearing
of the arrival of Capt. Edwards, and our unfortunate boat, run to
them [the convicts] with the glad tidings of their captain having
arrived; but one of them, starting in surprise, said, 'What Captain!

Dam'me, we have no Captain'; for they had reported, that the
captain and remainder of the crew had separated from them at
sea in another boat. This immediately led to suspicion of their
being imposters; and they were ordered to be apprehended, and
put in the castle. One of the men, and the woman, fled into
the woods; but were soon taken. They confessed they were
English convicts, and that they had made their escape from
Botany Bay.

31. Morrison, p. 199.
32. Hamilton, p. 165.
33. Morrison, p. 201.
34. *The Journals of Captain James Cook* on his Voyages of Discovery,
     p. 443.
35. Morrison, p. 201.
36. Hamilton, p. 169.
37. Morrison, p. 202.
38. Hamilton, p. 169.
39. Edwards, pp. 83-4.
40. Tench, p. 219.
41. Morrison pp. 205-6.
42. Clark, p. 306.
43. *Dublin Chronicle*, 21 July 1792.
44. Ibid.
45. *London Chronicle*, 7-10 July 1792.
46. Nepean to Boswell, quoted in Pottle, p. 23.
47. *London Chronicle*, 7-10 July 1792.
48. *Dublin Chronicle*, 21 July 1792.
49. *London Chronicle*, 10-12 July 1792.
50. *London Chronicle*, 30 June-3 July 1792.
51. Quoted in Pottle, p. 24.
52. Ibid., p. 26.
53. Ibid., p. 25.
54. Ibid., pp. 27-8.
55. Brady, p. 465.

2. INTO THE BLUE

1. Collins, vol. 1, p. 333.
2. Bligh to William Windham, 31 October 1807, HRA 1/6, p. 159.
3. BT, vol. 24, p. 5076.
4. BT vol. 24, see also Ritchie, pp. 116-117, 166 and HRNZ 1, pp. 484, 593.
5. HRNSW vol. 1, part 2, p. 565.
6. Collins, vol. 1, p. 360.
7. Macquarie to Bathurst, 31 August 1813, HRA 1/8, p. 85.
8. Cunningham, p. 286.
9. Ibid., p. 287.
10. Anonymous Account of a Convict Escape, ML MSS 5536.
11. Hunter to Portland, 10 January 1798, HRNSW vol. 3. p. 345.
12. *Sydney Gazette*, 22 May 1808.
13. Ibid.
14. *Calcutta Gazette*, 23 March 1809.
15. *Bombay Courier*, 20 May 1809.
16. Collins to King, 2 November 1805, HRA 3/1, p. 335.
17. Ibid.
18. General and Garrison Orders, p. 257.
19. Bligh to Castlereagh, 30 June 1808, HRA 1/6, p. 535.
20. *Sydney Gazette*, 22 May 1808.
21. BT 80, p. 588 (*Calcutta Gazette*, 23 March 1809).
22. BT 80, p. 590 (*Calcutta Gazette*, 24 August 1809).
23. *Sydney Gazette*, 2, 23 June 1810.
24. Tipping, p. 136.
25. Macquarie to Bathurst, 31 August 1813, HRA 1/8, p. 86.
26. *Sydney Gazette*, 29 May 1809.
27. *Sydney Gazette*, 30 January 1817.
28. Lieutenant-Governor Sorell to Macquarie, 15 May 1819, HRA 3/2, p. 386.
29. Governor-General to Hunter, 3 July 1800, HRA 1/3, pp. 22-3.
30. Mortlock, p. 59.
31. Cunningham, pp. 18-19.

32. Cheyne, p. 214.

33. *Report from the Select Committee on Transportation*, 1837, p. 262.

34. Marsden to Darling, 2 August 1830, HRA 1/15, p. 705.

3. THE CANNIBAL OF VAN DIEMEN'S LAND

1. *Hobart Town Gazette*, 25 June 1824.

2. Sorell to Cuthbertson, 8 December 1821, AOT CS01/133/3229.

3. Sorell to Sir George Arthur, 9 June 1824, HRA 3/4, p. 150.

4. Pearce, Narrative of the Escape .... DL MS 3. This is based on Pearce's interrogation by Rev. Robert Knopwood probably in January 1824. (A similar, but shorter version is held by the NLA at MS 3323.) Other contemporary sources for Pearce's escape are: (i) Deposition made before Lieutenant Cuthbertson headed 'Pearce's Narrative' and catalogued as 'Confession of Murder and Cannibalism', ML A1326. This appears to be the basis of the deposition placed before the Select Committee on Transportation 1837-38 ('Molesworth Report'). (ii) Pearce's Confession to Rev. Philip Conolly just before being executed. (iii) Pearce's Confession to the Keeper of Hobart Town Gaol, 20 June 1824 (reproduced in *Alexander Pearce of Macquarie Harbour* by Dan Sprod). Neither of the manuscript accounts (DL MS 3 and ML A1326) are in Pearce's hand, but appear to be transcriptions or reworkings of his own accounts as related to officials at different times. Except where otherwise indicated all further quotations concerning the escape are from DL MS 3.

5. Pearce, Confession to Rev. Philip Conolly.

6. According to Pearce's Narrative (ML A1326), Dalton did not leave with Brown and Kennely but was killed and eaten by the others.

7. Pearce, Confession to Rev. Philip Conolly.

8. Pearce's Narrative, ML A1326.

9. This encounter with Aborigines is not mentioned in other sources.

10. Pearce's Narrative, ML A1326.

11. *Hobart Town Gazette*, 11 January 1823.

12. Knopwood, p. 387.

13. Pearce, Confession to the Keeper of Hobart Town Gaol.
14. Ibid.
15. Ibid.
16. Ibid.
17. Ibid.
18. *Report from the Select Committee on Transportation*,
    Appendix (I) No. 56, p. 316.
19. *Hobart Town Gazette*, 25 June 1824.
20. *Report from the Select Committee on Transportation*, Appendix (1)
    No. 56, p. 316.
21. *Hobart Town Gazette*, 25 June 1824.
22. Ibid.
23. Pearce, Confession to Rev. Philip Conolly.
24. *Hobart Town Gazette*, 23 July 1824.
25. Phrenology: the study of the shape of a person's skull as the
    supposed indicator of his mental powers.

4. THE HEIRS OF MARY BRYANT

1. Bowes-Smyth, p. 90.
2. Bradley, p. 82.
3. White, p. 125.
4. Bowes-Smyth, p. 108.
5. Collins, vol. 1, p. 74.
6. Ibid., p. 406.
7. Hunter to the Duke of Portland, 10 January 1798, HRNSW
   vol. 3, p. 346.
8. Collins, vol. 2, p. 55.
9. Nagle, pp. 179-80.
10. Anderson, pp. 4-5.
11. Collins, vol. 1, p. 406.
12. Collins, vol. 2, p. 22.
13. *Sydney Gazette*, 13 July 1806.
14. Ingleton, p. 42.
15. *Sydney Gazette*, 13 July 1806.
16. Ibid.

17. Ibid.

18. De Vera.

19. Ormsby, M.L. 'Badger, Charlotte'. *Dictionary of New Zealand Biography*.

20. Fitzsymonds, Callaghan and Batman, p. 15.

21. Ibid, p. 16.

22. *The Surprising Adventures and Unparalleled Sufferings of Jane Turner, A Female Convict who made Her Escape from New South Wales.*

23. Turner, p. 6.

24. Cunningham, p. 315.

25. *Sydney Gazette*, 9 January 1830.

26. *Report from the Select Committee on Transportation*, 1812, p.112.

27. Ibid., p. 12.

5. THE COUNCIL OF SEVEN

1 . Brisbane to Under-Secretary Horton, 24 March 1825, HRA 1/11, p. 533.

2. *Australian*, 23 February 1827.

3. Ibid.

4. Ibid.

5. Ibid.

6. *Australian*, 14 February 1827.

7. Williams, p. 34.

8. Duke, Statement, ML A2226, p. 210.

9. Ibid.

10. Ibid., pp. 210-11.

11. Ibid., p. 211.

12. Williams, p. 35.

13. Ibid.

14. Duke, Statement, p. 211.

15. Williams, p. 35.

16. Ibid.

17. Spring: a line led from a vessel's quarterdeck to her anchor cable so that by hauling in or slacking it the vessel can be made to lie in any desired position.

18. Duke, Statement, p. 211.

19. *Sydney Gazette*, 16 February 1827.

20. Earle, p. 120.

21. *Sydney Gazette*, 16 February 1827.

22. Ibid.

23. Ibid.

24. Ibid.

25. Ibid.

26. Duke, Statement, p. 211.

27. Ibid.

28. *Sydney Gazette*, 16 February 1827.

29. Williams, p. 35.

30. Duke, Statement, pp. 211-12.

31. Williams, p. 36.

32. Duke, Statement, p. 212.

33. Williams, p. 36.

34. Duke, Statement, p. 212.

35. Ibid.

36. *Sydney Gazette*, 16 February 1827.

37. Sherrin, p. 332.

38. *Sydney Gazette*, 16 February 1827.

39. Earle, p. 121.

40. *Sydney Gazette*, 16 February 1827.

41. Minutes of the Executive Council, 15 March 1827, HRA 1/13 p. 158; Governor's Despatches, ML A1198, p. 648.

42. *Sydney Gazette*, 3 Mar. 1827.

43. Darling to Earl Bathurst, 12 March 1828, HRA 1/13, p. 157; Governor's Despatches, ML, p. 653.

44. Duke, Statement, p. 213.

45. *Monitor*, 16 March 1827.

46. Duke, Petition, HRA 1/13, p. 160.

47. Duke, Statement, p. 213.

48. Ibid.

6. WILD WHITE MEN

1. *Sydney Gazette*, 10 June 1804.
2. Ibid.
3. Ibid., 1 July 1804.
4. Ibid., 3 March 1805
5. Gunson, pp. 44, 45.
6. Ibid., p. 91.
7. *Report from the Select Committee on Secondary Punishment*, 1832, p. 40.
8. Watling, p. 28.
9. Phillip to Sydney, HRNSW, vol. 1. part 1, p. 146.
10. Ibid., p. 148.
11. Tench, p. 135.
12. Watling, p. 27.
13. Parker, p. 31.
14. Phillip to Sydney, HRNSW, vol. 1, part 1, p. 208.
15. Clark, 1 October 1788.
16. BT, vol. 18, p. 2411.
17. Bigge, p. 117.
18. *Sydney Gazette*, 16 December 1820.
19. Except where otherwise indicated all quotations regarding Buckley are taken from Morgan's *Life and Adventures of William Buckley*.
20. Bonwick, p. 7.
21. Quoted in Steele, p. 107. See AONSW SZ 29.
22. Ibid., p. 108.
23. Ibid., p. 109.
24. Fyans, pp. 254–5.
25. Ibid., p. 254.
26. Graham to Fyans, 6 September 1836, DL SP 196, p. 2.
27. Ibid., p. 4.
28. Ibid., p. 6.
29. Ibid., p. 6.
30. Ibid., p. 14.
31. Ibid., pp. 14-15.
32. Otter to Fyans, 27 August 1836. Reproduced in Gibbings, p. 105.

33. Fyans to the Colonial Secretary, 6 September 1836. Reproduced in Gibbings, p. 107.
34. Edward Deas Thompson, 2 April 1837. Reproduced in Gibbings, p. 115.

7. THE CRUISE OF THE *CYPRUS*

1 . Convict Indent: *Georgiana*.
2. Description enclosed with Dispatch from Arthur to Murray, 11 September 1829.
3. From 'Seizure of the *Cyprus* Brig in Recherche Bay', by Frank the Poet, in Ingleton, p. 129. (See also appendix of this book.)
4. Swallow, p. 3. This, Swallow's own account, is the most important source for the *Cyprus* story. Except where otherwise indicated all quotations are taken from it.
5. Pobjoy, Petition, 7 September 1829. Pobjoy was later to change his story and state that 'unperceived by the mutineers, [I] jumped overboard and swam ashore', *The Times*, 5 October 1830.
6. 'Extracts from Lady Jane Franklin's Diary', Royal Society of Tasmania — Papers, 1925.
7. Pobjoy, Petition, 7 September 1829.
8. *Hobart Town Courier*, 5 September 1829.
9. Pobjoy, Petition, 7 September 1829.
10. A ticket-of-leave was issued to a convict of good behaviour. It permitted him to work for himself and acquire property on condition of remaining in a specified district.
11. Quoted in Clune and Stephensen, p. 82.
12. *Hobart Town Courier*, 29 August 1829.
13. *Australian*, 3 September 1829.
14. Swallow's memory was faulty here. Brown's Christian name was actually William.
15. 'Williams' was an alias adopted by William Watts, a horsebreaker from Bristol who was working a seven-year sentence.
16. The *Cyprus* was the first Australian vessel to visit Japan.
17. *The Times*, 18 October 1830.
18. Ibid.

19. Ibid.
20. Ibid.
21. *The Times*, 14 October 1830.
22. 1bid.
23. *The Times*, 18 October 1830.
24. Ibid.
25. *The Times*, 19 October 1830.
26. *The Times*, 21 October 1830.
27. Ibid.
28. All quotations concerning the trial are taken from the report which appeared in *The Times* on 5 November 1830.
29. Swallow, Petition, p. 8.
30. Petitions of Convicts Appealing Against Sentences.
31. Robinson, p. 111.
32. Pretyman, p. 128.
33. *Hobart Town Courier*, 28 March 1834.

8. THE ADVENTURES OF JAMES PORTER

1. In fact there are several extant versions of Porter's autobiography. The best known was published in the *Hobart Town Almanac & Van Diemen's Land Annual for 1838*. It was written while he was a prisoner in Hobart Town Gaol and originally appeared in 1837 in the form of a petition to the Colonial Secretary. The Dixson Library, State Library of NSW, has two other more extensive manuscript versions (MSQ 604 and MSQ 168) which are very similar to each other without corresponding exactly. They were written in the early 1840s while Porter was languishing on Norfolk Island. Except where otherwise indicated I have relied on MSQ 604. In addition to the above there is a curious memoir titled *The Recollections of James Connor a Returned Convict* which was published in the Fife *Herald* in 1845. It has some striking similarities to Porter's narratives and it is worth noting that on the convict indent for the *Sarah* he is listed as James Connor, while James O'Connor was an alias he used in Chile. However, there are sufficient inconsistencies in this memoir to cast doubt on its authenticity. Possibly it is an amalgam of the

experiences of several convicts. Two years later a variant version appeared in Montreal under the title *Recollections of a Convict and Miscellaneous Pieces by Y-Le*.

2. This date is at odds with other dates that Porter mentions. For instance he says that in 1818 he was eighteen years old, making the year of his birth 1800 or 1801. To complicate matters further his convict record indicates that he was born in 1805.

3. Porter's convict record states that he was transported for burglary, which implies the robbery of a house rather than a boat.

4. A copy of his convict record (including the prison report) was enclosed with the Dispatch from Arthur to Stanley, 7 February 1834.

5. Backhouse, pp. 50–1.

6. The following story is taken from the version of Porter's memoirs at DL MSQ 168.

7. Evidence of the Board of Enquiry, March 1834.

8. The castaways had been landed on the southern shore of the harbour. They crossed to the north shore, three at a time on a homemade raft, and made their way along the coast to the Van Diemen's Land Company's base at Cape Grim which they reached on 25 January. By the time they got the news of the mutiny to Hobart the *Frederick* was long gone. Nevertheless Lieutenant Governor Arthur sent HMS *Alligator* in pursuit and warned the Residency in New Zealand, but it was all in vain.

9. Porter, Autobiography, DL MSQ 168.

10. Darwin, pp. 271–2.

11. Earlier in his memoir Porter mentions that he was known as 'Don Santiago O'Connor, my name being at that time James O'Connor'.

12. Porter, Autobiography, DL MSQ 168.

13. Chains: an iron link or bar held by a chain by which the shrouds (or rigging) are secured to a vessel's side.

14. *Hobart Town Courier*, 28 April 1837.

15. Porter, Autobiography, DL MSQ 168.

16. Colonial Secretary, In-Letters, AONSW 42/7314.

9. THE GENTLEMAN BUSHRANGER

1. Tench, p. 247.
2. HRNSW vol. 3, p. 195.
3. HRA series 3, vol. 1, p. 393.
4. HRA series 1, vol. 8, p. 250.
5. Convict Indent: *Mangles*.
6. Rogers, W.F. , p. 85. Except where otherwise indicated all further quotations are from Westwood's autobiography in this volume.
7. *Sydney Gazette*, 22 May 1841.
8. Lempriere, p. 69.
9. Booth, 30 March 1842.
10. *Hobart Town Courier*, 6 September 1845.
11. Cook, p. 178.
12. *Sydney Gazette*, 25 March 1804.
13. *Norfolk Island 1846: The Accounts of Robert Pringle Stuart and Thomas Beagley Naylor*, p. 83.
14. Ibid.
15. Ibid. p. 54.
16. Quoted in Hoare, pp. 196-7.
17. Cash, p. 154.
18. Ibid., p. 155.
19. Life of William Westwood, Suttor Family Papers, p. 76.
20. Rogers, Rev. Thomas. pp. 162-3.
21. Westwood to the Port Arthur chaplain.
22. *Australasian*, 1 February 1879.
23. Rogers, Rev. Thomas, p. 164.
24. Ibid.
25. *Australasian*, 1 February l879.
26. Price, 13 October 1846.

10. THE LAST OF NORFOLK ISLAND

1. Burn, p. 209.
2. Ibid., pp. 208-9.
3. Ibid., p. 209.

4. Ibid., p. 210.

5. Ibid., p. 211.

6. Hazzard, *Punishment Short of Death*, pp. 225–7.

7. Tasmanian Papers, vol. 223 (Convicts from N.Z. to Tasmania).

8. Ibid.

9. *Sydney Morning Herald*, 2 February 1855.

10. *Tasmanian Colonist*, 21 July 1853.

11. Price, p. 257.

12. Ibid.

13. *Moreton Bay Courier*, 2 April 1853.

14. Ibid.

15. Ibid.

16. Ibid.

17. Ibid.

18. Ibid., 16 April 1853.

19. Ibid., 14 May 1853.

20. Ibid., 26 June 1853.

21. *Tasmanian Colonist*, 21 July 1853.

22. Ibid., 30 January 1854.

23. *Illustrated Sydney News,* 11 February 1854.

24. *Hobart Town Advertiser*, 6 July 1855.

11. BY LAND AND SEA

1. *Report of the Commissioner on the Judicial Establishments of New South Wales and Van Diemen's Land*, p. 79.

2. *Report from the Select Committee on Secondary Punishments*, 1831, Appendix No. 4, p. 138. This figure only referred to convicts who had left the colony. It did not include those who were still illegally at large in the colony.

3 Harris, p. 12.

4. *Report from the Select Committee on Transportation*, 1837, p. 232.

5. *Report from the Select Committee on Secondary Punishments*, 1831. Evidence of E.G. Wakefield, p. 100.

6. Ibid.

7. *Report from the Select Committee on Transportation*, 1838. Evidence of John Barnes, p. 39.

8. Ibid. and Appendix (I) no. 56, pp. 310-12.

9. *Report from the Select Committee on Secondary Punishments*, 1832. Evidence of Allan Cunningham, p. 36.

10. HRNSW, vol. 4, p. 464.

11. *Sydney Gazette*, 22 December 1832.

12. Mitchel, p. 173.

13. Ibid., p. 175.

14. Breton, pp. 130-1.

15. Dillingham, p. 19.

16. Ibid.

17. Trollope, p. 354.

Bibliography

Unpublished Primary Sources

Anonymous Account of a Convict Escape between 1840 and 1844, ML MSS 5536.

Arthur, Sir George. Lt.-Governor's Despatches, Despatch to Sir George Murray, 11 September 1829, PRO CO 280/2.

Arthur, Sir George. Lt.-Governor's Despatches, Despatch to Edward Stanley, 7 February 1834, PRO CO 280/46.

Arthur, Sir George. Correspondence with John Walpole and other associated correspondence, 1834, AOT CSO1/700/15339.

Bligh, William. A Log of the Proceedings on His Majesty's Ship Providence, ML Safe 1/45.

Booth, Charles O'Hara. Memoranda to the Chief Magistrate, 26 & 30 March 1842, AOT CSO 22/19/799.

Bowes-Smyth, Journal of a Voyage to New South Wales in the Lady Penrhyn, 1786-89, ML Safe1/14.

Burn, David. Journal on New South Wales and Norfolk Island 1844, ML B190-2.

Cheyne, Andrew. Account of trading Voyages in the Western Pacific 1841-44, ML B1408.

Clark, Lieutenant Ralph. Journal 1787-1792. ML Safe 1/27.

Colonial Secretary — Letters, Warrants and Assignment Lists Received re Convicts Transported to Van Diemens Land 1842-46, ML Tasmanian papers vol. 37.

Colonial Secretary, Correspondence — Convicts, 1845, AONSW 4/2681, 4/2686.1.

Colonial Secretary, In-Letters, AONSW 42/4751, 42/7314, 43/1598, 45/6071.

Colonial Secretary, Letters Sent re Convicts, AONSW 4/3691.

Colonial Secretary, Papers re New South Wales 1799-1806, ML MSS 681.

Colonial Secretary's Papers, 1788-1825, ML FM4/10244.

Comptroller-General's Record Books of Convicts, AOT CON 31/48 p. 206, CON 35/1, p. 597, CON 16/1 p. 200.

Convicts from New Zealand to Tasmania, ML Tasmanian Papers vol. 223.

Convict Indents: *Castle Forbes*, AONSW COD 147; *Georgiana*, ML Tas. Papers, v.23 & v.24; *Argyle*, ML Tas. Papers, v.26; *Malabar*, AONSW COD 149; *Asia*, AONSW 4/4009; *Sarah*, ML Tas. Papers, v.26 & v.29; *Mangles*, AONSW Reel 908.

Cook, Thomas. The Exile's Lamentations, 1826-1841, ML A1711.

Easty, John. A Memorandum of the Transactions of a Voyage from England to Botany Bay in the Scarborough Transport, 1787-93, DL 374.

Evidence taken by Commissioner Bigge and Appendix to Bigge's Report, ML BT Vols. 1, 10, 11, 18, 24, 25.

Fyans, Foster. Reminiscences of Foster Fyans, ML FM4/2278.

General and Garrison Orders, ML A341.

Graham, John. The Humble Petition of John Graham Now in Hyde Park Barracks, 29 December 1836, DL SP196.

Graham, John. Letter to Captain Foster Fyans, 6 September 1836, DL SP 196.

Graham, John. Memorandum of the Real Facts — follows of John Graham &c. &c. &c., undated, ML Ag 72.

Hall, John. Petition and Memorial, 16 October 1829 & undated, AOT CSO 1/416/9354.

Latrobe, Charles. Despatch No. 5 to Secretary of State, 8 January 1847, PRO CO 280/205-206.

Life of William Westwood 1821-1846, Suttor Family Papers, ML MSS 2417/5 Item 10.

McTernan, James. Medical Journal on Sarah, ML PRO 3209.

McTernan, James. Papers re Mutiny on Sarah. ML Tasmanian Papers vol. 19.

Maitland Gaol Description Book, 1849-59, AONSW 2/2017.

Marsden, Rev. Samuel. Letter to D. Coates, 24 February 1827. BT 53.

Morrison, James. Journal on H.M.S. Bounty and at Tahiti 1792, ML Safe 1/42.

Newcastle Gaol Entrance Book, 1841-45, AONSW 2/2008.

Newgate Execution Register, PRO PCOM 2/190 f.51.

Noah, William. A Voyage to Sydney in New South Wales in 1798 and 1799 and A Few Remarks of the County of Cumberland in New South Wales, DL MSQ 49.

Pardon of Mary Bryant. Correspondence and Warrants Entry Book, PRO HO 13/9 (ML PRO 421).

[Pearce, Alexander]. Narrative of the Escape of Eight Convicts from Macquarie Harbour, September 1822, DL MSQ 3.

[Pearce, Alexander]. Pearce's Narrative or Confession of Murder and Cannibilism, 1823, ML A1326.

Petitions of Convicts Appealing against Sentences ... Include William Watts, Alexander Stevenson, John Beveridge, George Huntly, John Pobjoy and '4 members of the Jury', PRO Fp20 HO 17/40.

Pobjoy, John. Petition, 7 September 1829, AOT CSO 1/416/9354.

Pobjoy, John and Others. Petition, 7 September 1829, AOT CSO 1/416/9354.

Porter, James. Autobiography, DL MSQ 604.

Porter, James. Autobiography, DL MSQ 168.

Probation Books — Pestongee Bombangee February 1847, ML Tasmanian Papers vol. 53.

Price, Aaron. History of Norfolk Island from Period of Discovery to the Present Day, DL MSQ 247.

Rogers, W.F. Man's Inhumanity — Being a Chaplain's Chronicles of Norfolk Island in the Forties, ML C214 (includes William Westwood's autobiography).

Principal Superintendant of Convicts — Ticket of Leave Butts, 1846 — AONSW 4/4206.

Robinson, George Augustus. Journals 1829-34, ML A7024.

Scott, James. Remarks on a Passage to Botany Bay In Ship 1787, DL MSQ 43.

Sharland, Wiliam. Mr Sharland's Exploration to the Westward in 1832, ML C722.

Sharpe, Rev. T. Papers 1826-1841, ML A1502.

Swallow, William. Petition to Sir Robert Peel, 10 November 1830, PRO HO 17/59 Kp. 18.

Sydney, Thomas Townshend, Viscount. Papers, DL MSQ 522.

Tobin, Lieutenant George. Journal of H.M.S. Providence 1791-3, ML A562.

Woodriff, Daniel. 'Memo Book', ML C269.

Published Primary Sources

Backhouse, James. *A Narrative of a Visit to the Australian Colonies*, London, 1843.

Bigge, John Thomas. *Report of the Commissioner of Inquiry into the State of the Colony of New South Wales*, Adelaide, 1966. (Facsimile of 1822 House of Commons paper no. 148).

Bigge, John Thomas. *Report of the Commissioner of Inquiry on the Judicial Establishments of New South Wales and Van Diemen's Land*, Ordered by the House of Commons to be printed 21 February 1823.

Bigge, John Thomas. *Report of the Commissioner of Inquiry on the State of Agriculture and Trade in the Colony of New South Wales*, Ordered by the House of Commons to be printed 13 March 1823.

Boswell, James. *Letters*, vol. 2 (ed. C.B. Tinker), Oxford, 1924.

Bradley, William. *A Voyage to New South Wales, 1786-1792*, Sydney 1969 (facsimile edition of the original manuscript in the Mitchell Library).

Breton, Lieutenant *Excursions in New South Wales, Western Australia and Van Diemen's Land*, London, 1833.

Cash, Martin. *The Bushranger of Van Diemen's Land in 1843-44*, Hobart, 1911.

Collins, David. *An Account of the English Colony in New South Wales*, 2 vols. London, 1798, 1802. Reprinted Sydney, 1975.

[Connor, James]. *The Recollections of James Connor a Returned Convict containing an account of his sufferings in, and ultimate escape from New South Wales*, Cupar, Fife, 1845.

Cunningham, Peter. *Two Years in New South Wales*, London, 1827. Reprinted Sydney, 1966.

Darwin, Charles. *Diary of the Voyage of HMS Beagle* (ed. Nora Barlow), Cambridge, 1933.

Dillingham, Richard. T*he Dillingham Convict Letters* (ed. Harley W. Forster), Melbourne, 1970.

Earle, Augustus. *A Narrative of Nine Months Residence in New Zealand in 1827*, London, 1832.

Fitzsymonds, Eustace (ed.). *Callaghan & Batman: Van Diemen's Land 1825*, Adelaide, 1978.

Fitzsymonds, Eustace (ed.). *The Capture of the Frederick: Macquarie Harbour, Van Diemen's Land*, Adelaide, 1981.

Edwards, Captain Edward. 'Reports in the Voyage of H.M.S. *Pandora*' in *Voyage of HMS* Pandora, (ed. Basil Thomson), London, 1915.

Hamilton, George. '*A Voyage Around the World*' in *Voyage of HMS Pandora* (ed. Basil Thomson), London, 1915.

Harris, Alexander. *Settlers and Convicts*, London, 1847. Reprinted Sydney, 1966.

Historical Records of Australia, Series 1 & 3, Sydney, 1914-23.

Historical Records of New South Wales, Facsimile reprint, Sydney, 1978-9.

Historical Records of New Zealand, Dunedin, 1903.

Historical Records of New Zealand (ed. R. McNab), Wellington, 1908-14

King, Philip Gidley. *The Journal of Philip Gidley King, Lieutenant, R.N. 1787-1790*, Sydney, 1980.

Knapp, A. & Baldwin, W. *Newgate Calendar* vol. 3, London, 1825.

Knopwood, Robert. *The Diary of the Reverend Robert Knopwood* (ed. Mary Nicholls), Hobart, 1977.

Martin, James. *Memorandoms*, Cambridge, 1937.

Mitchel, John. *Jail Journal or Five years in British Prisons*, Dublin, 1864.

Mortlock, J.F. *Experiences of a Convict Transported for Twenty-One Years*, London, 1965.

Nagle, Joseph. *The Nagle Journal* (ed. John C. Dann), New York, 1988.

Newscuttings, ML Q 991/N.

Newspaper Cuttings, ML Q991/N.

Norfolk Island 1846: The Accounts of Robert Pringle Stuart and Thomas Beagley Naylor, Adelaide, 1979.

Pearce, Alexander. Confession to the Keeper of Hobart Town Gaol,

1824. Reproduced in Dan Sprod's *Alexander Pearce of Macquarie Harbour*, Hobart, 1977.

[Pearce, Alexander]. Confession to Rev. Philip Conolly in *Hobart Town Gazette*, 6 August 1824 and reproduced in John West's *History of Tasmania*, Sydney, 1971.

Pelham, Camden. *Chronicles of Crime or The Newgate Calendar*, London, 1841.

Porter, James. 'A Narrative of the Sufferings ... of the Convicts Who Piratically Seized the Frederick' in *Hobart Town Almanac & Van Diemen's Land Annual for 1838*.

Ritchie, John (ed.). *The Evidence to the Bigge Reports*, 2 vols., Melbourne, 1971.

Report from the Select Committee on Transportation, Ordered by the House of Commons to be printed, 10 July 1812.

Reports from the Select Committee on Secondary Punishments, Ordered by the House of Commons to be printed, 1831 and 1832.

Report from the Select Committee on Transportation ('Molesworth Report'), British Parliamentary Papers, vol. 3, 1837-8, Shannon (Ireland), 1968.

Rogers, Rev. Thomas. *Correspondence relating to the Dismissal of the Rev. T. Rogers From his Chaplaincy at Norfolk Island*, Launceston, 1849.

Tench, Watkin. *A Narrative of the Expedition to Botany Bay and A Complete Account of the Settlement at Port Jackson*, reprinted as *Sydney's First Four Years* (ed. L.F. Fitzhardinge), London, 1979.

Trollope, Anthony. *Australia and New Zealand*, Melbourne, 1873.

Turner, Jane. *The Surprising Adventures and Unparalleled Sufferings of Jane Turner, A Female Convict*, Doncaster, 1850.

The Van Diemen's Land Anniversary and Hobart-Town Almanack for the Year 1831.

Watling, Thomas. *Letters from an Exile at Botany Bay to his Aunt in Dumfries*, Sydney, 1945.

Westwood to the Port Arthur Chaplain, 8 October 1846, published in George Boxall, *The Story of the Australian Bushrangers*, London, 1899.

White, John. *Journal of a Voyage to New South Wales*, New York, 1971.

Williams, Henry. *Early Journals* (ed. L.M. Rogers), Christchurch, 1961.

Newspapers and Periodicals

The Australasian

The Australian

Birmingham Gazette

Bombay Courier

Calcutta Gazette

Calcutta Journal

Colonial Observer

Dublin Chronicle

Hobart Town Advertiser

Hobart Town Courier

Hobart Town Gazette

Illustrated Sydney News

London Chronicle

The Monitor

Moreton Bay Courier

Police Gazette; or Hue and Cry

Sydney Gazette

Sydney Herald

Sydney Monitor

Sydney Morning Herald

Tasmanian Colonist

The Times

Thesis

Jenkins, Lisa. 'Offending Lives: Subjectivity and Australian Convict Autobiographies 1788-1899', PH.D thesis, Stanford University, 2001. ML MSS 7107.

Secondary Sources

Alexander, Michael. *Mrs Fraser on the Fatal Shore*, Michael Joseph, London, 1971.

Anderson, Clare. 'Multiple Border Crossings: Convicts and Other Persons Escaped from Botany Bay and Residing in Calcutta', *Journal of Australian Colonial History*, vol. 3, no. 2, October 2001.

Australian Dictionary of Biography, vols 1 & 2, Melbourne, 1966-7.

Backhouse, James and Tyler, Charles. *The Life and Labours of George Washington Walker*, London, 1862.

Bonwick, James. *The Wild White Man and the Blacks of Victoria*, Melbourne, 1863.

Brady, Frank. *James Boswell: The Later Years 1769-1795*, New York, 1984.

Brand, Ian. *Penal Peninsula*, West Moonah, 1978.

Brand, Ian. *Sarah Island Penal Settlements*, Launceston, 1990.

Clark, C.M.H. *A History of Australia*, vols 1, 2 & 3, Melbourne, 1962, 1968 and 1973.

Clarke, Marcus. 'The Last of Macquarie Harbour' in *Stories of Australia in the Early Days*, London, 1897.

Clune, Frank and Stephensen, P.R. *The Pirates of the Brig Cyprus*, London, 1962.

Cook, Judith. *To Brave Every Danger*, London, 1994.

Cowan, James. *Hero Stories of New Zealand*, Wellington, 1935.

Crowley, Frank (ed.). *A Documentary History of Australia. Vol. 1. Colonial Australia, 1788-1840*, Melbourne, 1980.

Currey, C.H. *The Transportation, Escape and Pardoning of Mary Bryant*, Sydney, 1963.

David, Andrew. *The Voyage of HMS Herald*, Melbourne, 1995.

De Vera, M. (comp.), *An Australian Woman's Diary, 1985*, Sydney, 1984.

Dick, George. *The Bushranger of Bungendore*, Bungendore & District Historical Society.

Dictionary of New Zealand Biography, 2002, URL:http//www.dnzb.govt.nz/

Earnshaw, John. 'Thomas Muir Scottish Martyr', *Studies in Australian and Pacific History-No. 1*, Cremorne, 1959.

Flynn, Michael. *The Second Fleet. Britain's Grim Convict Armada of 1790*, Sydney, 1993.

Frost, Lucy and Maxwell-Stewart, Hamish (eds). *Chain Letters: Narrating Convict Lives*, Melbourne, 2001.

Gibbings, Robert. *John Graham Convict 1824*, London, 1956.

Gillen, Mollie. *The Founders of Australia*, Sydney, 1989.

Gray, A.J. 'Ann Smith of the Lady Penrhyn', *Journal of the Royal Australian*

Historical Society, vol. 43, part 5, 1957.

Gunson, Neil (ed.). *Australian Reminiscences & Papers of L. Threlkeld*, Canberra, 1974.

Hazzard, Margaret. *Punishment Short of Death: A History of the Penal Settlement at Norfolk Island*, Melbourne, 1984.

Hazzard, Margaret. *Convicts & Commandants of Norfolk Island 1788-1855*, Norfolk Island, c. 1978.

Hiddens, Les. *Stories of Exploration and Survival*, Sydney, 1996.

Hirst, John B. *Convict Society and its Enemies*, Sydney, 1983.

Hoare, Mervall. *Norfolk Island: An Outline of its History 1774-1981*, St Lucia, 1982.

Hughes, Robert. *The Fatal Shore*, London, 1987.

Ingleton, Geoffrey. *True Patriots All*, Sydney, 1952.

Julen, Hans. *The Penal Settlement of Macquarie Harbour*, Launceston, 1976.

King, Michael. *Moriori — A People Rediscovered*, London, 1989.

Knight, J.J. *In the Early Days*, Brisbane, 1895.

Kociumbas, Jan. 'Mary Ann, Joseph Fleming and Gentleman Dick: Aboriginal-Convict Relationships in Colonial History', *Journal of Australian Colonial History*, vol. 3, no. 1, April 2001.

Langhorne , George. 'Reminiscences of James Buckley' in *The Life and Adventures of William Buckley*, (ed. Tim Flannery), Melbourne, 2002.

Lempriere, T.J. *The Penal Settlements of Van Diemen's Land*, Launceston, 1954.

Masson, M. and Jameson, J.F. 'The Odyssey of Thomas Muir', *The American Historic Review*, vol. XXIX, no. 1, Oct., 1923.

Morgan, John. *The Life and Adventures of William Buckley*, Sydney, 1996.

Nobbs, Raymond (ed.). *Norfolk Island and its Second Settlement*, Sydney, 1991.

Parker, Henry. *The Rise, Progress and Present State of Van Diemen's Land*, London, 1833.

Pottle, F.A. *Boswell and the Girl from Botany Bay*, London, 1938.

Pretyman, E.R. 'Pirates at Recherche Bay or The Loss of the Brig *Cyprus*' in *Papers and Proceedings of The Royal Society of Tasmania*, vol. 88, 1954.

Roderick, Colin. *John Knatchbull*, Sydney, 1963.

BIBLIOGRAPHY

Shaw, A.G.L. *Convicts and the Colonies*, London, 1966.

Steele, J.G. *Brisbane Town in Convict Days 1824-1842*, St Lucia, 1975.

Sherrin, R.A. & Wallace, J.H. *Early History of New Zealand*, Auckland, 1890.

Smith, Bev C. *Shadow Over Tasmania*, Hobart, 1942.

Sprod, Dan. *Alexander Pearce of Macquarie Harbour*, Hobart, 1977.

Tipping, Marjorie. *Convicts Unbound*, Ringwood, 1988.

Tudehope, C.D. 'William Buckley', *The Victorian Historical Magazine*, vol. 32, no. 4,` May 1962.

West, John. *The History of Tasmania*, Launceston, 1852. Reprinted Sydney, 1971.

Index

Australian Navigators

Robert Tiley

In the mid-1700s Australia was a largely forgotten curiosity at the bottom of the world. Still only partly mapped by the Dutch explorers who had made a series of often disastrous visits in the previous century, it was regarded as too distant, too hostile and too much trouble.

Then came the Australian Navigators. Within a 40-year span, one of the bloodiest in European history, legendary explorers including D'Entrecasteaux, Cook, Marion, Bligh, Bass, Baudin and Flinders undertook the perilous journeys of exploration to the southern continent. They were dangerous enterprises, and of that illustrious company, only Bligh survived long enough to retire. What motivated this great burst of interest? Why did some succeed where others, particularly the French voyages, failed? Why were the French the first to publish a map of Australia's coastline, some of it named after their Emperor Napoleon?

In this intriguing book, Robert Tiley looks at the roots of the era in war-torn Europe and at the complicated aims of the backers who supported and promoted these expeditions. He shows how, in many cases, the Australian Navigators were pawns in their floating political world, carrying out missions whose underlying aims were often overtaken by political events, or destroyed by their own weaknesses. He also explores the thirst for scientific knowledge, and the effect that this had on the navigators and their journeys.

A great deal has been written on these explorers in weighty academic volumes. This book does not seek to emulate them, but instead to capture the spirit of the era and the personalities and ambitions of the individuals involved. They emerge fresh, convincing and compelling, as relevant now as they were then.

ISBN 0 7318 1118 6
Paperback
256 pp
234 x 180 mm

A Guide to Australian Folklore
From Ned Kelly to Aeroplane Jelly

Gwenda Beed Davey and Graham Seal

The term 'folklore' often makes people think of the past: bush songs, old tales, traditional beliefs and the like. But as this new book shows, folklore is just as much a part of modern life. *A Guide to Australian Folklore* is a major new guide to allusions, characters (real and fictional), events, places, beliefs and activities that constitute the folklore of the Australian peoples, past and present.

The book is presented in an easy-to-read A–Z form that will appeal to the general reader as well as specialists. Entries range from The Dog on the Tuckerbox and The Pub with No Beer to Gallipoli, The Wild Colonial Boy and the Tasmanian Tiger. It is a fascinating guide to Australia's character and traditions.

Much of the material in the guide is new or little known outside folk groups. The guide builds on more than 20 years of research and is the most comprehensive and authoritative work of its type. It is an indispensable reference for schools, colleges, government and corporate libraries.

ISBN 0 7318 1075 9
Paperback
320 pp
234 x 153 mm

The Washerwoman's Dream
Hilarie Lindsay

This is the remarkable story of an extraordinary life. Winifred Steger was born in England in 1882. To break the cycle of poverty her father takes part in a land grab and books a passage for his family to head for Australia, work the land and strike it rich.

Arriving in Australia, Winifred and her father find that their land grant is covered with a prison of prickly pear and is worthless. Faced again with poverty, endlesss backbreaking work and isolation in an unfamiliar country, Winifred's father spirals into depression and alcoholism, leaving Winifred emotionally alone. From skivvy in a bawdy house to a loveless marriage, Winifred battles almost insurmountable odds to maintain her dignity and sanity, finding solace as she creates fictitious scenarios to ease her hardship.

At the age of 26, she is forced to abandon her four small children. Finding work in a hotel bar, she meets and falls in love with an Indian man, Ali, who treats Winifred with respect and decency. She bears him three children and the small family travels to outback Australia where they run a camel line. A new phase begins in Winfred's life, taking her to places and meeting people she has only ever dreamed of.

The Washerwoman's Dream is an epic story that could easily be the stuff of fiction. Hilarie Lindsay has meticulously researched and reconstructed Winifred's life through her memoirs, newspaper articles, short stories, letters and 14 unpublished novels. This is an account of the amazing life of a forgotten Australian writer and a woman with an indomitable spirit.

Strongly recommended reading – *Australian Bookseller and Publisher*

ISBN 0 7318 1092 9
Paperback
356 pp
234 x 153 mm

The Murder of Nellie Duffy

Stephanie Bennett

In 1908, on Queensland's remote Carpentaria Downs station, the vibrant Nellie Duffy was found dead, her throat slit. Fanny Wilson, wife of the station manager, and Billy, an Aboriginal station-hand, were charged with the murder. The trial failed and the truth never surfaced. Newspaper headlines screamed of a high-level cover-up, and calls for a parliamentary inquiry went unheeded.

Who was responsible for killing this housekeeper-companion to Fanny Wilson? Among the many suspects was Fanny's husband, the station boss Henry Wilson, known to police via allegations of cattle stealing and cruelty to Aborigines.

For almost a century, the legend surrounding this callous murder has lingered, fuelled by tales of adultery, family secrets, racial exploitation, brutality and police bungling. In *The Murder of Nellie Duffy*, Stephanie Bennett narrates a fascinating tale and presents a compelling exercise in forensic reconstruction. Along the way she tackles the questions: What evidence was hushed up? Why do rumours that persist in the north tell a different story from the one the public was allowed to hear? Why was Nellie Duffy killed? Indeed, who killed her?

ISBN 0 7318 1117 8
Paperback
240 pp
210 x 135 mm